WINNING TEAM
PUBLISHING

45BOOKS.COM

ISBN: 978-1-7355037-3-8

Published in the United States by
Winning Team Publishing
www.45Books.com

Proudly manufactured in the United States of America

10 9 8 7 6 5 4 3 2 1

For more information on this and our other titles,
please visit our website:
www.45Books.com

THE COLLEGE SCAM

INTRODUCTION

Laying Out the Case

"Charlie, why didn't you go to college?"

People ask me this all the time. The fact is, I had planned to go to college. Like most of my high school classmates, I had bought into the mindset that says, "Of course, I'm going to college. It's just what you do. It's how you prepare yourself for life, right?"

I also felt pressure from everybody around me. During my senior year of high school, dozens of people asked me, "Where will you be going to college next year?" Not "*Are* you going?" but "*Where* are you going?"

I had my sights set on the U.S. Military Academy at West Point. When I didn't get an appointment to the Academy, I was really discouraged. But it turned out to be the best thing that ever happened to me.

My second choice was Baylor University. I visited the campus and met the president of the university. He asked me about my goals in life and I told him that I planned to build a youth organization. He liked my ideas and said, "It'll take a lot of time and hard work to get the organization off the ground. Why don't you take a year to focus on starting the organization? Once it's up and running, you can always come back to Baylor."

His advice made sense. Looking back, I'm amazed at his wisdom and honesty. Imagine—a university president encouraging me to pursue my life goals instead of trying to sell me on four years at his institution. That kind of honesty from a university official is rare.

> My gap year became a gap decade.

I would have had to take out a lot of student loans to go to Baylor. I wasn't eager to shoulder that much debt, so I took a gap year and focused on building Turning Point USA. The organization became successful in less than two years—so successful that going to college ceased to be a priority. My gap year became a gap decade.

Do I have any regrets about not going to college? No, none at all.

An Instant Focus Group

Full disclosure: I did take a couple of community college classes, so I can't technically say I never went to college. But I've never been a full-time college student and I've never taken out a student loan.

More full disclosure: though I have no regrets now, there was a time when I had plenty of regrets. I used to see all my friends from high school going to college and having good times. I would check out their Facebook and Instagram posts, and they were joining fraternities and sororities, going to football games, and really having fun.

I visited some of my friends on campus, and they asked me what I was doing. I explained that I was building a youth organization based on conservative principles. They'd give me a pitying look, and I could tell they thought I had taken my life on some weird tangent. I soon wondered if my gap year had been a mistake.

After about a year and a half, things began to change. Turning Point USA had started making inroads on campuses around the country. At the same time, my friends' postings on Facebook and Instagram took on a different tone. I thought, *Wow! What happened to all the fun these guys were having in college? They've all gained twenty-five pounds and they look stressed and miserable!*

I messaged with them, and they told me, "I hate college! This is awful! I don't know what I'm going to do with my life—and now I'm saddled with all this debt!"

And it hit me: there I was, just twenty years old, debt-free, and I knew exactly what I was going to do with my life—because I was already doing it. Turning Point was up and running, we had the support of donors, we were making payroll, and we were making a difference. Four years of college would have been a roadblock to my goals and would have left me deep in debt.

Okay, I didn't have a diploma to hang on my wall. But I had achieved all the success that college promises but rarely delivers.

Since the founding of Turning Point USA, I have visited with countless students and I've taken the pulse of college life. I've also interacted with countless students through my radio show and podcasts. I'm conducting an instant focus group with millions of college students. I hear their stories, their complaints, and their questions. I know what college students are saying and thinking.

And what I hear, again and again, is that college is a scam. Everybody knows it. The professors know it. The administrators know it. The board members and donors know it. Some will admit it in private—"but don't quote me," they say. Few dare to admit it out loud.

Students *especially* know that college is a scam. They know they're not getting real value for their tuition dollars. But they think they have no choice. They've been told they must go deep in debt to get their ticket punched so they can come out with a degree. And that degree, they've been told, is the key to a successful future. But it's all a scam.

> But of all students who attend college, only a tiny percentage end up in careers requiring a professional degree.

If the college industry were *only* a scam, that would be bad enough. But the college industry is much worse than that. As you'll soon see, so-called "higher education" has become corrosive to our culture and a threat to our future.

So we have to ask ourselves: Should young people go to college anymore?

The answer, for the vast majority of students in college (or considering college) is *NO!* There are some professions, of course, that require a college degree and even an advanced degree. If you're planning to become a doctor, lawyer, or engineer, then yes, choose your institution wisely and go to college.

But of all students who attend college, only a tiny percentage end up in careers requiring a professional degree. In fact, *more than 95 percent* of college students would be far better off, in terms of finances, career goals, and lifestyle, if they had never gone to college. I will document that claim in the chapters to come.

The Best—and Worst—Person to Write This Book

Let's get one thing out of the way right now: I am both the best and the worst person to write this book. I'm the best person to write it because I didn't go to college and I have succeeded precisely *because* I didn't go. I couldn't have accomplished what I did if I had gone to college. A four-year degree would have only held me back.

But I can hear it now—some critics will say, "Charlie Kirk has no business writing a book like this. He's never been to college. He doesn't understand the advantages of a college education. He doesn't know what he's talking about."

Let's cut that off at the pass. I founded Turning Point USA in 2012, and in less than a decade TPUSA has experienced phenomenal growth, establishing roughly a thousand campus chapters and activism hubs across the United States. With a $50 million annual budget, TPUSA is *the* dominant force in campus conservatism. I employ 160 recent high school and college graduates.

Few individuals have visited as many college campuses as I have. Since the founding of TPUSA, I have personally visited more than 150 college campuses, I speak at more than fifteen campuses per semester, and I have met with more college presidents than I can count. Thanks to all my conversations with students and faculty across the country, I have a *better* sense of what students are thinking, saying, and experiencing than most of the professors and administrators on their campuses.

So let me forewarn my critics: before you claim I don't know what I'm talking about, make sure you can back it up. Why? Because I will challenge you to a debate in the forum of your choice.

And when we debate, I will indict the college industry for the scam it is. I will put the college system on trial, and I will get a conviction in the court of public opinion—especially student opinion.

Now a special word for you as a student or parent: if you're thinking about going to college or sending your son or daughter to college, you need to keep reading. You need to reconsider the assumption that a university degree is a box you must check to achieve success in life.

Student, by the time you've finished this book, I think you'll be convinced that you should *not* go to college. Parent, by the time you've finished this book, I think you'll agree that you should *not* send your kids to college.

I'm living proof that you don't need a college education to make a difference. But you don't have to take my word for it. The data and the stories speak for themselves. I am indicting the college industry, and I will prove my case beyond a shadow of a doubt.

Anti-College = Pro-Education

Let me be clear: *I strongly believe in education.*

I believe that colleges and universities can play a role in a functioning, civil society. Historically, higher education has made an indispensable contribution to society. There are a few small, independent institutions that still offer a robust education in the Western philosophical tradition, the Great Books, and the U.S. Constitution. There are a few colleges that reinforce character, faith in God, and the responsibilities of American citizenship. The only college I can personally endorse is Hillsdale College in Michigan, but there are a few others. These institutions are performing the function that all colleges and universities should fulfill.

The overwhelming majority of colleges and universities have rejected Western culture, the U.S. Constitution, and any notion of character education. They are aggressively atheistic and anti-American. They have passed any possibility of reform. The pragmatic truth is that it's too late to turn this ship around.

Colleges and universities have ceased to be centers of learning. Instead of making students stronger, wiser, and better equipped to contribute to society, today's "higher education" industry leaves students debt-ridden, brainwashed, and incapable of rational thinking. Today, the best education is self-education. Some of the most highly educated people I've met have never attended a single college class—and some of the most irrational, ill-informed people I've met are those with the most formal education.

This is probably the most pro-education book you will read this year. In these pages, you'll learn how to become truly well-prepared and well-educated *without* going to college. You'll learn why the cost of a college education has skyrocketed by many times the rate of inflation. You'll learn who's behind the college scam and how they are ripping you off.

You'll understand the roots of the radical college indoctrination that is tearing our society apart at the seams. You'll learn, through anecdotes and unassailable facts, how a college education makes students morally and intellectually weak, intolerant of other viewpoints, and incapable of critical thinking and debate. And you'll learn why 41 percent of recent college graduates end up in careers that don't require college degrees.

I love learning. I love exploring ideas. And because I have such a deep respect for *real* education, I am committed to taking down the college cartel. I'm committed to de-funding the college industry.

Indoctrination isn't education. Trapping a generation of young people in debt-slavery isn't education. Handing your sons and daughters over to corrupt administrators and radical professors isn't education. But that is what the college cartel has become, and that is what this book will expose.

Breaking a Cherished Institution

Of all the battles I have fought—and there have been many—challenging America's irrational attachment to the four-year college system has been the most turbulent. Many people put me in a political category because of my beliefs, and for most issues that's fair. But when it comes to criticizing and critiquing college, I have found that just as many Republicans as Democrats are defensive of this broken education machine.

Since I began questioning the college regime as corrupt and broken, I have encountered a wall of resistance from people from all walks of life who are unprepared or unwilling to face the core issue. Many people feel an understandable sense of loyalty and sentimental attachment to their alma mater. But since

I've never gone to college, I have no reason to feel protective of a system that has become an incredibly expensive credentialing exercise.

There are many "thought crimes" one can commit in today's America. If you dare question the medical industrial complex or the technocratic scientific elite, you'll be vilified by the propagandists on television and the smear artists who call themselves journalists. But the theme of this book may well top the list of "thought crimes" one can commit. I intend to break apart a cherished institution, a bedrock of society that has been a birthright and a rite of passage for generations of Americans.

As I'll make clear in this book, not all colleges are equally corrupt or involved in this scam. If every college had a mission statement like that of Hillsdale College, for example, my criticism would be quite different. If every school had a president like Hillsdale's Dr. Larry Arnn, a leader who unapologetically contends for truth, liberty, and the development of good character, then my critique would be mostly about job placement and the cost of college.

Unfortunately, only a handful of colleges are focused on objective truth, beauty, and traditional morality. At most colleges, you'll pay exorbitant tuitions to be indoctrinated in the idea that there is no God, no truth, no meaning in life—and at the end of four years, you'll have no useful job skills upon which to build a career.

The word "education" comes from the Latin word meaning "to lead forth." The word conveyed an image of leading young people forth from a cave of ignorance into the sunshine of understanding and wisdom. The cave, of course, refers to Socrates's "Allegory of the Cave" in Plato's *Republic*—an allegory on the nature of perception and truth.

Do our colleges and universities "lead forth" today's young people toward a future where they love and respect this land of freedom and opportunity? Do our colleges and universities "lead forth" young people on a journey to improve their souls and appreciate justice, truth, and all that is good? These are fundamental questions, and the answer, overwhelmingly, is *No*. In fact, students are being led deeper into the dark cave of ignorance and false belief.

I can anticipate another accusation my critics will make: "Charlie Kirk runs a campus-based organization, Turning Point USA. His marketplace is colleges and universities. That's where he goes to speak. That's where his audience is. If colleges and universities didn't exist, Turning Point USA couldn't exist. Now he says that the college industry should be dismantled and students should stay away from higher education. That's the height of hypocrisy!"

No, there is absolute consistency between the message of this book and the message of Turning Point USA. Our organization exists to counter the corrosive and destructive influence of our so-called "higher education." Young people enroll in college completely unaware that they are walking into a buzz saw of indoctrination, intellectual bullying, and an intense pressure to conform to a Marxist, anti-American mindset.

Turning Point USA exists to support conservative students in a hostile environment, and to teach the value of liberty and the free market system on campus. TPUSA is trying to rescue students who are already caught up in the college scam, and to prevent them from being ruined, emotionally and intellectually, by the college industry. Consistent with that goal, this book seeks to prevent future students from being drawn into the intellectual and moral sausage grinder that is the college industry.

Most important of all, through this book I hope to restore respect for people who did not go to college. For years, non-college-graduates have been treated as "less-than." In the coming chapters, I'll expose this elitist snobbery and prove that many people without a degree have made a much better life choice than their college-educated counterparts.

Putting the College Industry on Trial

In this book, I'm putting the college industry on trial. I will lay out a ten-count indictment, along with all the evidence. Here's the case I will make:

COUNT 1:

COLLEGES AND UNIVERSITIES ARE RUNNING A SCAM.

The college industry promises students an education that will prepare them for a rewarding career. For the overwhelming majority of students, that promise is a lie. A 40 percent dropout rate is proof that the college system is failing to deliver on its promises. Because this fraudulent industry is heavily subsidized by the federal government, it is a scam not only on students, but taxpayers as well.

COUNT 2:

A COLLEGE EDUCATION IS RIDICULOUSLY OVERPRICED.

The cost of a college education has been artificially inflated to an absurd level. Student loan debt is crushing students and their parents, robbing people of the dream of homeownership and a financially secure future. I will show how federal funding of the student loan industry is driving the cost of education through the roof, and threatens to destabilize the American economy.

COUNT 3:

UNIVERSITIES HAVE BECOME OBSCENELY RICH AT STUDENT AND TAXPAYER EXPENSE.

These institutions have become "hedge funds with universities attached," and they now exist primarily to amass bloated endowments. They exist to provide make-work jobs for academics and administrators, such as "deans of diversity, equity, and inclusion." Who gets the bill for the universities' obscene profits? Students, parents, and taxpayers.

COUNT 4:

COLLEGES DO NOT EDUCATE ANYMORE.

Students go through the college system and come out the other end not having learned anything at all. Testing shows conclusively that students do not improve their critical thinking skills in college. Employers overwhelmingly say, "We can't hire college grads. They're not equipped to hold down a job." Contrary to repeated claims, a college education does not increase career earnings of most graduates.

COUNT 5:

COLLEGE RUINS THE ABILITY TO THINK AND REASON.

So-called "higher education" teaches students to abandon common sense, logic, and reason. I will give example after example of professors and students who had taken leave of their senses as a direct result of "higher education." I will show you a list of the truly ridiculous courses offered at universities—courses that promote lunacy on campus.

COUNT 6:

COLLEGE INDOCTRINATES STUDENTS AND REPRESSES SPEECH.

Universities used to open students' minds and widen their horizons. Today, universities weld minds shut. Radical professors engage in "grade activism" (giving students extra credit for extracurricular protesting and other actions), punishing nonconforming students with failing grades, and more. Radical students persecute their nonconforming peers through "cancel culture" and threats. Students quickly learn to conform—or else.

COUNT 7:

COLLEGES AND UNIVERSITIES BREED VIOLENCE AND HATE.

Violence against conservative, pro-America students is commonplace on campus. Some administrations have sided with violent campus radicals instead of protecting the rights of the peaceful minority. Through story after story, I will introduce you to students who have been physically assaulted and threatened with death for peacefully exercising their First Amendment rights on campus.

COUNT 8:

COLLEGES AND UNIVERSITIES HAVE BEEN INFILTRATED BY SUBVERSIVE FOREIGN GROUPS.

The rise of anti-Israel groups like Jewish Voice for Peace and Students for Justice in Palestine has created an atmosphere of anti-Semitism and anti-American hate on many campuses. And the on-campus presence of Confucius Institutes has enabled Communist China to infiltrate American universities on a massive scale, threatening national security.

COUNT 9:

COLLEGES AND UNIVERSITIES HAVE UNLEASHED WAVES OF WOKE, ANTI-AMERICAN ACTIVISTS.

All the destructive ideas that are now eating away at the foundation of America originated on college campuses or were spread on college campuses: Critical Race Theory, Intersectionality, Wokeism, Antifa, Defund the Police, White Fragility, Speech Codes, Cancel Culture, "Anti-Racism," The Green New Deal, and on and on.

COUNT 10:

MANY PROFESSORS ARE LEFTIST RADICALS BENT ON INDOCTRINATING STUDENTS.

Through story after story from the Professor Watchlist, I will show that college is a massively hostile environment for students who do not conform to the leftist groupthink of academia.

That's my ten-count indictment. I will make the case, count by count, then I will submit the case to you for a decision. You are the jury. You will examine the evidence. You will reach a verdict. And I have full confidence in your verdict.

Read with an open mind. Listen to these stories. Weigh these facts. Set aside the assumptions and expectations that have been imposed on you by the culture. Then make up your own mind.

Are you ready for a fresh new look at your future, your children's future, and the future of society? Then turn the page and buckle up.

Here . . . we . . . go.

1

THE GAME IS RIGGED AGAINST YOU

COUNT 1:

Colleges and Universities Are Running a Scam.

Sarah Rose Attman is the founder of Sarah Rose Public Relations. She was named by *Adweek* as one of the top "30 Under 30" PR professionals in America. A few years ago, she wrote a piece for the *Huffington Post* titled "I Learned Nothing in College."

In the piece, she adds some nuance to that statement. She didn't literally learn *nothing*—she did have two English professors who helped improve her writing skills and self-confidence. But aside from those two professors, she concluded, college "was a colossal waste of time. My memories are a vague blur of hanging out with friends and cramming for exams—forgetting all the information on my way out the door."

Attman refers to her diploma as "that little slip of paper that says you graduated," and adds that, with few exceptions, employers don't really care where you went to school. "When I interned at NBC," she recalls, "the head recruiter told us that she never looked at GPAs or read cover letters. Yikes."

College didn't do Attman's friends much good, either. Her best friend, she writes, was an acting major in college but now works in the financial sector. Another friend, who majored in economics, is now a yoga instructor. If you surveyed your own circle of college-grad friends, you'd probably find that most of them got little, if any, career benefit from college.

As a millennial, Sarah Rose Attman finds it kind of quaint that, in the past, people went to college to *learn*. One of her parents' friends told her that, during his college days, he was so busy studying he had no time for socializing. Attman's response: "Wow!"

But her complaint about college is not so much that it's a waste of time (though it is). She fears that college does serious damage to young souls. College, she writes, is "a breeding ground for a toxic, misogynistic, elitist social culture. A place where self-esteem goes to die. Think Greek parties with themes like 'CEOs and Office Hoes.' Think date rape cover-ups and roofies. Is it any surprise that young men and women go off to school and fall into deep depressions or attempt suicide?"

Sarah Rose Attman is a college grad who is unusually honest about the great college swindle. She saw through the scam, she survived it, and her message to you and others contemplating college is clear and simple: "I learned nothing in college."[1]

Not "Where?" but "Why?"

This brings us to Count 1 of our ten-count indictment of the college industry: *"Colleges and universities are running a scam."* Whether you know it or not, the college industry is a game that is rigged against you. The rules of the game are:

1. **You go deep into debt.**
2. **You spend four years (at least) going through the motions of getting an education.**
3. **At the end of the process, you get a piece of paper called a diploma.**
4. **You spend the next ten or twenty years paying off the debt.**

Most people assume they have to play the game to have a good career. But that assumption is crumbling. Young people are asking, "What am I getting in exchange for the debt I'm taking on? Will four years of college advance my career in any meaningful way? Is there a better way to have a high-paying career?"

If you're a young person facing the future, the first question you should ask yourself is not *"Where* should I go to college?" but *"Why* should I go to college?"

There are some professions that require a college degree. But there are other good jobs—plumbers, electricians, commercial pilots, and police officers, to name a few—that offer a high income with no college degree required.

So do you really need to go to college? If you're only going because your friends are going or because your parents expect you to or because you haven't figured out what to do with your life—those are bad reasons. Before you waste four years of your life and take on a crushing burden of debt, you should set some clearly defined life goals.

Seldom, if ever, are high schoolers encouraged to think this way about their future. When parents, teachers, or friends ask you where you're going to college, the unspoken assumption is, "Everybody goes to college." If you disrupt that assumption by replying, "I'm not going to college," or, "I haven't decided if college is for me," you'll get responses of shock and disbelief.

Parents, teachers, and guidance counselors need to change the way they talk to young people about their future and about college. They need to stop asking "where" and start asking "why." We need to give young people permission to consider non-college options. We need to give students permission to say, "I'm not going to college unless I can justify the time and expense."

> If you're a young person facing the future, the first question you should ask yourself is not "Where should I go to college?" but "Why should I go to college?"

Where did the "everybody goes to college" assumption come from? It can be traced to the decades from the 1960s through the 1990s, when there was a much higher correlation between a college degree and a good-paying career. But the world has changed. The job market has changed. Universities are very different from what they used to be. Yet our cultural assumptions have not kept up with changing times.

To break through that assumption, I always ask high school seniors, "What do you want to do with your life?" Frequently, the answer is, "I don't know. I'm hoping to figure it out while I'm in college." That's a terrible answer. It's the height of irrationality to say, "I don't know what I want to do with my life, but I'm going to borrow a ton of money, go to college without any plans or goals, and figure it out along the way."

No one should never enter college in the desperate hope of finding a life goal. To succeed in college, you must sit down and ask yourself, "What do I want out of life? What do I want to accomplish? What am I passionate about? What do I excel at? What gives me a sense of satisfaction and joy in life?"

You won't succeed in college—or in life—unless you have clearly defined goals. Decide what you want to do with your life, and if your goals don't require a college degree, then *don't go to college*.

There's so much beauty and richness in the world outside of college. You can pursue the world of ideas and opportunities on your own terms, without taking on debt. If, after a few years, you discover you need to go to college to achieve your goals, to acquire a skill, to pursue a profession, then go for it.

> If your goals don't require a college degree, then don't go to college.

But goals *must* come first. Know where you are going and what you must do to get there. That may mean going to college or going to a trade school. It may mean starting your own business or joining the work force instead of going to college. Whatever your goals, aim high and pursue those goals with everything you've got.

Above all, ask yourself the "why" question: "*Why* should I go to college?" That question will keep you from wasting tens of thousands of dollars, not to mention four prime years of your life.

How the Scam Works

The word "college" comes from a Greek word that means "partnership"—a collaboration or project from which both parties benefit. Are colleges partnering with their students—or exploiting them? Do colleges treat their students as valued future members of a free society—or are they widgets in a revenue-generation scheme that devalues their future at the expense of the profit margins of the leviathan?

According to the National Center for Education Statistics in 2020, the *six-year* graduation rate for full-time undergrads seeking a bachelor's degree is 62 percent. That means that, even if you give a student an extra two years to complete a four-year degree, only 62 percent achieve that goal; 38 percent fail to graduate. More than half of all students take on tens of thousands of dollars in student debt—and that includes the 38 percent who end up with no degree to show for it.[2]

Who is to blame for the high college dropout rate? Some would put all the blame on the students—but that makes no sense. After all, colleges screen applicants very carefully. They use transcripts, testing, and essay questions to ensure that the students they admit have what it takes for academic success. In fact, according to EducationData.org, four out of ten college dropouts left school with a GPA of 3.0 or higher. And 39 percent of dropouts said that their college didn't give them their money's worth.[3]

If the national graduation rate is 60 percent and the failure rate is 40 percent, then clearly the college industry is one of the worst industries in America at delivering its product. What if a restaurant only satisfied 60 percent of its patrons and the other 40 percent went hungry? What if your phone only delivered 60 percent of your texts and connected 60 percent of your calls? What if your car only started 60 percent of the time? What if the internet or the electrical grid only operated 60 percent of the time? You would be outraged and militant. The high dropout rate alone is proof that the university system is failing its students.

Yet we accept the abysmal performance of the college cartel as normal. We don't raise a whimper of protest over being gouged for tens of thousands of dollars over a piece of paper of questionable (and diminishing) value. We all know the college industry is ripping us off, yet we accept it because we don't see any way around it.

I can tell you from personal experience that some of the best employees we've hired at Turning Point USA never went to college. We hire both college graduates and non-graduates at TPUSA, and those who went to college and those who didn't are almost indistinguishable from each other. They demonstrate roughly the same level of competence and leadership skill. In fact, I salute our college graduate employees for surviving the corrosive and hostile campus environment without being ruined as employees.

As an employer, I can tell you that a college degree doesn't mean anything to me. If you list your college degree on your résumé, I won't hold it against you—but it won't give you any advantage. I believe many employers now take a similar position because they see that the college industry is a scam.

To understand how the college scam works, we have to look at the big picture. The scam is driven not only by universities and colleges, but also by the federal government and lending institutions. Together, these institutions form an oligopoly—an economic arrangement in which a small number of players control the market.

The federal government unleashes a flow of cheap, easy-to-get money, which triggers an inflationary cycle. As Jenna A. Robinson of the James G. Martin Center for Academic Renewal explains, "If the government gives money to students to spend on education, then students will be able and willing to spend more on that product. Universities, knowing that the funds are available, raise tuition without worrying about whether students can afford it. An ugly cycle ensues."

The result is that universities are awash in money and have no incentive to rein in tuition costs. Why would universities ever cut tuitions or improve their product if their students always pay in full, regardless of whether they get any value from their education? (And, as we'll see in chapter 4, most students get no value whatsoever from a college education.) FAFSA (Free Application for Federal Student Aid) keeps flooding the system with Pell Grants and student loans, subsidizing a bloated and corrupt system, and perpetuating the college-inflationary cycle.

It's a scam on students—and a scam on taxpayers. The college industry scoops up billions of dollars and (in most cases) delivers a worthless educational product in return.

The Myth of "Reform"

Because the failures, abuses, and corruption of the college industry are so obvious and well known, there have been numerous attempts to reform the system. For example, in 2019, Senator Marco Rubio of Florida introduced the Leveraging Opportunities for Americans Now (LOAN) Act to eliminate student loan interest and replace it with a one-time financing fee that borrowers would repay during the term of the loan. Payments would be based on the borrower's income to prevent working-class Americans from being saddled with payments they cannot afford. Senator Rubio also introduced the Student Right to Know Before You Go Act to enable students, families, and taxpayers to better understand the costs of a college education.

Though well-intentioned, Rubio's legislative efforts only tap-dance around the problem. They don't get to the root of the Great College Swindle. This is typical of every attempt at so-called "reform" of the college system. Everybody says, "We need to reform the system," but their proposals are either too weak or too unfair or they create more problems than they solve.

There are many college "reform" ideas floating around today: eliminate standardized testing; eliminate letters of recommendation and application essays; consider grades and merit only; do away with preferences for "legacy" students (children of alumni); and on and on. But these reform ideas only nibble at the edges of the problem. The *real* problem is that the entire system is corrupt from top to bottom.

We are way past any possibility of reform. The university industry is corrupt through and through. No one will stand up and say, "Stop this cultural madness!" The students, parents, and taxpayers who pay for the system won't say it because they don't think there's any way around it. The academics, politicians, and financiers won't say it because they *are* the problem.

So who will tell the truth about the college scam? Only someone who has no stake in the college system. Only someone who succeeded *without* a college degree. Only someone who has nothing to lose. Only someone who's willing to make hamburger out of sacred cows.

Are There Any Exceptions?

I can hear the objections already: "Hold it right there, Charlie! What about Christian colleges and conservative liberal arts colleges?"

For those who must have a college degree for their chosen profession, I always recommend Hillsdale College in Michigan. Hillsdale offers an excellent education in science, mathematics, economics, medicine, law, and more. The school maintains high academic standards, it's affordable, and students study the Greek, Roman, and Judeo-Christian foundations of Western civilization. They read Socrates, Plato, and Aristotle, and they learn about the great ideas on which our culture is based. Hillsdale students also learn why America is a special place, why freedom is worth preserving, and why they should be good citizens of the United States.

But Hillsdale is not merely an exception—it's practically unique. Hillsdale doesn't take government money and is not part of the Great College Swindle.

As for Christian colleges, yes, there are definitely some great Christian schools. But you need to research them carefully. Some Christian colleges that were theologically conservative and philosophically strong just a few years ago have veered off course in recent years. Many have compromised their standards and beliefs to win approval from the secular world. Some have even begun teaching "woke" social justice ideology.

It would be outside the scope of this book for me to list which Christian colleges remain faithful and which have gone downhill. If you are considering a Christian college, investigate it thoroughly. Visit the campus. Talk to the students and faculty. Sit in on classes. Subscribe to the campus newspaper.

Remember that Yale, Harvard, Princeton, and Oxford were all founded as theologically conservative Christian institutions of higher learning. Today they are all dogmatically hostile to the Christian faith. No Christian college or university is immune to the temptation to defect from the faith.

Never assume that a school with a great reputation is still living up to its legacy. If you really must go to college to pursue your calling and profession, make sure that institution is worth the investment of your time and money.

An Essential Life Experience?

You might be thinking, *Okay, I agree, the college system is a scam. But there's more to college than getting an education. What about a once-in-a-lifetime experience? People tell me that my college years will be the best years of my life. I'll make lifelong friends and make a lot of good memories.*

If that's your thinking, let me ask you this: Is it worth taking on a six-figure debt to have a "once-in-a-lifetime experience," and "make lifelong friends"? If you want to take on debt to be indoctrinated by Marxist professors, attend some forgettable football games, and endure your roommate's weird habits, go ahead—it's your money and your future. But to me, the fear of missing out on the "once-in-a-lifetime experience" of college is a bad reason to squander four years of your life and a boatload of money.

You might also be thinking, "What about the networking? At college, I'll meet a lot of people who will help me up the ladder of success."

I call this the "fallacy of networking." This seems like a super-expensive way to meet people in the hope that they might help your career at some unknown time in the future. You shouldn't view college as a debt-financed networking system. You must decide: Is this a good investment of four years of my life and a huge pile of borrowed money?

Networking is nothing more than building career-related relationships. The best place to network is not on a college campus but out in the real world. And the best way to network is to identify people who are connected to your career field, meet likeminded people over social media, join online communities related to your field, be outgoing and helpful to others, and make friends wherever you go. That kind of networking pays—and it doesn't cost you a dime.

Avoiding Responsibility—and Adulthood

Many young people see college as a way to live free of responsibility for four years. For many students, college is their first experience living away from home—unsupervised. It's "pretend adulthood" with all of the freedom and none of the responsibilities that come with being a real grown-up. College students can get blackout drunk, hook up with girls or boys, and live off their student loans for four years. I will stipulate that, yes, it's a lot of fun to live without rules or responsibilities. But long-term, it's not good for the student and not good for society.

People often say you gain maturity in college. You're out of the family nest, you're spreading your wings, you're learning to fly, you're getting your first experience of the real world, right? Wrong.

College is the opposite of the real world. You don't become more mature in college. In fact, the opposite is true. Maturity comes from taking on responsibility. Lack of responsibility breeds immaturity. Most of the high school seniors I've met are far more mature than most of the college seniors I've met—and I've met plenty of both. Why is this? It's because high school seniors have much more responsibility and accountability in their lives. They're accountable to parents and teachers.

The college experience makes students less likely to behave responsibly. They're away from home and unaccountable to parents. Their professors don't take roll or hold them accountable to study. The college environment tolerates and even promotes bad moral behavior.

College used to be a place that encouraged young people to grow up and become intellectually and emotionally strong. Today, entering college means entering a prolonged adolescence. Instead of building mental and physical muscles to help you shoulder the burdens of life in the real world, college coddles and softens its students. It weakens your spirit and atrophies your muscles. College students are less prepared than ever to live in a changing, stressful, unpredictable world. The students who graduate from college today are angry, mentally inflexible, and too emotionally fragile to watch the nightly news without retreating to a "safe space."

Most of the students I talk to on college campuses are less prepared to enter the real world at age twenty-two than they were at age eighteen. (I'm talking about the general campus population, not Turning Point USA members; the reason they're involved in TPUSA is that they are serious about life and their responsibilities as citizens.)

Most college students know nothing about personal finance or budgeting or the crushing load of debt they'll be shouldering as they leave college. They have no idea what it has cost them to get that piece of paper.

Campus life promotes irresponsible eating and weight gain. Students have a name for the weight gain that results from life on campus: the "Freshman 15." Some people claim it's a myth, but it's very real.

A four-year study of college students, published in 2012, found that 70 percent of student participants gained weight—an average of 5.3 kg or 11.7 pounds. Not quite 15 pounds, but close. The percentage of student participants ranked as overweight or obese grew from 18 percent to 31 percent. Researchers concluded, "The increasing prevalence of obesity and normal weight obesity among this college population suggests the need for additional health promotion strategies on college campuses." I have a better suggestion: avoid college and stay trim.

It's easy to understand why students gain weight at college, especially during their freshman year. While living at home during their high school years, most students had nutritious, balanced meals provided for them. Arriving at college, students face unlimited choices: junk food, fast food, sugary soft drinks, and midnight pizza. Students generally keep their mini-fridge stocked with millions of calories to keep them going through late-night study sessions. Stress-induced cravings lead to binge eating. Many students take up drinking alcohol for the first time in their lives—and alcohol is rich in calories.

So you tell me: Does college make people more mature—or less? Does college make people stronger—or more weak-willed and undisciplined? There's really no question. College is a net-negative for most young people. The majority of young people would be better served to go from high school straight into the workforce, the military, technical school, or some other productive pastime.

People Who Say "Enough Is Enough"

We have just examined Count 1 of our ten-count indictment of the college industry: *"Colleges and universities are running a scam."*

Students and parents know it's a scam—yet many young people willingly sign up to be sheared like sheep so they can say, "I went to Harvard," or so their parents can say, "My kid goes to Yale." They're willing to be swindled by the college cartel just so they can claim some hollow bragging rights.

But there are some people who are willing to stand up and say, "Enough is enough."

Take, for example, Trina Thompson. She graduated from New York's Monroe College with a degree in information technology. Her 2.7 GPA was the equivalent of a B-minus average, which meant that she was a good, but not exceptional, scholar. After graduation, she spent three months applying for jobs but getting nowhere. She searched through the college's recruiting website for job openings, then made phone calls and sent out cover letters and résumés. Only two employers responded, and neither response led to a job offer.

Finally, she filed suit against Monroe College in Bronx Supreme Court, alleging that the school's Office of Career Advancement failed to help her find full-time employment. She sought $70,000 in reimbursement for her tuition and $2,000 compensation for the stress she suffered in her three-month job search.

Thompson claimed the college failed to help her get job interviews as promised. She said, "They're supposed to say, 'I've got this student, her attendance is good, her GPA is all right—can you interview this person?' They're not doing that."

Unable to afford an attorney or even the filing costs, Thompson filed a "poor person order," exempting her from paying the court fees. She lost the case.

I can't say whether Trina Thompson's case had merit or not, but I applaud her for trying to recover reimbursement and damages from the college industry. I don't know what kind of education Monroe College offers. But I do know that the college industry as a whole is wasteful, outrageously expensive, and doesn't keep its promises. In short, the college industry is a scam.

We need more people like Trina Thompson, people who will stand up to the system and say, "I've been scammed and abused by the college cartel. All this time and expense—for what? For a lot of broken promises? For a piece of paper to hang on my wall? All so that a lot of academics and bankers and politicians can get rich?"

That's just the first count of the indictment. Wait till you see the *second* count.

2

THE OBSCENE COST OF A DIPLOMA

COUNT 2:

A College Education Is Ridiculously Overpriced.

The *Wall Street Journal* recently ran a story headlined, "Over 60, and Crushed by Student Loan Debt." It's true. Borrowers in their sixties owe $86 billion in student loan debt—an average of $33,800 per borrower, according to the credit-reporting firm TransUnion. Some 40,000 retirees are having their Social Security checks garnished to pay off student loans. How can people nearing or beyond retirement age be struggling with student loan debt?

Some are paying off loans they took out for their own job retraining after the 2008 recession. Many more are paying off loans for their children's college education.

One such parent, profiled by the *Journal*, is sixty-year-old Christopher Raymond of North Danville, Vermont. He taught high school history for thirty-two years before retiring from the teaching profession. When he was in his late forties, his daughter was accepted to a very expensive private college in Pennsylvania, so Raymond and his wife took out Parent Plus loans. A few years later, Raymond's son was accepted to the University of Maine—so, more loans.

Raymond and his now-ex-wife owe around $136,000 in student loans. His monthly payment is $1,100 (about a quarter of his after-tax income) and his ex-wife's monthly payment is about $800. When big expenses arose, such as roof and stove repairs, he had no emergency fund to cover the costs, and had to take out a personal loan. These expenses forced Raymond to come out of retirement and take a job at an airport merely to service the debt—a debt he expects to be paying on well into his seventies. He calls that debt "a very dark cloud that's always in the back of my mind."

Christopher Raymond's experience is far from unique. The *Wall Street Journal* grimly observes:

> The borrowing buildup has upended the traditional arc of adult life for many Americans. . . . Seniors are finding they have to work longer, holding onto positions younger adults might otherwise receive. They're relying on credit cards and personal loans to pay for basic expenses. People 65 and older account for a growing share of U.S. bankruptcy filers, according to the Consumer Bankruptcy Project; unlike most consumer loans, student debt is rarely dischargeable in bankruptcy.

Take special note of that last line: "student debt is rarely dischargeable in bankruptcy." If you are considering taking out student loans right now, that statement should chill you to the marrow. Consider this: in bankruptcy, you can discharge almost every other form of debt imaginable—car loans, credit card debt, even gambling losses. But by law, you are saddled with student loan debt for as long as it takes to pay it off. That's why student loan debt can keep you living on the ragged edge of insolvency for decades or even the rest of your life.

They Just Want Your Money

This brings us to Count 2 of our ten-count indictment of the college industry: *"A college education is ridiculously overpriced."*

Tuition costs are insane—yet keep rising much faster than the rate of inflation. Because college costs are so outrageously high, few people can afford to go to college without incurring student loan debt. And even if you go bankrupt, it is almost impossible to discharge student loan debt.

Think about it. There are only a few categories of debt that cannot be discharged through bankruptcy: alimony and child support, judgments for willful and malicious injury to others, judgments for death or personal injury due to driving under the influence—and student loan debt. If you are struggling to pay your student loans, you're in the same category as a deadbeat, a scofflaw, or a criminal. Why is that?

There have been a number of changes to the bankruptcy code over the years, most notably the Bankruptcy Abuse Prevention and Consumer Protection Act of 2005 (BAPCPA). Lending institutions, working through lobbyists, pressured politicians of both parties to make it harder for people to discharge debts through bankruptcy. The bill passed both houses with bipartisan support and was signed into law by President George W. Bush.

Under BAPCPA, it became practically impossible to discharge student loan debt, even if you are going through a Chapter 7 (complete liquidation of assets) bankruptcy. In order to discharge the debt, you must prove to the bankruptcy court that repaying the loan would cause you "undue hardship." And it's almost impossible to meet the standard of "undue hardship" unless you are so severely disabled or so old that it would be impossible for you to find employment. You must show that repaying the loans would make it impossible to maintain a "reasonable standard of living"—and most courts consider living in your parents' basement "reasonable."

> Student loan debt cannot be discharged. If you take out a student loan, expect to be married to that loan until it's paid off.

So, for all intents and purposes, student loan debt cannot be discharged. If you take out a student loan, expect to be married to that loan until it's paid off.

When you start repaying your loan, you will send your payments to a loan servicing company (such as Navient, FedLoan, Sallie Mae, or Nelnet). That company is paid through federal contracts and commissions for collecting the debt. The loan servicing companies have no incentive to show you any leniency, to save you any money, or protect you from fraud or abuse. They don't care if you got a good education for a great career—or if you got ripped off. They have no reason to offer you lower payments or more convenient terms. They just want their money, and they want you to keep paying as much as possible for as long as possible.

To maximize their income, these companies use a small portion of their profits to pay lobbyists and make political donations. The goal of these donations is to keep lawmakers on their side—and keep a mountain of student loan debt on your back. Student debt service companies spent more than $4 million lobbying Congress in 2020 alone. That's a lot of money—but in Washington terms, that's chump change. It shows that a lobbyist can buy a congressman or senator for mere tens of thousands of dollars, and the result will be millions of dollars in profits for those companies.

Seth Frotman, executive director of the Student Borrower Protection Center, explains, "The student-loan lobby claims to support students and their families. But the reality is that executives are profiting enormously off of a broken system that leaves so many borrowers crippled in debt. Over the decades, we've seen a revolving door of lobbyists peddle policies designed to exploit the pursuit of the American dream."

In 2010, President Obama signed legislation making the federal government, not banks, the lender of choice for most students. This legislation unleashed a flood of taxpayer money to enrich universities and colleges while driving up tuitions and student loan debt. Colleges and universities know they can jack up tuitions with impunity because they will get paid no matter what.

$150,000, Even $300,000 of Debt for What?

Washington Post columnist Michelle Singletary shared a letter she had received from a reader, asking for advice. The reader, a woman in her late fifties, explained:

> I am financially secure and could retire today with no problems. My friend is recently divorced and in a terrible financial mess. She lost her house, has no job and her husband is not paying the support he is supposed to pay. She has student loan debt of about $150,000 that, according to her, is in an

income-based repayment plan. She was living with her parents, but they are moving into a nursing home. They have to sell the home, so now she is homeless. . . .

She called me sobbing that she has nowhere to go. She begged me to take her in.[4]

Michelle Singletary replied that, before inviting the friend to come live with her, the reader should take precautions to make sure she didn't get stuck financially. Singletary's advice was sound, as far as it went. But if I had received such a letter, I would have zeroed in on the phrase "student loan debt of about $150,000." What?

Singletary completely ignored a question that seems blindingly obvious: How can a person have $150,000 worth of education and still be destitute and homeless? If a college education is as valuable as it's touted to be, shouldn't she have the skills to haul down a six-figure income? Why did such a highly educated person have to live with her elderly parents—and later become homeless?

My friend Sergio Gor graduated from the George Washington University, where the undergrad tuition for 2021–2022 is $59,780 for one academic year—and that number goes up annually.[5] Sergio doesn't regret attending GWU, but he had a clear vision of what he wanted to do in politics and he went on to work in the United States Senate and for President Donald Trump. He feels his experience prepared him well for a professional career in the political world. But he points out that a student should not attend a school like GWU without a clear sense of his or her professional career goals.

"When you consider your tuition, room, and board," Sergio told me, "that diploma is going to cost you a minimum of a quarter of a million dollars. That's a lot of money—and it's a lot of debt if you must take out four years of student loans. I know a lot of people who couldn't get the jobs they wanted and ended up in completely different industries. And that amount of debt is just for a bachelor's degree. If you're pursuing a masters or a doctorate, you're piling up even more debt."

In July 2021, the *Wall Street Journal* published a lengthy and shocking exposé on the higher education racket, with a special focus on the Columbia University film program. According to the *Journal*, recent graduates of the Columbia film program carried a median debt of $181,000. Yet two years after earning a master's in filmmaking, half were earning less than $30,000 a year.

One of those Columbia film grads, twenty-nine-year-old Zack Morrison, is carrying almost $300,000 of student loan debt. Though he landed a studio job in Hollywood, he only earns between $30,000 and $50,000 a year, which he supplements with side gigs as a photographer and videographer. He told the *Journal*, "There's always those 2 a.m. panic attacks where you're thinking, 'How the hell am I ever going to pay this off?'"

Another Columbia film grad, Patrick Clement, attended community college in California, earned a bachelor's degree at the University of Kansas, and graduated with a master's from Columbia in 2020. His debt load: $360,000. That's right, more than a third of a million dollars for a master's degree alone. As of July 2021, he was making an independent film while teaching at a community college and running an antique store.

And then there's Matt Black, who graduated from Columbia in 2015 with a master's in film. He left school owing $233,000 in student loans. In 2021, he still owed $331,000—almost $100,000 more than his original debt. He's on an income-based repayment plan, and when he can't make payments, the interest keeps accruing. His most lucrative year as a writer-producer brought in $60,000. He describes his finances as "calamitous," adding, "We were told by the establishment our whole lives this [an Ivy League education] was the way to jump social classes." He considers himself "hobbled for life" by debt. Marriage and home-ownership seem permanently out of reach.

One Columbia film student, Paul Carpenter, who graduated in 2018, said that the university offered emergency grants to international students. But when Carpenter and other American students ask for financial help, the University told them to "go and take more loans."

The *Journal* concluded, "Highly selective universities have benefited from free-flowing federal loan money, and with demand for spots far exceeding supply, the schools have been able to raise tuition largely unchecked."[6] Many students have no idea what a huge financial obligation they've taken on. Some of our most prestigious universities are taking advantage of naïve young people in a way that's not just inexcusable—it could be viewed as criminal fraud.

Here's a suggestion for anyone who wants to get into filmmaking. Forget the master's degree from an elite university. Go to the library and read every book you can find on filmmaking. Then go to YouTube.com and search "filmmaking." You'll find hundreds of videos on every aspect of filmmaking, including interviews with some of the greatest moviemakers in Hollywood. You'll get a college-level education absolutely free.

Buy some used camera equipment, lights, boom mikes, and even a drone, plus some state-of-the-art digital editing software. Now you can make commercials and independent films, build up your portfolio, and submit it to film producers. If your work is impressive, no one will ask where you went to film school. You'll be on your way.

Attending film school is a way of pretending you are moving toward a film career when you are really putting off adulthood for four years. Colleges and universities excel at making students feel like they're accomplishing something when they're just spinning their wheels and avoiding reality.

A Threat to Our Way of Life

In 2019, *Business Insider* and Morning Consult surveyed 4,400 Americans who had carried student loan debt, including 1,207 identified as millennials, age 22 to 37. The survey found that 44 percent felt that their investment of time and money in a college education had *not* been worthwhile; 53 percent felt their college education *had* been worthwhile. Respondents who were still making payments on their student loans generally felt worse about having gone to college than those whose loans were paid off.

Why are so many Americans dissatisfied with their decision to go to college? *Business Insider* asked Richard Vedder, professor emeritus of economics at Ohio University, for an explanation. He said, "The rewards for college have expanded and grown from 1985 to a little after 2000 and sort of leveled off in the past decade. . . . [The] advantage of a degree today is less than it was 10 years ago, because of the rising cost. The return on investment has fallen."[7]

The American dream was built on a foundation of freedom and opportunity. Debt crushes freedom and limits opportunity. Today, college graduates are struggling—and failing—to achieve their dreams while straining to scale a mountain of student loan debt. The high cost of "higher education" is killing the American dream.

Those costs are also harming the economy, according to a 2017 study by the Federal Reserve Bank of New York. That study—the first to quantify the damage to the U.S. economy from college-related debt—found that student debt had doubled from 2009 to 2017 at the same time homeownership among Americans aged 28 to 30 had sharply declined. The drop in homebuying impacted not only the real estate market but related industries—home furnishings, home repairs, landscaping and gardening supplies, and so forth. The study found that as much as 35 percent of the drop in homeownership could be attributed directly to student loan debt.

The Federal Reserve Bank study concluded that about 360,000 Americans would have owned a home in 2015 *if they had not been prevented from homebuying because of student loan debt.* In other words, for many Americans, a college education delays or prevents the achievement of homeownership. A college education harms a young person's financial prospects—and the U.S. economy.

The study also concluded that the downward trend in homebuying among millennials is bound to continue as tuition costs spiral, increasing the level of student loan debt. At the time of the 2017 study, student loan debt stood at $1.4 trillion. By 2021, that figure topped $1.6 trillion. The trend will undoubtedly continue, with more and more Americans locked out of the homebuying market. And remember, homeowning has historically been the primary avenue for acquiring wealth in America.[8]

People who fall behind on student loan payments suffer severe consequences. Defaulting on student loans can wreck your credit score and result in wages and tax refunds being garnished. But few people realize that, in some states, a student loan default can cost you your professional license and your career.

A report in the *New York Times* "identified at least 8,700 cases in which licenses were taken away or put at risk of suspension" because of student loan default. The *Times* added that the analysis probably underestimated the number of default-related license suspensions. The report cited one case in which a nurse in Nashville, Tennessee, began experiencing epileptic seizures. As a result, she was temporarily unable to work. The lost wages caused her to get behind on her loan payments, which led to the suspension of her license. As a result, she was unable to return to nursing, yet she still must pay off the loans.[9]

Such stories are all too common. Laws intended to motivate people to keep up their loan payments catch them in a vicious cycle that robs them of their careers. They went to college to earn a better future, but the high cost of a diploma *robbed them* of their future.

Since the *New York Times* report, many states have changed their laws to eliminate these drastic punishments from their education debt laws. But several states, including Florida, Minnesota, South Dakota, and Tennessee, can still lift your professional license or your driver's license if you have defaulted on student loans.[10]

A college education, long touted as the doorway to career success, has actually been *proven* to be a roadblock for many to the American dream, homeownership, and a career. The college cartel and the student loan industry are harming young people, hindering their financial mobility and prosperity, roadblocking their careers, and damaging the American economy.

Debt "Forgiveness"?

As an attempt to solve the student loan debt crisis, Senators Elizabeth Warren of Massachusetts and Bernie Sanders of Vermont have put forward a scheme of "student loan forgiveness." These legislative proposals fail to address the spiraling *cost* of a college education. In fact, their proposals would fuel and incentivize even *more* tuition inflation. Warren's plan would have canceled $50,000 in debt for students with a household income less than $100,000. Sanders' $2.2 trillion plan would have canceled all student loan debt regardless of income.[11]

In January 2020, Senator Warren was in Grimes, Iowa, campaigning for the Democratic presidential primary. She stood in the photo line when a man walked up to her and said, "I just wanted to ask one question. My daughter is getting out of school. I've saved all my money. She doesn't have any student loans. Am I going to get my money back?"

"Of course not," Warren said.

"So you're going to pay for people who didn't save any money and those of us who did the right thing get screwed? My buddy had fun, bought a car, and went on all the vacations. I saved my money. He makes more than I did. I worked a double shift, worked extra. And my daughter has worked since she was ten. So, you're laughing at me. Yeah, that's exactly what you're doing. We did the right thing and we get screwed."[12]

> The Warren and Sanders schemes don't actually "forgive" the debt. Only the lender can truly forgive a debt. Warren and Sanders would use taxpayer money to pay off the unpaid debt.

Senator Warren stammered uncomfortably, but had no answer for the man's accusation. Because he was exactly right. This is what the Warren and Sanders "debt forgiveness" plans really mean: if you have already paid off your student loans, or if you saved up for years to avoid taking out loans, or if you went to a less expensive, less prestigious college to be fiscally responsible—too bad, it sucks to be you. In fact, as a taxpayer, you now get to help pay off the student loans of everyone who's debt will be "forgiven."

I put "forgiven" in quotation marks because the Warren and Sanders schemes don't actually "forgive" the debt. Only the lender can truly forgive a debt. Warren and Sanders would use taxpayer money to *pay off* the unpaid debt. The lenders would get paid. The universities would get paid. The borrowers would receive the benefit—and the taxpayers would get stuck with the bill.

In July 2021, Democrats were putting enormous pressure on President Joe Biden to issue an executive order "forgiving" all federal student debt. Even

Senate Majority Leader Chuck Schumer was urging Biden to wave his pen and cancel $1.7 trillion of student debt by executive fiat. In response, House Speaker Nancy Pelosi held a news conference and announced that President Biden didn't have that power under the Constitution.

"The president can't do it," she said. "That's not even a discussion. People think that the President of the United States has the power for debt forgiveness. He does not. He can postpone, he can delay, but he does not have that power. That has to be an act of Congress."[13]

Debt—and Regret

We've looked at the evidence in support of Count 2 of our ten-count indictment of the college industry: *A college education is ridiculously overpriced."* We've seen people of all ages, even retirement age, who are crushed by student loan debt. Loan servicing companies rarely offer lower payments or more convenient terms. Instead, they extract as much money from borrowers as they possibly can.

The obscene cost of a college education is destroying the American Dream and preventing hundreds of thousands of Americans from owning a home and achieving success. Government officials promise to enact student loan "forgiveness"—a promise they don't have the legal authority to keep.

And there's another factor that is driving up the insane cost of a college education: college rankings, such as the rankings published annually by *U.S. News & World Report.* These rankings promote corruption in cost inflation in the college industry and doing serious harm to college students.

The corrupting influence of college rankings was highlighted in December 2020 when Temple University's Fox School of Business and Management agreed to a $700,000 settlement with the Department of Education. Temple was accused of falsifying information to improve its ranking on the *U.S. News and World Report* list. The Department of Education stated:

The Department believes that, to increase enrollment, grow revenue, and harm competitors, Temple's Fox School knowingly, intentionally, and substantially misrepresented the nature of certain of its educational program by advertising the false rankings by *U.S. News and World Report* thousands of times via online portals, social media, fully wrapped buses and newsstands, highway billboard signs, and advertisements at airport terminals, on trains, at train stations, in magazines, in newspapers, and on television and radio.

LiberalArtsColleges.com concludes, "Falsified information is the dirty little secret of college rankings. In order to rank higher on the list, a growing number of colleges are willing to lie about enrollment numbers, graduation rates, and test scores."

U.S. News and World Report reportedly changes its criteria on an annual basis, possibly to shuffle the standings from year to year and sell more magazines. The rankings are largely based on subjective opinion and untrustworthy self-reporting by colleges and universities. The rankings are not based on how much debt a school inflicts on its students, how affordable a school is, how much schools pay for faculty and administration salaries, whether or not a school is top-heavy with administrators and deans, how much financial assistance a school offers low-income students, and other factors relating to the cost of education.

CBS News reports that the rankings system has distorted the admissions and scholarship process at many schools:

Schools care deeply about inching up *U.S. News'* college rankings and this is reflected in how they spend their money. Institutions have been focused on devoting more of their revenue to attract students with higher test scores, class rankings and grade point averages. That's to impress the rankings king.

Consequently, public and private colleges and universities have been pouring a growing amount of money into merit scholarships for affluent students at the expense of students who desperately need financial help.

The *U.S. News and World Report* rankings do not measure how many graduates land good-paying jobs, nor do they measure whether students are learning anything. The ranking criteria exclude excellent colleges like Hillsdale College in favor of legacy schools with name recognition like Princeton, Harvard, and Yale—schools that are increasingly becoming centers of indoctrination instead of education.

The ranking system contributes to the upward spiral of college costs. The higher a school scores in the rankings, the more incentive it has to jack up tuition and fees. If you *must* attend college to pursue your chosen profession, I recommend you trash your copy of *U.S. News and World Report*. Apply your own personal criteria and common sense, then choose the school that is best for you, not a school touted by some magazine editor.

Above all, take a clear-eyed look at your future. If you can have a good career and make a good living without sacrificing a ton of money and four years of your life—then your choice is obvious.

In 2019, CNBC interviewed a number of college graduates who were struggling to make payments on student loans. One was Jarret Freeman, who carried about $50,000 of student debt. "I think that it's so engrained in your head that you have to go to college, that college is the next step after graduation," he said. "I think in hindsight, I see that college is not for everyone."

That is the sadder-but-wiser voice of experience. That is someone who has learned the hard way about the obscene cost of a college education.

3

WHERE DOES ALL THE MONEY GO?

COUNT 3:

Universities have become obscenely rich at student

and taxpayer expense.

In July 2020, during the coronavirus pandemic, Harvard University announced it was charging full tuition for online classes. I tweeted on July 6, "Why is Harvard still charging a full undergraduate tuition rate of $49,653 despite holding all classes online? They have a 41 BILLION dollar endowment. Why are they still ripping students off?"

The same day, *Slate* columnist Jack Shafer tweeted: "Harvard is the new University of Phoenix."[1] And *New Yorker* writer Caitlin Flanagan tweeted, "Harvard suckers customers into paying for the world's most expensive MOOC [massive open online course]."[2] When both Charlie Kirk and liberal columnists agree that Harvard students are being fleeced, the world should take note.

> When both Charlie Kirk and liberal columnists agree that Harvard students are being fleeced, the world should take note.

It's as if we're all characters in the Hans Christian Anderson folktale "The Emperor's New Clothes." Harvard, the emperor of American universities, is strutting around in all its pride and vanity, charging exorbitant tuition for a series of Zoom calls. For years, no one has dared to point out the obvious: a Harvard education is a rip-off. But the pandemic exposed Harvard's swindle so completely that commentators on both left and right pointed fingers and shouted, "The Emperor has no clothes!"

If a Harvard education is a scam, what about all the other over-priced colleges and universities across the nation? Before the pandemic, college costs had been rising at a rate of 3 to 5 percent on average, faster than the rate of inflation, faster than the rise of family income. Some colleges and universities announced a tuition freeze during the 2020 pandemic and economic crisis, while a smaller number announced discounts or tuition cuts.

But several major institutions—notably Stanford, Yale, Amherst, Brown, Dartmouth, Rice, Wellesley, and Grinnell College—boosted their tuitions sharply in 2020, about 4 to 5 percent, even though classes were overwhelmingly taught online.[3] These pandemic-era tuition hikes took a toll on student and family budgets. In 2020, student loan debt exceeded $37,500 per student —and outstanding student debt totaled nearly $1.6 trillion (source: the Federal Reserve Bank of New York).[4]

As the pandemic took its toll on the world, greedy universities continued to gouge students for a Zoom-class learning experience. One that some would argue cost universities less while they charged their students the exact same tuition.

A Hedge Fund with a University Attached

This brings us to Count 3 of our ten-count indictment of the college industry: *"Universities have become obscenely rich at student and taxpayer expense."*

The wealth of a university or college is determined by the size of its endowment—the legal structure the institution uses to manage and perpetuate its financial holdings, investments, and real estate holdings. The ten wealthiest universities in the United States (as of the end of fiscal year 2020) are, from first to tenth:

HARVARD UNIVERSITY, MASSACHUSETTS

Endowment: $41,894,380,000 ($41.9 billion)

YALE UNIVERSITY, CONNECTICUT

Endowment: $31,108,248,000 ($31.1 billion)

STANFORD UNIVERSITY, CALIFORNIA

Endowment: $28,948,111,000 ($29.0 billion)

PRINCETON UNIVERSITY, NEW JERSEY

Endowment: $25,944,300,000 ($26.0 billion)

MASSACHUSETTS INSTITUTE OF TECHNOLOGY

Endowment: $18,381,518,000 ($18.4 billion)

University of Pennsylvania

Endowment: $14,877,363,000 ($14.9 billion)

Texas A&M University

Endowment: $12,720,529,611 ($12.7 billion)

UNIVERSITY OF NOTRE DAME, INDIANA

Endowment: $12,319,422,000 ($12.3 billion)

UNIVERSITY OF MICHIGAN—ANN ARBOR

Endowment: $12,308,473,000 ($12.3 billion)

COLUMBIA UNIVERSITY, NEW YORK

Endowment: $11,257,021,000 ($11.3 billion)

(Source: U.S. News & World Report, September 2021)[5]

Some of the universities on this list have endowments that are larger than the entire gross domestic product of such nations as Latvia ($38.1 billion), Estonia ($33.2 billion), Iceland ($26.8 billion), and Zimbabwe ($25.8 billion).[6] These universities are crazy-rich, and getting richer all the time, thanks to taxpayer-financed federal subsidies and ever-rising tuitions.

College students have always griped about inedible cafeteria food, not enough parking, sloppy roommates, and being nickeled and dimed by student fees. But in recent years, student complaints have been increasingly focused on the soaring cost—and diminishing value—of a college education. Textbook prices climb faster than the rate of inflation. Many professors double-dip by publishing their own textbooks, then requiring students to buy them.

Outrageous profit has replaced education as the mission of today's universities. Astra Taylor, cofounder of the Debt Collective, wrote in *The Nation* that an institution of higher learning is best described as "a hedge fund with a university attached." She quoted a Malcolm Gladwell tweet: "I was going to donate money to Yale. But maybe it makes more sense to mail a check directly to the hedge fund of my choice."

Taylor tells the story of Dartmouth University board chairman Stephen F. Mandel Jr., who is also founder and president of the hedge fund Lone Pine Capital. Lone Pine managed Dartmouth's investments. Dartmouth trustees, Taylor wrote, "were blasted, in a widely cited open letter, for recycling a portion of their 'sky high fees' back to the university as 'donations' for which they were often rewarded by having a building named in their honor."[7]

Dartmouth is far from unique in having ethically conflicted hedge fund managers on its board. The result of these cozy financial arrangements is that universities pile up mountains of cash from tuitions and donations, then Wall Street places hedge fund managers on university boards. The hedge fund managers approve self-dealing investment schemes with university funds. Meanwhile, tuitions continue to soar, students take on more and more debt, and the value of a college diploma plummets.

To keep the money spigot flowing, the hedge funds send their lobbying arm, the Managed Funds Association, to Congress to lobby for "student debt relief" legislation to soak the taxpayer and funnel *more* federal money through the universities to the hedge fund tycoons.

It almost seems as if amassing huge piles of cash is the primary function of the university—and "education" is merely an afterthought.

Where It All Goes

Writing in *The Atlantic* in 2018, Cornell-educated journalist Amanda Ripley makes what (at first glance) appears to be an indictment of the college cartel:

> Today, the U.S. spends more on college than almost any other country, according to the 2018 Education at a Glance report . . . [from] the Organization for Economic Cooperation and Development (OECD).
>
> All told, including the contributions of individual families and the government (in the form of student loans, grants, and other assistance), Americans spend about $30,000 per student a year—nearly twice as much as the average developed country. "The U.S. is in a class of its own," says Andreas Schleicher, the director for education and skills at the OECD, and he does not mean this as a compliment. "Spending per student is exorbitant, and it has virtually no relationship to the value that students could possibly get in exchange."[8]

But Ripley goes on to explain away the cost of a college education in America. She suggests, for example, that because "college is a service delivered mostly by workers with college degrees," that service will inevitably become more expensive as the cost of a college degree rises. She completely fails to understand that the vast infusions of federal cash are the real driving force behind tuition inflation.

Ripley accurately notes that many universities are accepting a disproportionately large number of out-of-state and foreign students at inflated tuition rates. As a result, in-state students, whose families pay taxes in that state, are elbowed aside and unable to get into the school of their choice. She points to Purdue University, which cut its in-state student rolls by 4,300 while adding 5,300 out-of-state and foreign students, who pay *triple* the in-state tuition. Instead of educating the young people of their own communities, many universities now greedily compete for privileged, affluent out-of-state and foreign students.

She briefly observes that American colleges spend "a startling amount of money on their nonteaching staff"—from librarians to counselors to fund-raisers to food-service workers to "diversity-and-inclusion managers" and on and on.[9] But she really doesn't dwell on this factor enough.

In 2012, Nobel laureate neurobiologist David H. Hubel of Harvard Medical School (HMS) wrote an opinion piece for the *Harvard Crimson* titled "A Top-Heavy Administration?" He recalled that when he came to HMS in the 1950s, the school was directed by one dean and one assistant dean. By 2012, the list of HMS deans was a page and a quarter long, and included nine academic deans, one executive dean of research, a dean of faculty affairs, a dean of medical education, a dean of graduate education, a dean of clinical and translational research, a dean of students, a dean of diversity and community partnership, a dean of academic and clinical affairs, nine administrative deans, and a four-person council of academic deans.

Hubel added that the one-and-a-quarter-page list of HMS deans was dwarfed by the *sixteen pages* which listed the deans of Harvard's Faculty of Arts and Sciences (FAS). Nearly a decade later, as this book goes to press, the list is undoubted much longer.

David H. Hubel recalled a conversation with Henry Rosovsky, Harvard's Dean of FAS from 1973 to 1984. Hubel said, "I asked him how many deans of various kinds there were [at FAS] when he held the office. He held up an index finger, 'one,' and he pointed to himself, 'me.'"

Hubel concludes that while there are many reasons for the soaring cost of a college education, a chief cause is administrative bloat. "The administration's growth has outrun that of the University," he writes, adding, "The next time that Harvard undergraduates and medical students ask themselves why their fees are so high, they could estimate the annual salaries and expenses of the various deans, their secretaries, and assistants—and do some arithmetic."[10]

In her piece for *The Atlantic*, Amanda Ripley wrongly concludes that the solution to skyrocketing college costs is for "a centralized government authority" to step in and impose price controls on colleges and universities. But the problem is not that there is too little government control. It's that there is *too much government money* in education. Government is the problem, not the solution.

Government, doing the bidding of lobbyists, has opened the floodgates of money via the federal student loan system. The system is already rigged to make the universities, lenders, lobbyists, and politicians rich. Who in that corrupt system has any motivation to use the "centralized government authority" to cap tuitions? That notion is as fanciful as calling upon Santa Claus, Superman, and the Tooth Fairy to team up and solve the problem.

Let's get real. You cannot fix a corrupt government system with more corrupt government intervention. The college cartel is simply unfixable.

A Student-Led Counter-Offensive?

I give 330 speeches a year, record two podcasts a day, and host a three-hour daily radio show. I have my finger on the pulse of America and I have a good idea of what people are saying and thinking across the country. One claim I often hear, especially from older members of my audience, is, "Students are lazy and don't know how to work hard. They should get a job and stop complaining about how expensive and difficult life is. Life was hard for my generation, so I don't have any sympathy for these young complainers."

> To accuse today's young people of being lazy or spoiled is not entirely fair.

I have to admit that I used to make similar statements myself. But I now realize that this is an overgeneralization and an unfair characterization of students. To accuse today's young people of being lazy or spoiled is not entirely fair. After all, the Great College Scam is unconscionably expensive. And this scam really does make life difficult for today's students in ways never before seen in American history. The current model of college victimizes an entire generation of young people.

From the time a toddler enters kindergarten, that child is bombarded with college propaganda. By the time they reach the fourth grade, students are continually told, "You need to apply yourself in school so you'll be able to go to college and have a successful life." When they reach high school, no one asks *if* they are going to college but *where*.

> At the same time, students are inundated with loan offers—and what eighteen-year-old can resist the offer of all that money for just a few mouse clicks?

At the same time, students are inundated with loan offers—and what eighteen-year-old can resist the offer of all that money for just a few mouse clicks? And the lenders don't even require parental consent. So young people are enticed into a long-term debt agreement, seduced into borrowing money they don't have at interest rates they can't afford to study subjects that don't matter to prepare them for jobs that will never exist. From then on, they are shackled in a twenty-first-century form of indentured servitude.

Then, along comes Senator Bernie Sanders, the socialist from Vermont, with a nakedly transactional promise to trade taxpayer dollars for student votes. The cost of so-called "student debt forgiveness" would bankrupt the country— but students don't understand the meaning of fiscal responsibility. After all, no one ever mentions such matters at college. They figure that Bernie Sanders is a United States Senator and he was almost the Democratic Party's presidential nominee, so he must know what he's talking about

I can understand why many conservatives say, "Students only want free stuff—that's why they want debt forgiveness. That's why they support Bernie." But I can also understand why many debt-burdened students find Bernie's hollow promises so attractive. Few students have the economic education and maturity to understand that the government can't simply print mountains of money and make their debt go away.

Bernie Sanders should be censured by the Senate for preying on the naïveté of college students. We should all be fiercely opposed to student debt forgiveness. It would be a scam on the taxpayer and an injustice toward those (like myself) who didn't go to college—and an even worse injustice toward those who worked their way through college without accumulating debt. After all, why should those who made financially prudent decisions be taxed and penalized to pay off the debts of others? Why should the American taxpayer pay higher taxes to finance Bernie Sanders's vote-buying scheme?

Sanders postures as a kind of secular Moses—a socialist liberator who would set all students free from bondage to soul-crushing debt. Well, Bernie Sanders may have been around since Moses, but students need to know that he's no liberator. His promise to give students something for nothing is political huckstership, nothing more.

Bernie has struck a nerve with college-age people. Students today know they've been victimized by a voracious trillion-dollar money machine—and they want to be compensated for being seduced into a financially ruinous decision. Their support for Bernie and his policies is rooted in their resentment toward the college cartel for selling them into bondage.

I don't agree that they deserve to be rescued from their bad decisions by the taxpayers. But I do sympathize with them and I think it would be a mistake to simply condemn their motives. Instead, I would encourage political leaders on the right to understand these students, embrace their energy and anger toward the college cartel, and enlist them in a counter-offensive to right the wrongs that have been done to them in the name of "higher education."

Student loan forgiveness? Absolutely not. But telling students who the *real* villains are in the Great College Scam? Holding the college system accountable for hiking tuitions to insane heights while sitting on massive endowments? Working to defund these rich, oppressive institutions by divesting and diverting donor funds? Yes, absolutely, let's do it—and the sooner the better.

Student Loan Oppressors

According to *U.S. News & World Report*, the average tuition in 2021–2022 for a private college is $38,185; average tuition for an in-state public college is $10,388. So a four-year college education would cost, on average, between $41,000 and $152,000.[11] That would make a college diploma the most wildly overpriced piece of paper you own.

A bachelor's degree used to offer proof to a potential employer of a candidate's ability to read and comprehend, think and reason, learn and grow, and communicate effectively. Today, employers know that many college graduates can barely read their own diplomas, which in turn drops the value of a bachelor's degree to nearly zero.

Michael Arceneaux is a Houston-based, *New York Times* bestselling essayist. His 2018 collection *I Can't Date Jesus* reflects on his early years as a young black gay man growing up in a Catholic family. His 2020 book *I Don't Want to Die Poor* deals largely with his struggle to survive the crushing burden of student loan debt.

"The first time I got one of my now-many student loan debt collection calls, I was mortified," Arceneaux wrote. "Me? Behind on a payment? No, no, no."

He feared late payments impacting his credit, upsetting his chances of owning a house or taking a vacation. He also feared being hounded by creditors for years to come. He was ready to sacrifice anything to make his payments on time. But when his employer was slow paying his summer wages, Arceneaux couldn't make his loan payments. "It was so easy to fall back behind," he wrote. "The system was designed this way."

He began ignoring the calls from his "student loan oppressors." This only prompted the lenders to start calling his mother, who had cosigned his loans.

Whenever Arceneaux would get some cash, he'd call the lender. The first question the lender would ask is if he would like to pay the entire outstanding balance. "I try not to laugh," he wrote. "Do you think I called to give you that much? If I did, I would have paid online, fool. No, this call is to perform damage control with what I have to offer. But cute of you to be that optimistic given your line of work." No, he didn't say that out loud, but he thought it as he politely offered to make the minimum payment, about $800.

The person on the phone would inevitably ask why he had fallen behind on his payments. "The question enrages me every single time, but I have to maintain my composure. . . . I try not to be rude to people who haven't been rude to me."

Arceneaux recalled that he tried to refinance once, but gave up when he realized that all of the refi companies were trying to make his situation worse. "One company in particular made an offer to somehow expand my debt from a 12-year repayment structure to a 30-year one without decreasing the monthly payments by any significant figure."

He concluded, "I stuck with the devil I had come to know."[12]

Arceneaux's term for the student loan system, "student loan oppressors," is perfectly appropriate. The system *is* oppressive and deliberately designed to keep students in debt for as long as possible.

The universities, the lenders, the lobbyists, and the politicians all get rich while the student remains trapped for years or decades in involuntary servitude to the oppressors. You can't reform a system like this. The people who have the power to fix the system have no interest in doing so. The only way We the People can fix this corrupt system is to defund and depopulate it by refusing to take part in it.

> The student loan system is oppressive and deliberately designed to keep students in debt for as long as possible.

To sum up Count 3 of our ten-count indictment of the college industry, we have asked the question, *"Where does all the money go?"* The answer is that universities, lenders, and politicians have become obscenely rich at the expense of students and taxpayers. So you have to ask yourself: "Do I want to continue propping up this scam? Do I really want to impoverish myself and take on a crushing weight of debt to enrich the corrupt, exploitative 'education' cartel?"

It's not time for your verdict yet. We have seven more counts of the indictment to examine.

4

WHAT DOES ONE EVEN LEARN IN COLLEGE?

> COUNT 4:
>
> **Colleges do not educate anymore.**

I used to enjoy visiting college campuses incognito. I looked like a college student, so it was easy to blend in. I would sit in on big lecture classes at Stanford or Harvard and other schools. I'd hear what the professors had to say about economics or political science or journalism. They don't take roll and they don't care who's there and who's not. If you look like a college student, you can learn a lot about what is being taught in those courses.

For a while, I thought it might make an amusing documentary to send a young person on campus with a hidden camera to secretly audit classes. The documentary would show how easy it is to get a college education—everything but the diploma—completely free of charge.

But as I sat in on those classes, I quickly saw a flaw in my documentary idea—there was as much indoctrination and misinformation being handed out in those lecture halls as there was genuine education. I sat in on dozens of classes filled with dangerous postmodern ideas, Critical Race Theory, Marxism, and more.

I thought, *So this is "higher education." This is what I've been missing by not going to college?*

In much the same way that ice cream manufacturers shrink the size of their carton an ounce or two every few years to disguise the price inflation of their product, the education industry has been shrinking the size of its product while increasing the cost. Colleges and universities keep shortening the school year, even as they raise tuition costs faster than the rate of inflation. In 1914, the average college class was in session 204 days per year. In 1939, 195 days per year. In 1964, 191 days per year. In 1996, 156 days per year. Today, the average academic year is 150 class days.[1] The ultimate insult to our intelligence came during the pandemic in 2020 when the number of classroom days at many institutions dropped to zero yet the tuition continued to rise.

At the same time colleges and universities are giving us fewer days in class, they are dumbing down the curricula. George Leef of North Carolina's James G. Martin Center for Academic Renewal offers this assessment:

> On the whole, students get surprisingly little value from college. Standards are low and the curriculum is weak. Many faculty members are more concerned with being popular than with sound education. . . .
>
> Low achievement in high school means that many students will enter college with poor skills, but with the expectation that they'll receive high grades for minimal work. To keep those kids happy and paying, most colleges have decided to accommodate their desires.[2]

To extend our ice cream analogy, colleges and universities are not only shrinking the package, but they are replacing the real cream, sugar, and vanilla extract with skim milk, saccharine, and tasteless fillers. They keep charging more and more for an increasingly inferior educational product.

An Indictment of Fraud

This brings us to Count 4 of our ten-count indictment of the college industry: *"Colleges do not educate anymore."* Students literally go through the college system and emerge having learned nothing at all. As a result, employers are concluding, "We can't hire college grads. They can't do the job. College has ruined them as potential employees."

A few years ago, the chancellor and football coach at the University of North Carolina-Chapel Hill were fired. The chair of the school's African Studies department was indicted for felony fraud—though the criminal charge was dropped because of his cooperation with the investigation. What happened at UNC Chapel Hill?

Well, it seemed that as many as 200 classes listed by the African Studies department either didn't exist or were only taught on an irregular basis. Predictably, many of these courses were very popular with UNC athletes, many of whom could barely read or write. As University of Tennessee law professor Glenn Harlan Reynolds observed in *USA Today*, UNC's "'students' who are functionally illiterate strike at the very point of college, which is, supposedly, to educate."[3]

How did UNC get away with offering a phantom African Studies department, year after year, without anybody detecting the scam? Where was the administrative oversight? Why didn't anyone get suspicious about a catalog full of nonexistent college courses? Kevin Carey, director of the Education Policy Program at the New America Foundation, offers two possible explanations:

> UNC Chapel Hill is not a coherent undergraduate institution. It's a holding company that provides shared marketing, finance and physical plant services for a group of autonomous departments, which are in turn holding companies for autonomous scholars who teach as they please. This is the only possible explanation for the years-long, wholly undetected operation of the African and Afro-American Studies Department credit fraud scam. Or, rather, it's the only possible explanation other than a huge, organization-wide conspiracy in which the university administration, department, and football team colluded to hand out fake grades to hundreds of athletes.[4]

The facts allow only those two alternatives: either UNC Chapel Hill was a sprawling collection of profit-driven fiefdoms and the right hand didn't know what the left was doing—or it was a completely corrupt conspiracy. Take your pick.

Who gets burned by the Chapel Hill fraud? Well, the students and parents who spent their life savings or borrowed tons of money certainly get burned. But what about the employers who trusted that a Chapel Hill grad had a proven ability to read, understand, communicate, work hard, and add value to a company? They get burned as well.

By the way, according to CNN, this scandal went on for 18 years. CNN further continued, UNC Chapel Hill admitted to thousands of students taking fake "paper classes" and advisers funneling athletes into these programs to inflate their grades. Do you think any of their grade got corrected after nearly 2 decades of this scam? Though UNC Chapel Hill was forced to stop offering one fraudulent product—nonexistent classes—it is almost impossible to guess how one would correct thousands of grades over so many years.

How much would you bet that this kind of fraud is limited to one campus of one university in the state of North Carolina? The truth is that most "higher education" being peddled today is fraudulent. Think that's an over-the-top claim? Keep reading. I'll show you.

No Improvement

In 2011, the University of Chicago Press published a book that leveled a shocking accusation at so-called "higher education" in America. Titled Academically Adrift: Limited Learning on College Campuses, the book was written by sociologists Richard Arum of New York University and Josipa Roksa of the University of Virginia. The authors analyzed standardized test data provided by the Collegiate Learning Assessment (CLA). The test data was based on a representative sample of 2,300 undergraduates from twenty-four colleges and universities. The students took the CLA exam at the beginning of their freshman year in fall 2005 and again at the end of their sophomore year in spring 2007.

The study found that, after two years of college, 45 percent of students showed no meaningful improvement in key measures of writing ability, critical thinking, and complex reasoning. Authors Arum and Roksa turned up surprising statistics that help explain why so many students got so little out of college. Half of the students in the study never took a single course requiring as much as twenty pages of writing during the most recent semester. One-third were not required by any course to read forty pages per week. The students in the study were not being challenged to study hard or learn very much.

In recent years, many education reformers have focused on trying to raise graduation rates. But getting more college students to graduate without attempting to better educate them is mere credentialism. Richard Arum warned against this sham approach to education in an interview: "It's not the case that giving out more credentials is going to make the U.S. more economically competitive. It requires academic rigor."[5]

Poorly motivated students deserve some of the blame. Arum and Roksa point out that some students select the easiest courses and prefer hanging out over studying—and that's why they get nothing out of college. But these are precisely the kinds of young people I've been saying have no business being in college. They have no life goals or career plans. They don't want to learn or grow or be challenged. They just want to check the boxes and get the piece of paper.

You might think that in the decade since Academically Adrift was published, colleges and universities might have improved their educational product. But no, they haven't.

Wasted Money, Stolen Years

In June 2017, the *Wall Street Journal* published a report titled "Exclusive Test Data: Many Colleges Fail to Improve Critical-Thinking Skills." The report was based on an extensive study of students at 200 American colleges. The study examined the results of tests taken by students in their freshman and senior years, between 2013 and 2016—a full four-year span of college experience. The test used was an updated version of the CLA known as the Collegiate Learning Assessment Plus (CLA+).

"The results," the *Journal* concluded, "are discouraging. . . . At some of the most prestigious flagship universities, test results indicate the average graduate shows little or no improvement in critical thinking over four years." The results were not all bad. The *Journal* noted, "Some of the biggest gains occur at smaller colleges where students are less accomplished at arrival but soak up a rigorous, interdisciplinary curriculum."[6]

The most accomplished and improved students tended to be at schools where there is *no focus* on faculty research, sports programs, graduate programs, or on-campus amenities—schools that place a *primary* emphasis on teaching young people how to think. So if you really must go to college and you're really there to *learn*, you're much better off at a no-name school with a solid academic tradition and a strong core curriculum than at one of the "prestige" campuses.

The *Journal* stated that its findings appear to be "a sign of the failure of America's higher-education system to arm graduates with analytical reasoning and problem-solving skills needed to thrive in a fast-changing, increasingly global job market. . . . International rankings show U.S. college graduates are in the middle of the pack when it comes to numeracy and literacy and near the bottom when it comes to problem solving."[7]

The report also cited a survey by PayScale Inc. which showed that *fully half* of all employers they surveyed complain that college grads simply aren't prepared for the workplace. The most often-cited reason college grads are poor hires: they lack critical-reasoning skills. We have to ask ourselves: How do so many students slide through the halls of academia, grab a diploma after four years, yet show zero improvement in their ability to reason and solve problems? Clearly, that diploma is *prima facie* evidence of a fraudulent education.

As sociologist Josipa Roksa laments, "Students basically spend four years in college, and they don't necessarily become better thinkers and problem solvers. Employers are going to hire the best they can get, and if we don't have that, then what is at stake in the long run is our ability to compete."[8]

According to CLA+ test results, three-fourths of seniors at the University of Louisiana at Lafayette demonstrated "basic" or "below basic" mastery—the two lowest of five CLA+ rankings. The *Journal* interviewed one graduate of that school who happened to be working in a Lafayette coffee shop. "I wasn't as focused as I should have been," the barista admitted, "but in a lot of classes, we just watched videos and documentaries, and then we would talk about them. It wasn't all that challenging."[9]

The *Academically Adrift* and *Wall Street Journal* studies are an indictment of the entire "higher education" scam. With few exceptions, colleges and universities are guilty not merely of failure, but of fraud. These schools are guilty of wasting the money of these students and their parents—and stealing years of their lives, years that could be more productively spent in the job market or a trade school.

Can You Spot the False Premise?

"To succeed in America, you must get a college degree," wrote Gawker's Hamilton Nolan. "To get a college degree, you must go into a soul-crushing amount of debt. And what do you get for all that money? Not learning. College kids don't learn stuff."[10]

Did you spot the false premise in that statement?

Let's look at another statement, this time from Amanda Ripley, writing in *The Atlantic*. See if you can find the fallacy: "If American colleges are not adding obvious and consistent academic value, they are adding financial value. Americans with college degrees earn 75 percent more than those who only completed high school. Over a lifetime, people with bachelor's degrees earn more than half a million dollars more than people with no college degree."[11]

I hope you've got your critical thinking cap on and you spotted these errors in logic: "To succeed in America, you must get a college degree." "Americans with college degrees earn 75 percent more than those who only completed high school." Both statements falsely assume that a college degree causes graduates to be financially successful, and that success is impossible without a degree. This assumption is clearly false.

Our own government is responsible for perpetuating this myth. For example, the United States Census Bureau's document "The Big Payoff: Educational

Attainment and Work-Life Earnings" states, "This report illustrates the economic value of an education, that is, the added value of a high school diploma
or college degree. It explores the relationship between educational attainment
and earnings . . ."[12] Similarly, the U.S. Bureau of Labor Statistics document
"Employment Projections: Education Pays" displays a graph of "Earnings and
Unemployment Rates by Educational Attainment, 2020." Here's the data from
that graph:

	Median usual weekly earnings	Unemployment Rate
DOCTORAL DEGREE	$1,885	2.5%
PROFESSIONAL DEGREE	$1,893	3.1%
MASTER'S DEGREE	$1,545	4.1%
BACHELOR'S DEGREE	$1,305	5.5%
ASSOCIATE'S DEGREE	$ 938	7.1%
SOME COLLEGE, NO DEGREE	$ 877	8.3%
HIGH SCHOOL DIPLOMA	$ 781	9.0%
LESS THAN A HIGH SCHOOL DIPLOMA	$ 619	11.7%[13]

> A college degree has no magical ability to transform you into a high achiever.

Clearly, there is a statistical correlation between
one's level of education and lifetime earnings. But
does that mean that a college education *causes* higher
lifetime earnings? On the surface, these statistics *seem*
to confirm the claim made by Hamilton Nolan: "To
succeed in America, you must get a college degree."

The statistics also seem to confirm Amanda Ripley's claim that even though
American colleges are "not adding obvious and consistent academic value,
they are adding financial value." But think about it: If students aren't learning
anything, if college adds no "academic value" to their lives, how does college add
"financial value" to their lives? If colleges don't teach, what is this mysterious

alchemy that magically transforms college grads into high earners?

A college degree has no magical ability to transform you into a high achiever. We need to remember this simple principle of logic: "Correlation does not imply causation." The mere fact that two variables *appear* to be correlated does not prove that one *caused* the other. In most cases, *a college degree does not cause higher earnings.*

Yes, the more education people have, the more they earn. But the *real* reason college-educated people earn more is obvious once you think about it: *The kind of people who are the likeliest to succeed in life are also the kind of people who are the likeliest to succeed in college.*

High-achievers are focused, goal-oriented, clear-thinking, problem-solving people. High-achievers tend to go to college. Why? Because their parents, peers, and society have convinced them that they need a college degree to succeed in life. So they go to college, they get their degree, then they go out into the world and earn a significant income.

Did college add "financial value" to their lives? In most cases, no. According to the Federal Reserve Bank of New York, only 27 percent of college graduates end up in a career related to their college major.[14] So don't expect that Sociology or Art History major to boost your lifetime earnings.

And let's be clear: professional and doctoral degrees are obvious exceptions to this rule. If you are intently focused on a career in medicine, law, engineering, or some similar profession, *higher education can add both academic and financial value to your life.* Just be prepared for the added price tag for all those post-grad studies.

> Don't be fooled. Instead, consider carefully whether college will add real value to your life.

But most college grads don't have to go to college to succeed. They would succeed financially, college or no college. But because they bought the myth that "to succeed in America, you must get a college degree," they wasted four years of their lives, got their ticket punched, and went on to successful, lucrative careers. If they had shrugged off the myth and skipped college, most would have achieved the same results four years earlier and *without* taking on a crippling load of debt.

The notion that a college degree is going to magically increase your earnings over your career is a lie that colleges tell you. Don't be fooled. Instead, consider carefully whether college will add real value to your life. Think critically and logically about your future, then make an informed choice.

What about STEM?

If you want a college education that delivers *real* return on your investment, forget about majoring in the Humanities, Liberal Arts, History, or Sociology. Those majors won't improve your critical thinking ability, nor will they enhance your lifetime earnings. And unless you plan to become an academic and teach future generations how to be easily offended and perpetually angry, don't even *think* about the "grievance majors" like Women's Studies, Gender Studies, or Ethnic Studies.

However, there are still areas of emphasis in American universities that frequently deliver a bang for your education buck. I'm speaking of the STEM fields—Science, Technology, Engineering, and Mathematics. If you want a career in a STEM-related field, you've picked a field where many universities in the United States still excel—at least for now.

An international study, led by Prashant Loyalka of Stanford's Graduate School of Education, compared computer science students in four countries. The study revealed that undergrad computer science programs at American schools turn out better-skilled students than equivalent programs in Russia, India, and China. Published in 2019 in the Proceedings of the National Academy of Sciences, the study is based on a two-hour standardized test developed by the Educational Testing Service. It was administered to 551 students in Russia, 364 students in India, 678 students in China, and 6,847 college seniors in the United States.

Loyalka concluded, "Our results suggest that the U.S. is doing a great job at least in terms of computer science education compared to these three other major countries."[15]

In March 2021, the National Research University Higher School of Economics published the results of the Supertest, an international test of engineering students in the United States, Russia, India, and China. The Supertest (developed by Stanford University and partner universities in Russia, China, and India) tracked the performance of more than 30,000 engineering and computer science undergrads in those four countries. The students were tested three times—at the beginning, the midpoint, and the end of their four-year course of studies. The exam tested their mastery of critical thinking, physics, and mathematics.

The Supertest found that U.S. students showed the most improvement over four years, especially in critical thinking skills. Igor Chirikov of the Center for Studies in Higher Education at U.C. Berkeley explained the Supertest findings: "As the students progress in their studies, their critical thinking skills remain approximately the same in Russia and India, but significantly decrease in China. On the contrary, American students show improvement."

Chirikov suggested that the poorer performance of the Chinese students might be explained because China's undergrad education emphasizes lectures and China's instructors "are not as demanding as in Russia and India."[16] I'm not persuaded. I think it's more likely that the oppressive Communist system in China discourages critical thinking and encourages slavish conformity of thought.

That same Marxist-inspired tyranny and pressure to conform pervades the woke liberal arts, humanities, and sociology departments of American colleges and universities, which is why critical thinking is dead in most of American academia. The Supertest results suggest that the STEM departments of U.S. colleges and universities have largely been spared from the woke madness that has infected the rest of American academia. So, at least for now, a STEM concentration is one of the few areas of a college education that could add both academic and financial value to your life.

But be warned: even STEM education is under assault by the "woke" social justice cabal. The University of California San Diego recently posted job openings for professors and assistant professors of chemistry and biochemistry, with the requirement that applicants must be able to "design and teach undergraduate courses that align with the African American Studies Minor (AASM) and the Black Diaspora and African American Studies Major." Candidates should not apply unless they have conducted research or service to advance the "anti-racism, anti-oppression, equity, and justice" agenda. There are comparable requirements for those seeking to teach engineering or computer science.[17] Translation: if you want to teach science at UC San Diego, you must also be able to teach that America is racist and oppressive, that white people have racism encoded in their DNA, and the entire American system must be torn down.

If you want a high-quality STEM education, investigate thoroughly and choose your school wisely. I guarantee UC San Diego isn't the only university injecting "woke" leftist dogma into their curriculum. (In chapter 5, we'll take a closer look at how "wokeness" has infected and corrupted the teaching of biology and medicine at major universities.)

Consider, too, that your STEM education will have no value unless you end up in a STEM-related career—and very few college graduates do. Of the roughly 2 million students who graduate from college every year, only 18 percent graduate in a STEM-related major, according to the National Center for Education Statistics.[18] And are you ready for this? According to the U.S. Census Bureau's American Community Survey, *only half* of all college grads with STEM degrees are employed in STEM occupations—and almost a third of STEM workers do not have a bachelor's degree (15 percent have an associate degree, 14 percent have attended some college, and 3 percent have no college).[19]

Even though China's STEM students lag behind American college students in terms of critical thinking skills, China is redoubling its efforts to produce a highly educated workforce of scientists, technologists, engineers, and mathematicians. Writing in *Inside Higher Ed*, Elizabeth Redden observes, "The U.S. share of global science and technology activity has shrunk in some areas even as . . . China and other Asian countries have invested in science and engineering education and increased their research spending. . . . When it comes to the number of science and engineering degrees awarded, China has caught up quickly, and on some measures it outperforms the U.S."[20]

One sign of Communist China's single-minded obsession with outperforming the United States is the Gaokao, China's national college entrance exam. This standardized test is taken by China's students in their final year of high school. Parents and teachers put enormous pressure on students to prepare for the Gaokao. Some parents even take a months-long leave of absence from their jobs to help their children study for the exam. The intense stress of the Gaokao frequently leads to teen depression and suicide. A poor showing on the exam can bring shame on the student's family. A high score, however, is a ticket to a prestigious university in China and the prospect of a successful career.

Many Chinese parents, when they know their student is unlikely to perform well on the Gaokao, send their student to the United States for a less challenging (i.e., dumbed down) liberal arts education. As Peggy Blumenthal of the Institute of International Education explained to *Science* magazine, parents who want to shield their children from the "pressure cooker" of the rigid Chinese higher education system find an American liberal arts education to be "an attractive alternative." American colleges and universities give Chinese families "a unique opportunity to shop" for a school, based on the institution's reputation and cost.

What does that say about the value of a liberal arts education in the United States? It tells me that Chinese students who can't hack a rigorous STEM education in China have figured out how to get an easy-peasy degree: simply attend an American college. These Chinese students and their parents are playing the same credentialism game that many American students play: just go along with the scam and get your ticket punched.

This is further evidence of the worthlessness of most American "higher education."

Ruining a Generation

Russell Ronald Reno III holds a BA from Haverford College and a doctorate in philosophy from Yale University. He taught theology and ethics at Creighton University from 1990 to 2010. Today, R. R. Reno is the editor of the ecumenical religious journal *First Things* magazine. Despite his Ivy League education and his long association with academia, he wants nothing to do with the current crop of graduates from elite schools.

"Why I Stopped Hiring Ivy League Graduates" is the title of a June 2021

piece Reno penned for the *Wall Street Journal*. "I'm not inclined to hire a graduate from one of America's elite universities," he wrote. "That marks a change. A
decade ago, I relished the opportunity to employ talented graduates of Princeton, Yale, Harvard and the rest. Today? Not so much."

In the fall of 2020, Reno looked into the campus unrest and the student
strike at his alma mater, Haverford College. The school had become, in his
words, "a progressive hothouse." During a Zoom meeting for Haverford undergrads, he saw students displaying "thin-skinned narcissism and naked aggression" which college officials met with "self-abasing apologies." The experience
convinced Reno that students today are not being prepared to function as team
members in an organizational environment. They are too easily triggered, too
quick to "panic over pseudo-crises," and too eager to make "inflammatory accusations."

Reno acknowledges that woke student activists are a minority on campus,
not representative of most of the student body. However, there was no one on
campus willing to stand up against the shrill and abusive activists. Were the un-
woke majority cowed into silence out of fear of being called "racists"? Why did
the majority timidly acquiesce to the bullying behavior of the loud minority?

As an employer, Reno wants people in his organization who will stand firm
on their principles and demonstrate strong leadership. He finds that most students at elite Ivy League schools have learned to keep their convictions to themselves—and some seem to "manifest a form of post-traumatic stress disorder."

Are there any colleges Reno does recommend? "My rule of thumb," he
writes, "is to hire from institutions I advise young people to attend. Hillsdale
College is at the top of that list, as are quirky small Catholic colleges such as
Thomas Aquinas College, Wyoming Catholic College and the University of
Dallas."[21]

Reno describes a conversation he once had with a student from an Ivy
League school that advertised itself as a training ground for the world's future
leaders. The student told him, "The first thing you learn your freshman year is
never to say what you are thinking."[22] In other words, this young student was
not learning to lead. He was learning to go along to get along, to blend in, to be

a timid follower.

Our so-called "elite" universities aren't training future leaders. They aren't educating. They are ruining an entire generation of young people.

The notion that "to succeed in America, you must get a college degree" is a myth. The evidence shows that the only difference between a high school graduate entering the workforce and a college graduate entering the workforce is that the college graduate has lost four years and tens of thousands of dollars.

There was a time, before I founded Turning Point USA, when I thought I was missing out on an important life experience by not going to college. I felt left out because my friends went to college and I didn't. But now I'm running an organization with a $50 million budget that is making a difference in America. We receive thousands of applications for jobs and internships, and we have to turn most applicants away. I know that if I had gone to college for four years, Turning Point USA would not exist.

If you're a high school senior, your guidance counselors and school administrators have your whole year programmed for you. They're going to send you to a College Fair, introduce you to college recruiters, tell you how to fill out your FAFSA and transcript release forms, push you to apply for financial aid and scholarships, and more. No one will ask you *why* you should go to college. Instead, they will hurry you along toward the future *they* have picked out for you.

> When you break away from the norm, when you throw off everyone else's expectations for your life, when you go out on your own and take full advantage of all the opportunities that America affords—the sky's the limit.

When you break away from the norm, when you throw off everyone else's expectations for your life, when you go out on your own and take full advantage of all the opportunities that America affords—the sky's the limit. It's not easy to be your own person and move out from the herd. You must take risks, and a risk means you might fail. But it also means you might roll the dice and win big.

Knowing what you know now, what's the best way to prepare for a bright future? The standard four-year stint in college—or . . . ?

You have a decision to make.

5

THE LUNACY OF COLLEGE

> **COUNT 5:**
>
> **College ruins the ability to think and reason.**

In July 2021, biologist Carole Hooven, who teaches Human Evolutionary Biology at Harvard, appeared on *Fox & Friends* on the Fox News Channel. She stated that on many campuses, it's becoming increasingly important to defend science from "woke" activists. She said it's important that science instructors be able to make the obvious statement that biological sex is real, and that terms like "male," "female," and "pregnant women" have precise scientific meanings.

Hooven was frustrated that "ideology has been infiltrating science." She said, "The ideology seems to be that biology really isn't as important as how somebody feels about themselves, or feels their sex to be. The facts are that there are in fact two sexes—there are male and female—and those sexes are designated by the kind of gametes we produce."

She noted that it's important to be considerate of the feelings of transgender people. "We can treat people with respect and respect their gender identities and use their preferred pronouns," she said, "so understanding the facts about biology doesn't prevent us from treating people with respect."

Despite the compassion Hooven displayed toward trans individuals, her statements angered Laura Simone Lewis, director of the Diversity and Inclusion Task Force at Harvard's Department of Human Evolutionary Biology. Lewis tweeted, "I am appalled and frustrated by the transphobic and harmful remarks made by a member of my dept in this interview with Fox and Friends."

In a follow-up tweet, Lewis added, "I respect Carole as a colleague & scientist. But this dangerous language perpetuates a system of discrimination against non-cis people within the med system. It directly opposes our Task Force work that aims to create a safe space for scholars of ALL gender identities and sexes."[1]

Laura Simone Lewis is afflicted with a college-induced obsession that renders the academic mind incapable of grasping common sense and scientific fact. In Lewis's thinking, scientifically accurate terms such as "male," "female," and "pregnant women" constitute "dangerous language."

I call this kind of thinking "the lunacy of college."

This brings us to Count 5 of our ten-count indictment of the college industry: *"College ruins the ability to think and reason."* So-called "higher education" teaches students to abandon common sense, defy science, and embrace a delusional view of reality.

A Pandemic of Lunacy

A college campus is a laboratory of lunacy. No idea is too radical, irrational, or downright insane for academia to disseminate.

You've probably heard of the "Grievance Studies Affair," a hoax designed by James Lindsay, Peter Boghossian, and Helen Pluckrose. The purpose of the project was to expose the absurdity of academic thinking in several supposedly "scientific" fields, such as race, gender, queer, and fat studies. Over a 12-month period in 2017 and 2018, Lindsay, Boghossian, and Pluckrose wrote twenty academic papers and submitted them to peer-reviewed academic journals. They deliberately larded the papers with bogus ideas, obvious illogic, and academic jargon, dressing up the most outrageously nonsensical claims in scholarly clothes.

Their hoax was amazingly successful. By the time the three authors were outed by a *Wall Street Journal* report in October 2019, seven of the fake papers had been accepted by peer-reviewed journals, seven more were being reviewed for publication, and only six were rejected.

One paper, published by *Gender, Place & Culture,* claimed that dog parks are "petri dishes for canine 'rape culture'" and called for a greater awareness of "the different ways dogs are treated on the basis of their gender and queering behaviors, and the chronic and perennial rape emergency dog parks pose to female dogs." [2] The paper posed the question, "Do dogs suffer oppression based upon (perceived) gender?"[3]

Another paper, accepted by *Affilia: Journal of Women and Social Work*, was titled "Our Struggle Is My Struggle: Solidarity Feminism as an Intersectional Reply to Neoliberal and Choice Feminism." The paper consisted of a chapter from Adolf Hitler's *Mein Kampf* reworded in radical feminist jargon. James Lindsay believes it was just days away from being published when the *Wall Street Journal* exposed the hoax.[4]

Yet another paper attacked "Western astronomy" as sexist and asserted that physics departments should include "feminist and queer astrology" as a normal part of teaching the science of astronomy. The paper was undergoing peer review at the time the hoax was exposed, and according to an account by Lindsay, Boghossian, and Pluckrose in *Areo*, the reviewers "were very enthusiastic about that idea."[5]

Academia's fascination with insane theories and absurd ideas is far from harmless. Much of it is rooted in destructive Marxist doctrines and neo-racist Critical Race Theory. Why is America so deeply divided and coming apart at the seams? The prime culprit, in my view, is the college regime, which I call "the educational industrial complex." Bad ideas are manufactured in academia, accredited in academia, and propagated through academia. College graduates take these bad ideas and spread a pandemic of lunacy throughout our culture.

Colleges serve as the perfect incubator for newly formed, loyal left-wing voters. Harvard University is a perfect example. The institution was once widely respected as a forum for robust discussion and debate, where issues could be studied from a variety of perspectives. Today, the students and faculty at Harvard are completely consumed by racial and gender politics—and only the most extreme far-left viewpoints are tolerated. One must simply look at the professors employed at these elite schools to decipher their political leanings.

Coasting on its reputation as the top university in the world, Harvard is relevant today only because the public hasn't caught on to the disparity between the reputation and the reality of Harvard. A truly great institution should produce free thinkers and courageous risk-takers. Instead, Harvard churns out cookie-cutter radicals and think-alike dogmatists to populate American media, government bureaucracies, and top law firms. Elite universities use their position of influence to spread radical woke politics into every corner of American life.

Where did Anthony Fauci acquire the medical authority and credibility to impose a lockdown on America and arguably mislead the public? College. Let us not forget his misleading statements to Congress on gain of function research. Where did Somali-born Ilhan Omar learn to seemingly hate the country that saved her from the Dadaab refugee camp in Kenya? College. Where did Alexandria Ocasio Cortez learn that America must be bankrupted and evidently obliterated from within? College. Where did Nikole Hannah-Jones, the author of *The 1619 Project*, spread her revisionist history prior to joining the *New York Times*? College. Where was Barack Obama first inspired with a goal of fundamentally transforming America? College. Where was Hillary Clinton converted from a Goldwater Girl to a Saul Alinsky radical? College. Where was Critical Race Theory spawned? College.

> The college campus has become one of the most corrosive forces in American society today.

You get the point. The long list of dangerous movements and bad ideas that vex and divide America today originated on college campuses. The college system long ago ceased to be a force for enlightenment and instruction in America. Instead, the college campus has become one of the most corrosive forces in American society today.

"Woke" Science

Journalist Katie Herzog has reported extensively on the LGBTQ+ community. In July 2021, she wrote a multi-part series that was posted on the Substack blog, *Common Sense with Bari Weiss*. Herzog's investigative piece focused on the spread of "woke" ideology into the nation's leading medical schools and teaching hospitals. Herzog reports that professors in many medical schools now deny the undeniable facts of human biology to avoid being canceled as "transphobic" by their radical activist students.

Herzog cites the story of an endocrinology professor at a medical school in the University of California system who paused in mid-lecture to issue a frightened and groveling apology. "I don't want you to think that I am in any way trying to imply anything," the professor said, "and if you can summon some generosity to forgive me, I would really appreciate it. Again, I'm very sorry for that. It was certainly not my intention to offend anyone. The worst thing that I can do as a human being is be offensive."

What did the professor do that was so "offensive"? The professor explained: "I said 'when a woman is pregnant,' which implies that only women can get pregnant and I most sincerely apologize to all of you."

That's right. The professor said, "when a woman is pregnant." The professor apologized for stating a scientific fact of human biology: women get pregnant. Pregnancy is a function of the female anatomy. People with male anatomy, by definition, do not get pregnant.

But this professor was forced to abjectly apologize for stating, truthfully and accurately, a fact of nature. University professors are now trembling with fear, terrified of being canceled and hounded out of their careers for stating what is obviously, scientifically true. They are victims of college lunacy.

What is the supposed basis for the claim that concepts like "male," "female," and "pregnant woman" have no place in medical school? Herzog quotes a university instructor, lecturing on transgender health, who explains "woke" science this way: "Biological sex, sexual orientation, and gender are all constructs . . . that we have created." All other mammals on the planet are divided into two sexes, male and female. But human beings, according to "woke" ideology, are actually sexless. Biological sex is just an idea that human beings made up in their own minds.

It takes a lot of college education to believe an idea so manifestly stupid. Ordinary human beings would never develop such as psychotic worldview on their own. People have to be brainwashed into it. And this brainwashing takes place on college campuses.

Herzog cites a case reported in the *New England Journal of Medicine* in 2019. A thirty-two-year-old transgender man showed up in the hospital with severe abdominal pain. The patient, who was obese, told the triage nurse that he had stopped taking his blood pressure medication. The nurse, who not been told that the "man" she was examining was biologically female, misdiagnosed the problem.

It turned out that the patient's abdominal pains were, in fact, labor contractions. The patient was having a baby—and wasn't even aware of being pregnant. The doctors and nurses were shocked, the patient was stunned—and the baby was delivered dead. The baby might have been saved if the triage nurse had been given accurate biological information about the transgender patient.

The denial of scientific reality is epidemic in university medical schools. Many professors live in fear of saying the wrong (i.e., medically accurate) thing. And the "woke" professors will happily cancel a colleague who, for example, uses the term "breast-feeding" instead of the bizarre "woke" term "chest-feeding." Professors who do not use "woke" terminology are accused of the Orwellian-sounding crime of "wrongspeak."

Katie Herzog learned many of these stories from a medical student she identifies only as "Lauren." Herzog concludes:

> This hypersensitivity is undermining medical training. And many of these students are likely not even aware that their education is being informed by ideology.
>
> "Take abdominal aortic aneurysms," Lauren says. "These are four times as likely to occur in males than females, but this very significant difference wasn't emphasized. I had to look it up, and I don't have the time to look up the sex predominance for the hundreds of diseases I'm expected to know. I'm not even sure what I'm not being taught, and unless my classmates are as skeptical as I am, they probably aren't aware either."

Other conditions that present differently and at different rates in males and females include hernias, rheumatoid arthritis, lupus, multiple sclerosis, and asthma, among many others. Males and females also have different normal ranges for kidney function, which impacts drug dosage. They have different symptoms during heart attacks: males complain of chest pain, while women experience fatigue, dizziness, and indigestion. In other words: biological sex is a hugely important factor in knowing what ails patients and how to properly treat them.[6]

There's a very good chance that, in the near future, the doctor who treats you are your spouse or your child will have been indoctrinated in the "woke" dogma that biological sex is merely a human-made construct. Good luck with the medical treatment you receive . . . you're going to need it.

Canceling SpongeBob

Many college-educated people see racism in the most innocent places. Take, for example, University of Washington sociocultural anthropology professor Holly Barker.

In 2019, *The Contemporary Pacific: A Journal of Island Affairs* published a 10,000-word essay by Barker titled "Unsettling SpongeBob and the Legacies of Violence on Bikini Bottom." That word "unsettling" (or "unsettle") is "woke" academic jargon with a double meaning: it suggests unsettling people (making them feel uncomfortable) and unsettling a place ("decolonizing" that place by removing the "settlers"). Academics say that we need to "unsettle ourselves" by "deconstructing" our "colonial mentality."

Professor Barker wrote this scholarly paper to show that *SpongeBob SquarePants*, an animated comedy series that premiered on the Nickelodeon network in 1999, promotes "racism" and "violence." Understand, *SpongeBob* is a children's show set in a fictional underwater city called Bikini Bottom. There is a real-life coral reef in the Marshall Islands known as Bikini Atoll. *SpongeBob*'s fictional Bikini Bottom is supposedly located at the bottom of the lagoon enclosed by Bikini Atoll.

You may know that Bikini Atoll is where, in 1946, the U.S. government removed 167 indigenous Bikinians before using the site for a series of nuclear tests. The Bikinians suffered greatly due to hunger and radioactive fallout. Professor Barker wants the world to be aware of the plight of the Bikinian people, and that's a noble goal.

But it's lunacy to blame *SpongeBob SquarePants* for increasing the suffering of the Bikinian people. Yet that's exactly the bizarre claim Professor Barker makes: "SpongeBob's presence on Bikini Bottom continues the violent and racist expulsion of Indigenous peoples from their lands . . . that enables U.S. hegemonic powers to extend their military and colonial interests in the postwar era."

Barker claims that the fictional characters in Bikini Bottom constitute an "occupation" of the *real* Bikini Atoll, which she sees as an act of "symbolic violence." She writes, "Although the U.S. government removed the people of Bikini from the atoll above the surface, this does not give license to SpongeBob or anyone else, fictitious or otherwise, to occupy Bikini."[7]

Of course, it's impossible for cartoon characters to "occupy" the real-life Bikini Atoll in any way. In fact, the characters are sea creatures, indigenous to the ocean bottom. SpongeBob is a sea sponge. Patrick is a sea star. Squidward is a squid. They aren't occupying anything. They belong in the sea.

SpongeBob SquarePants was created by marine science educator Stephen Hillenburg to make kids (and their parents) laugh. He named his fictional setting "Bikini Bottom" not because he wanted to "occupy" the Bikini lagoon, but because "Bikini Bottom" is a funny, slightly risqué play on words, evoking the lower half of a two-piece swimsuit. (The bikini swimsuit was unveiled in July 1946, four days after the first atomic bomb test at Bikini Atoll, and was named for the test site.)

The *SpongeBob* show is not about colonization or nuclear tests or racism or violence. It's just a funny kid's show—and Professor Holly Barker needs to grow a sense of humor. But that's what academia does to academics. It removes their sense of humor, their sense of perspective, and their common sense.

"Woke" academics are always looking at the most inoffensive aspects of our culture and finding reasons to be aggrieved. The college system has trained students to find offensive racism in something as innocent as a children's TV show—or even an apple pie . . .

Canceling Apple Pie

Raj Patel is the ultimate "woke" academic. Raised in London, he studied philosophy, politics, and economics at Oxford, earned a master's at the London School of Economics, and had a Ph.D. from Cornell in 2002. He has been a visiting scholar and researcher at Yale, U.C. Berkeley, and the University of Texas at Austin.

When Raj Patel looks at an apple pie, all he sees is a symbol of racism and oppression. Why? Because apple pie is an unofficial symbol for America—and when you read the piece he wrote for The Guardian in 2021, it's clear that he isn't the biggest cheer leader for America. The piece is titled, "Food Injustice Has Deep Roots: Let's Start with America's Apple Pie." The opening paragraph drips with sarcasm:

> Resting on gingham cloth, a sugar-crusted apple pie cools on the window sill of a midwestern farmhouse. Nothing could be more American. Officially American. The Department of Defense once featured the pie in an online collection of American symbols, alongside Uncle Sam and cowboys.[8]

Patel proceeds to tell us that apples are not "particularly American" because they were first domesticated in Asia. Apples spread around the world through ancient trade routes, which he associates with "a vast and ongoing genocide of Indigenous people."

And the recipe for apple pie? That's not American either. It's really an adaptation of the English pumpkin pie recipe, says Patel. When the English came to the New World, they brought apple trees with them as "markers of civilization, which is to say property."[9]

There, Patel tips his hand. Karl Marx summed up his *Communist Manifesto* in a one phrase: "Abolition of private property."[10] So Patel's hatred of the humbly delicious American apple pie is rooted in Marxism and his loathing of private property rights.

Next, Patel attempts to trash the reputation of a great American hero, John Chapman, who called himself Johnny Appleseed. Let me tell you about Johnny Appleseed—then I'll show you how Raj Patel deceptively summed up his life.

Johnny Appleseed (1774–1845) was a devoutly Christian missionary for the New Church. He traveled widely, introducing apple trees to Pennsylvania to Illinois and even parts of Canada. He got his seeds from the pulp left over from cider mills and he established apple nurseries in various towns.

Going from town to town, he would preach the gospel to adults, tell Bible stories to children, and often receive food and lodging in return. He showed kindness to the Native American tribes, and they considered him eccentric but harmless, and believed he was protected by the Great Spirit.[11] Johnny Appleseed was so kindhearted toward animals that he would douse his campfire at dusk to prevent mosquitoes from flying into the flames.

That's the true story of Johnny Appleseed. Here's the Raj Patel revisionist history version: "John Chapman, better known as Johnny Appleseed, took these markers of colonized property [apple trees] to the frontiers of U.S. expansion where his trees stood as symbols that Indigenous communities had been extirpated."

In one sentence, Patel recasts a true American hero as a villain.

Next, Patel tries to make us feel guilty about the sugar in an apple pie. He tells us that the sugar trade in the 1700s was connected to the slave trade, which is true. But what does that have to do with the sugar we buy at the grocery store today? How are you and I responsible for events that happened three centuries before we were born?

Patel goes on in the same vein. He wants us to feel guilty for everything from a slice of apple pie to a tuna sandwich—products that come from the free market. The free market has created more jobs and lifted more people out of poverty than all of Raj Patel's favorite socialist programs combined. The free market has raised the standard of living for billions of people around the world.

Indoctrinated in the twisted dogmas of Karl Marx, Raj Patel looks at a slice of apple pie and sees only capitalist exploitation. He writes of "the horrors of international trade: violence, exploitation, poverty and profit," and concludes that "Capitalist logic is everywhere the same. . . . The apple pie is as American as stolen land, wealth and labour. We live its consequences today."[12]

Normal people don't think this way. They don't view reality through the distortion lens of Marxist dogma. They see reality as it is.

In college, students learn to twist the truth and cover up historical facts to make an invalid point sound plausible. They learn to stretch logic to the breaking point and pretend to find connections where there is no connection. That is how a brainwashed academic is able to slander the humble apple pie as a symbol of racism and colonialism.

Of course, apple pie is not the real target of this leftist's creed. It's only a stand-in. What leftists like Raj Patel really seek to destroy is America, freedom, and the free market economic system.

Canceling Capitalism

In June 2021, *Washington Post* opinion writer Christine Emba published a column titled, "Is It Time to Limit Personal Wealth?" Emba's bio at the *Post* website says that she has a degree in public and international affairs from Princeton University, and that she is a columnist "focused on ideas and society." She has also worked for the *New Criterion* and the *Economist Intelligence Unit*. Missing from her *Post* bio is her Robert Novak Journalism Fellowship, which The Fund for American Studies awarded her in 2018. The stated purpose of The Fund for American Studies is to "win over each new generation to the ideas of liberty, limited government and free markets."[13] Clearly, The Fund for American Studies failed to win over Christine Emba.

In her *Washington Post* piece, Emba expresses unhappiness that many millionaires (she cites Warren Buffett, Elon Musk, and Jeff Bezos) pay a lower tax rate than working-class people. She wrote, "ProPublica calculated that from 2014 to 2018, the 25 richest Americans paid taxes equal to only 3.4 percent of their gain in wealth." Emba makes a good point: our tax laws do contain many unjust loopholes that allow many millionaires and billionaires to get away with paying little or no income tax.

But then Emba veers off into Crazyville with this statement: "Every billionaire is a policy failure."

Wait, what? *Every* billionaire? She wants a world without *any* billionaires?

Does she know that a super-billionaire—Jeff Bezos—owns the *Washington Post* and pays her salary? Who would pay her to write such ridiculous drivel if there were no billionaires in the world?

Without any grasp of the implications of her ideas, Emba says she wants to do away with "wealth inequality." She explains:

> You must have rich people to have an economy. Rich people build businesses that employ people.

Instead of debating tweaks at the edges of our tax system, what we should be doing is stretching ourselves to imagine a world . . . where billionaires are impossible. Doing so would require a revised conception of what is good and what is fair, an approach focused less on what is "allowed" and more on what is "enough."[14]

It really takes no imagination to picture a place where billionaires are impossible. That place already exists. It's called North Korea. It's a place where there are no billionaires, there's no economy, there's nothing to eat, and there's no quality of life. You must have rich people to have an economy. Rich people build businesses that employ people. After all, when was the last time a poor person offered you a job?

Billionaires don't just hoard all their money in a bank vault and roll around in it like Scrooge McDuck. Billionaires put their wealth to work, and that wealth circulates throughout all levels of the economy. If there were no billionaires, Christine Emba would have to scratch her opinion pieces into the bark of a tree and beg people to come read it.

She advocates a philosophy called "limitarianism." According to this notion, society would set a "wealth line" over which no one would be able to earn. Everyone's income would be capped—and any earnings that exceeded the "wealth line" would go to the government. An idea this stupid could only come from—let me guess—a *university?* That's right. The notion of "limitarianism" was hatched by philosopher Ingrid Robeyns, director of the Fair Limits Project at Utrecht University in the Netherlands. Ideas this bad can *only* come from the mind of an academic.

The principle of "limitarianism," of course, is nothing new. It's been around for a long time under the label "Communism." But because Christine Emba of the *Washington Post* is the product of a Princeton University education, she thinks she's discovered a wonderful new idea that would lead us to Utopia.

Emba writes with childlike naïveté. She says that billionaires such as her boss, Jeff Bezos, may be talented, smart, and hard-working, "but it's doubtful they work that much harder than everyone else," as if "hard work" determines what people should earn. She doesn't seem to understand that entrepreneurs are people who put their capital at risk, who work eighty hours or more per week, who pay themselves last, and are entitled to a return on investment. She seems to view entrepreneurs as thieves and wonders why they should be "allowed to keep as much as they can grab."[15]

She suggests that capping the earnings of entrepreneurs would not stop them from innovating. Really? People would continue to put their money at risk and work long hours after you have slammed a lid on their profit incentive? Again, this is a childishly naïve view of both human nature and economics.

I honestly don't blame Christine Emba for holding these impractical views. She had the misfortune of being indoctrinated at Princeton University. This Marxist lunacy is concocted by academics who have never held a real-world job and never started a business. Academics live in a bubble of theory and unreality where you could eliminate the rich and Utopia would magically appear. It takes a college degree to believe such nonsense.

A Lunatic Course Catalog

To understand why a college education makes people incapable of rational thought, just look at some of the weird and pointless courses you can take at our nation's most prestigious universities. I have verified most of these classes at the universities' official websites. Some examples:

At Harvard you can take such courses as "Languaging and the Latinx Identities," "Chocolate, Culture, and the Politics of Food," and "Friendship as Way of Life."[16] Tufts University in Massachusetts offers a course called "Demystifying the Hipster."[17] At the University of South Carolina, you can study "Lady Gaga and the Sociology of Fame."[18] At UC Santa Barbara, the History Department and the Environmental Studies Program teamed up to present "The History of Surfing."[19]

The University of Wisconsin at Madison has offered a course called "Elvish," a study of the fictional language J. R. R. Tolkien invented for his *Lord of the Rings* trilogy.[20] If you want even *more* made-up languages, the University of California at Santa Cruz offers "Invented Languages, from Elvish to Esperanto," which also includes the Klingon language from the *Star Trek* universe. [21]

For more than a decade, Occidental College in Los Angeles has offered a course called "The Phallus" in its Department of Critical Theory and Social Justice. The college describes the course as "feminist and queer takings-on of the phallus" involving such topics as "the meaning of the phallus, phallologocentrism, the lesbian phallus, the Jewish phallus, the Latino phallus, and the relation of the phallus and fetishism." In recent years, the course has been retitled "The Phallus & The Siren: Gender Portrayals in Pop Culture."[22]

Occidental College also deconstructs fairy tales in its Department of Critical Theory and Social Justice. The course is called "Mother Goose to Mash-Ups: Children's Literature and Popular Texts." The course description asks the burning questions, "Why did the London Bridge fall down? Is Rub-a-Dub-Dub really about bath time? Why didn't an old man live in a shoe? Who is more imperialist, Babar or Peter Pan? Is Tinky Winky gay?" The course answers these questions through the lens of "gender, race, culture, and nation" with an emphasis on Critical Race Theory.[23]

Oberlin Experimental College in Ohio offers a course in "Cryptozoology," the study of creatures that only exist in urban legend—Chupacabra, Bigfoot, Yeti, the Loch Ness Monster, and the like. Oberlin also offers a course in "Spongebobology," the study of SpongeBob SquarePants.[24]

Evergreen State College in Olympia, Washington, offers a bachelor's in "Somatic Studies," in which you learn to holistically connect your mind to your body.[25] The University of Connecticut claims to be one of only two or three universities in the nation to offer both bachelor's and master's programs in "Puppet Arts." Puppetry classes are so popular that the school must limit enrollment.[26]

California's Santa Clara University offers a course called "The Physics of Star Trek," which claims to offer scientific explanations for the Starship *Enterprise*'s "warp drive" and matter transporter ("Beam me up, Scotty").[27] And Michigan State University offers a pop-culture-themed psychology course called "Surviving the Coming Zombie Apocalypse" (with the slogan "In times of catastrophes, some people find their humanity, while others lose theirs"). [28]

The University of Pennsylvania has offered a course called "Wasting Time on the Internet" under the Department of English. The online course description asks, "Could we reconstruct our autobiography using only Facebook? Could we write a great novella by plundering our Twitter feed? Could we reframe the internet as the greatest poem ever written? Using our laptops and a wifi connection as our only materials, this class will focus on the alchemical recuperation of aimless surfing into substantial works of literature."[29]

In its 2021 course catalog, U.C. Santa Cruz offers a course called "Trajectories of Justice: Standing Rock, Climate Change, and Trump's Potential Impeachment." Understand, this course is offered *after* President Trump has already been impeached twice and is out of office. The course description reads: "Enables students to become expert on the potential impeachment of

Donald Trump in the context of progressive American history, emphasizing his Neglect of Duty regarding global climate change through the lens of The Native Uprising against the Dakota Access Pipeline."[30]

Like all major universities, U.C. Santa Cruz is a hotbed of Critical Race Theory. Here are a few of the many courses that employ this destructive Marxist analysis of society: "Disability Studies" ("a focus on feminist and critical race approaches to disability"), "Feminist Critical Race Studies" ("argues for the necessity of combining feminist and critical race studies"), "Organizing for Water Justice in California" ("investigates, imagines, and practices movement toward water justice in California using feminist, Indigenous, and critical race theory"), "Politics of Space, Time, and Matter" (an amalgam of "indigenous studies, queer studies, afrofuturism, borderland studies, critical race studies, decolonial studies, disability studies, feminist science studies, and new materialisms"), and "Feminist Games" ("intersectional feminist games, transfeminist games, and queer feminist games will be created by students in this course . . . building on critical theories of race, gender, sexuality and algorithms"). [31]

That's just a brief, quirky selection among the many Critical Race Theory courses offered at UCSC. They are typical of the kinds of oddball courses offered at all major universities. (We'll take a close look at Critical Race Theory in chapters 9 and 10.)

The list of wacky courses, past and present, goes on and on: "To Hogwarts, Harry: An Intensive Study of Harry Potter Through the British Isles" (Central Michigan University), "Politicizing Beyoncé" (Rutgers), "The Sociology of Miley Cyrus" (Skidmore College), "California Here We Come: The O.C. & Self-Aware Culture of 21st Century America" (Duke), [32]"Wordplay: A Wry Plod from Babel to Scrabble" (Princeton), " 'Oh, Look, a Chicken!' Embracing Distraction as a Way of Knowing" (Belmont University), "Theory and History of Video Games" (Swarthmore), "Physics for Future Presidents" (UC Berkeley), "Zombies in Popular Media" (Columbia College, Chicago), "Cyborg Anthropology" (Lewis & Clark College), "Biology of Jurassic Park" (Hood College), "Joy of Garbage," (Santa Clara University), "How to Watch Television" (Montclair State), "The Textual Appeal of Tupac Shakur" (University of Washington), and "The American Vacation" (University of Iowa).[33]

This list just scratches the surface of countless college courses that are wacky or worthless or intended to brainwash the unwary.

Academia and the Arsonist-in-Chief

During the COVID-19 pandemic, Dr. Anthony Fauci (Chief Medical Advisor to the President) and the bureaucracy of the Centers for Disease Control were given extraordinary authority over American society. On their orders, businesses and churches were shuttered, commerce was halted, and property owners were forcibly prevented from collecting legally owed rent, driving many into bankruptcy. At the root of all this unconstitutional oppression was what I call "the Cult of Science"—a fanatical and misplaced worship of Science with a capital S. The high priest of this cult is Dr. Fauci and the mantra of this cult is "follow the science."

The Cult of Science is rooted in the worship of higher education, which is intertwined with the history of Progressive thought. Progressivism originated at Johns Hopkins University, where the radical ideas of Georg Wilhelm Friedrich Hegel and German historicism took root in the nineteenth century. Hegel taught that history unfolds in stages, and that we are moving inexorably toward a utopian state of justice, reason, and peace. Put simply, the lie of progressivism is that things must continue to "move forward" through a process Hegel called dialectic history, a linear and continuous progression toward perfection on earth.

Every leading leftist and most college academics embrace some form of Hegelianism. Hegel was the primary influence on Karl Marx, the father of Communism. In fact, Marx was the president of a German youth movement, the Young Hegelians, before he became an author and social commentator. The reason progressivism and Marxism have such an affinity for each other is that both are deeply rooted in Hegelianism, the view of history as inevitable progress.

One American president serves as an archetype of what colleges produce: Woodrow Wilson. He is the only president to earn a doctorate—a PhD in political science from Johns Hopkins University. It was at Johns Hopkins that Wilson was influenced by Hegelianism, and he quoted Hegel in his 1887 essay "The Study of Administration."[34] Wilson was a quintessential academic, having taught at various colleges before becoming president of Princeton University in 1902. A committed segregationist, he worked to keep black Americans out of the university.

Until Barack Obama, Woodrow Wilson was the most anti-American president ever elected. Wilson's election was something of a fluke. After serving as governor of New Jersey, he ran as the Democratic nominee in 1912. The Republican vote was split between his two opponents, Republican incumbent William Howard Taft and third-party candidate Teddy Roosevelt, representing the Bull Moose Party. With the Republican vote divided, an unpopular progressive academic, Woodrow Wilson, became president with a mere plurality of the vote.

President Wilson was the Arsonist-in-Chief of the American system of government. He blow-torched the principle on which America was founded, and was the first president to openly reject the founding fathers and the principles of the Declaration of Independence. In a 1911 speech in Los Angeles, he said, "If you want to understand the real Declaration of Independence, do not repeat the preface."[35]

Wilson meant that he approved of the Declaration's list of grievances against King George III, justifying the Revolution—but he rejected the principles of the preface, including this ringing proclamation of human rights: "We hold these truths to be self-evident, that all men are created equal, that they are endowed by their Creator with certain unalienable Rights, that among these are Life, Liberty and the pursuit of Happiness." As a progressive and a segregationist, Wilson believed it was his right to reject the Declaration's pronouncement of God-endowed human equality. His dismissive response to the preface of the Declaration: "The question is not whether all men are born free and equal or not. Suppose they were born so, you know they are not."[36]

Wilson gave us some of the most destructive laws in American history. He devised the unelected, unaccountable fourth branch of government, the administrative state. Wilson was a creature of the academy and saw himself as leading a wave of progress that would rid America of its antiquated ideas (including the principles of its founders) and boldly usher in a new phase of progressivism.

The Woodrow Wilson presidency had a major and lasting impact on American politics—and on American attitudes toward higher education. Ever since the election of the scholarly Woodrow Wilson, Americans have demanded to know each candidate's level of education and where he or she went to college. Beginning in the 1960s, we saw our government increasingly overrun by Boston-based, Kennedy-allied Harvard graduates. Today it's almost unheard of that a major leader in American politics would not have strong ties to an elite Ivy League institution.

On the current Supreme Court, all but one member attended either Harvard or Yale Law School (the lone exception is Amy Coney Barrett, who graduated from, and taught at, Notre Dame Law School). Since the creation of the Supreme Court in 1789, 115 people have served on the high court, of whom 32 have studied at Harvard or Yale.

As we have increasingly demanded that our leaders be college-educated, and even Ivy League-educated, has the wisdom and effectiveness of our leaders noticeably increased? Is the highly educated Woodrow Wilson an improvement over the unschooled and self-educated Abraham Lincoln? Has the current crop of government leaders, with their advanced degrees from elite institutions, made America stronger, more secure in its borders, and its people more free? Have the hordes of radicals unleashed upon our nation by the college system helped to the unify America—or have they set our cities ablaze with rage and hatred?

Has the college system made America better and stronger? Or has it shoved America down the slippery slope of decline and destruction?

In this chapter, you've seen the avalanche of absurd classes that are offered in colleges and universities. And you've seen the tortured logic, the revisionist history, and the "woke" academic denial of reason and scientific fact. That's my case for Count 5 of our ten-count indictment of the college industry: *College ruins the ability to think and reason.*

It's not time for your verdict yet. We have just five more counts to go.

6

HOW THEY TRY TO SHUT US UP

COUNT 6:

College indoctrinates students and represses speech.

In the fall of 2019, faculty, students, and staff at the University of Nevada, Reno, circulated a petition titled "Concerning White Nationalism on the University of Nevada, Reno Campus." It stated, "We are deeply alarmed by your administration's inadequate response to the presence and impacts of Turning Point USA (TPUSA) on our campus."

The petition claimed that TPUSA had engaged in "white nationalist tactics" and complained about the arrest of a student who had screamed at our TPUSA volunteers and tossed their table upside-down. The petition added, "TPUSA is waging a campaign to recruit students at colleges and universities nationwide. They have significantly increased their activity over the past years and months." Yep, recruiting students is kind of what we do.

The petition went on to libel our organization, falsely linking us to racist and white nationalist groups that have no affiliation with TPUSA whatsoever. The truth is that TPUSA stands for bedrock American principles of life, liberty, and the pursuit of happiness, the principles of the Bill of Rights, the power of free market economics. We preach values of strong moral character, honesty, integrity, and a willingness to listen to our ideological opponents and reasonably debate them.

But our opponents refuse to talk to us. They try to silence us. They overturn our tables and circulate a lying petition against us, accusing us of "racist, sexist, anti-Semitic, and anti-LGBTQ rhetoric"—rhetoric, they claim, that could "escalate into physical violence, including gun violence." This libelous document was signed by 1,590 people, including one politician:

"Kamala Harris, Presidential Candidate."

In October 2019, during the Democratic presidential primary, then-Senator Kamala Harris made a campaign stop at the UNR and signed the petition.

This is the same Kamala Harris who compared the agents of U.S. Immigration and Customs Enforcement to the Ku Klux Klan.[1] This is the same Kamala Harris who, according to the *New York Times*, fought hard against overturning wrongful convictions obtained through perjured testimony and evidence tampering.[2] This is the same Kamala Harris who, according to the *Washington Post*, made a sick and disgusting joke about a prisoner who begs for "a morsel of food please."[3]

I consider Kamala Harris's signature on that libelous petition a badge of honor. My Christian faith teaches me to consider myself blessed when people insult me and falsely accuse our organization—but I'll still speak out for truth and accountability. When I heard that she had signed that document, I told Matthew Boyle on *Breitbart News Sunday*, "We completely and wholeheartedly reject this accusation by Senator Harris. We demand a total and unequivocal apology and retraction."

I also called upon Senator Harris to visit with the young leaders of TPUSA's Black Leadership Summit, our Young Women's Leadership Summit, our Teenage Student Action Summit, and our Latino Summit. Instead of ignorantly smearing our organization, she should come meet our young women leaders and our young leaders of color. She should find out what our organization is about, and how our young people love their country, love the Constitution, and loved their liberty.

Kamala Harris never retracted or apologized for her signature on that petition. That's okay, I wasn't holding my breath. Two weeks after her appearance at the University of Nevada, Reno, I spoke to an audience on the same campus— an audience *twice* the size of hers.

A Free Speech Problem

The University of Texas at Austin has a free speech problem.

In October 2018, when I was scheduled to speak at Texas State University, I heard about attacks against a conservative student group at UT Austin, forty minutes north of Texas State. The attacks resulted from a controversy over the Brett Kavanaugh confirmation hearings. A woman named Christine Blasey Ford had leveled unsubstantiated claims that Kavanaugh had sexually assaulted her in the 1980s. The issue was being hotly debated on many campuses.

At UT Austin, half a dozen members of Young Conservatives of Texas (YCT) set up a table with signs that read "Confirm Kavanaugh" and "Change Our Mind"—an open invitation for debate. The conservatives were saying, in effect, "This is what we believe about Judge Kavanaugh. Come talk to us, debate us, and persuade us if you can."

The YCT group set up a display at around 11 a.m. About an hour later, the conservatives were surrounded by an estimated 150 leftist students who jeered, mocked, and shouted expletives. Through it all, the conservatives remained respectful. Campus police showed up and tried to keep the mob from turning violent.

One female student snatched a sign and ripped it in pieces. Then she ripped another sign in pieces. The crowd called the YCT students "rape apologists" and chanted "We believe survivors!" and "YCT off UT!" plus a few unprintable slogans. After two hours, the conservative students folded up their table and campus police escorted them to safety.

I decided to visit UT Austin myself and see if anyone would be willing to debate me. I arranged to arrive on October 24, and the TPUSA chapter put up posters advertising my appearance. Before my arrival, vandals took down the TPUSA posters and replaced them with posters intended to insult me. One had a photo of me with the words: "Charlie Kirk: Bankrolling Campus Fascism Since 2012."

The local TPUSA chapter had set up a tent on the West Mall Rally Space.

A protest group staged a noisy demonstration nearby, chanting, "No Kirk, No KKK, No TPUSA." Even though the noise was annoying, I was still able to have reasonable, cordial conversations with about twenty left-leaning students.

I would ask the student to pick a subject—health care, immigration, the economy, anything at all. I wanted them to feel they were being treated with respect, and I didn't want them to feel blindsided. Campus police let people talk, shout, and chant, but stepped in quickly when a student threw water at a TPUSA videographer.

For some reason, leftists feel threatened by the offer of a cordial exchange of views. Where do leftist students get the idea that bullying behavior is an appropriate way to respond to opposing views?

Could it be that they learned it in their college classrooms?

Minds Welded Shut

This brings us to Count 6 of our ten-count indictment of the college industry: *"College indoctrinates students and represses speech."*

Maddison Meeks is typical of countless TPUSA students across the country. She explains her core principles this way: "I'm not shy about my defending my beliefs. . . . One thing I always try to do is present my views in a civil manner. . . . I support the free market system, not just when it comes to businesses and markets, but also the free marketplace of ideas, which allows us to discuss issues and find common ground and develop solutions."[4]

During the 2018 Fall Welcome at the University of Colorado Boulder, Meeks and two other Turning Point USA volunteers set up a table for the school's Be Involved Fair. Their table was one of scores of tables on the quad. Maddison's table advertised an upcoming "Pizza and Politics" event and offered stickers with such slogans as "This Laptop Was Brought to You by Capitalism" and "Big Government Sucks." During their four hours of tabling, Maddison and her friends signed up more than 100 students for the email newsletter.

As they were closing up shop, Maddison and her friends decided to visit the

Socialists of America table. Maddison had emailed the group a couple of times, hoping to set up a debate between the socialists and Turning Point USA. The socialists had never replied, so Maddison wanted to introduce herself and make the offer in person.

One problem: Maddison and her friends wore T-shirts with the slogan "Socialism Sucks." So, as the TPUSA delegation approached the Socialists of America table, she said, "Please ignore our T-shirts. We honestly just want to introduce ourselves and ask you a question—"

A young man behind the table yelled, "Get the f*ck out of here!"

Maddison tried to explain that she just wanted to talk to them about arranging a debate, but the angry young socialist would only reply in words of four letters or less. Maddison and her friends gave up and walked away.

Obviously, the "Socialism Sucks" T-shirts were not a great conversation starter. But I doubt the conversation would have gone smoothly if their T-shirts had merely said "I Love America." Leftists have no interest in pitting their ideas against ours in an open debate. Maddison would have welcomed a conversation with a young socialist—and from her side, at least, it would have been a civil conversation.

> Where do young leftists learn to fear and despise opposing viewpoints? They learn it in the classroom.

I've gone to scores of campuses to set up a table on the quad and visit with young progressives. They do a lot of shouting, very little talking, and hardly any listening. Where do young leftists learn to fear and despise opposing viewpoints? They learn it in the classroom.

A college campus is where inquiring young minds go to be welded shut.

A Bernie Mug and the *Communist Manifesto*

Maddison Meeks wrote a piece for *The College Fix* on the mistreatment of conservative students on American campuses. She said, "I have been called a terrorist, a fascist pig, a conservative bimbo and a brainwashed conservative." She interviewed some of her conservative student peers and related their experiences.

At the University of Pittsburgh, Chloe Chappell applied for academic credit for her internship with the Pennsylvania Republican Party. Chloe's advisor denied her application, saying, "That's not a real internship." Students received credit for internships with left-leaning groups, no problem. But Chloe had to appeal to her dean to get her advisor's decision reversed.

When Bridgette Custis was a junior at Merrimack College, she avoided speaking up in her sociology class. The professor drank coffee from a Bernie Sanders mug and taught from the *Communist Manifesto*. He noticed the conservative stickers on her laptop and called on her (even though she hadn't raised her hand) to explain to the class why she had a negative opinion of Communism. She replied that in a Communist society, people have no incentive to work, so goods become scarce, the economy fails, and everyone suffers.

The prof told her she was wrong and that *true* Communism had never been tried. He concluded, "You and your people are *the worst* thing to happen to this country. America is not and never has been great."[5]

Conservative students routinely have their grades docked, are singled out for humiliation, and are deprived of their free speech rights by leftist administrators and faculty. The abuses take place daily in elite Ivy League schools and in little regional colleges. Many conservative students survive by keeping their heads down and keeping their ideas to themselves. But a few courageous students dare to challenge the status quo.

Conform to Our "Diversity" or Else

Ryan Lovelace is a journalist who covers politics for the *Washington Times*. A few years ago, when he was a student journalist at Butler University in Indianapolis, he gained national attention when he wrote an opinion piece about indoctrination at his college. He described how his political science professor, in the syllabus for "Political Science 201: Research and Analysis," instructed her students "to write and speak in a way that does not assume American-ness, maleness, whiteness, heterosexuality, middle-class status, etc., to be the norm."

Lovelace told his dean that this statement "presumes every student who walks through the door is a racist or misogynist."

The dean replied, "There's nothing about a college education that guarantees you won't be made uncomfortable."[6]

But Lovelace wasn't complaining about feeling "uncomfortable." He was concerned that the professor's expectation that he disavow his own identity had created an atmosphere that was both "offensive and hostile to any student's ability to learn." He explained:

> As a student at an institution predominantly focused on the liberal arts, I expected to hear professors express opinions different from my own. I did not expect to be judged before I ever walked through the door, and did not think I would be forced to agree with my teachers' worldviews or suffer the consequences.
>
> Being judged and forced to act a certain way is antithetical to how any institution of higher education should conduct itself.[7]

Ryan Lovelace's opinion piece went viral. It was shared and linked across the internet and featured on the *Wall Street Journal*'s "Best of the Web Today." Sean Hannity touted the piece on Fox News. Rush Limbaugh quoted from the piece on his radio show.

In the wake of this media scrutiny, Butler's president, James Danko, sent a campus-wide email with the heading "Affirming Our Guiding Principles." Danko stated that "inclusive language is encouraged and supported at Butler University" and vaguely suggested that Lovelace's article had caused "various individuals at Butler" to be subjected to "hateful language." Danko didn't contact Ryan Lovelace to ask if *he* had been subjected to "hateful language" (he had).

Lovelace was summoned to meetings with "a professor, a department head, multiple college deans, and the provost of the university." More than a hundred Butler professors attacked Lovelace's piece on an all-campus listserv. The faculty staged an "inclusivity teach-in" during which at least one professor called Lovelace a "racist." One attendee accused Lovelace of "plagiarism" because he had quoted (properly, with quotation marks and attribution) from the syllabus. Others who attended said that Lovelace should "burn in hell."[8]

Despite harassment and pressure for him to leave school, Lovelace persevered and graduated from Butler. The experience undoubtedly prepared him well for a career as a conservative journalist. He had hoped to persuade Butler decision-makers to rethink their definition of "inclusivity" and "diversity," and consider making Butler University a place that welcomed a *true* diversity of viewpoints.

The administration and faculty made it clear it was not going to happen.

A Survivor of Yale

In 1951, William F. Buckley helped establish the modern conservative movement with the publication of his book *God and Man at Yale*. In his foreword, Buckley described the leftist indoctrination that prevailed at Yale in those days:

> I propose, simply, to expose what I regard as an extraordinarily irresponsible educational attitude that, under the protective label "academic freedom," has produced one of the most extraordinary incongruities of our time: the institution that derives its moral and financial support from Christian individualists and then addresses itself to the task of persuading the sons of these supporters to be atheistic socialists.[9]

Buckley also observed that conservative students and faculty members at Yale were vastly outnumbered by leftists and Marxists: "The conservatives, as a minority, are the new radicals."[10] In the seven decades since Buckley wrote those words, leftist groupthink at Yale has only grown more oppressive—and conservatives have been more viciously persecuted.

Meet Aryssa Damron. She's a graduate (and survivor) of Yale University. She is now a columnist for Townhall.com and a guest commentator for Fox News.

In 2015, while an undergrad at Yale, Damron was interviewed on Fox News by Tucker Carlson. The subject was Yale's invitation to Black Lives Matter agitator DeRay McKesson to address Yale Divinity School. During the interview, Tucker asked Damron what it was like to be a conservative student at Yale. She replied that she had been harassed for her political beliefs and told by classmates she shouldn't be at Yale.

Damron didn't hesitate to wear conservative slogans and symbols on her apparel—and those symbols led to her being targeted and taunted. "I have been called a bigot from across crowded hallways," she said, "simply because of what I was wearing. I had someone tell me last year they could not live with me because I was too conservative."[11]

So much for the "open-mindedness" and "diversity" of the left.

After her appearance on Fox News, the harassment intensified. The Yale students' Facebook page, "Overheard at Yale," seethed with personal attacks against Damron, including demands that she withdraw from Yale. Not a single person dared to confront her face-to-face, but the online attacks were relentless and included doxing (publishing her private information online) and death threats. She told *Vanity Fair*, "I did get physical threats to the point where my mom was like, 'Do you need us to hire someone?'"[12]

Aryssa Damron didn't feel completely alone at Yale. She estimated that there were up to fifty conservative students at Yale. Several classmates approached her in private to offer encouragement—but they were scared, saying, "Don't tell anyone I agree with what you said."[13]

Yale has been hostile to conservatives for more than seven decades, as William F. Buckley has documented. And Yale is even more aggressively intolerant toward conservatives today. So what viewpoints *does* Yale tolerate?

Yale Covers Itself with Shame

In June 2021, Bari Weiss broke a story on her Substack platform about a psychiatrist who lectured at Yale's Child Study Center in April of that year. Weiss had received a recording of the lecture delivered by Dr. Aruna Khilanani, who is in private practice in New York City. The talk was titled "The Psychopathic Problem of the White Mind." Yale had invited Khilanani to participate in "Grand Rounds," a weekly mental health discussion for Yale faculty and staff.

Weiss posted the entire recording to her Substack page, along with quotes from Khilanani's lecture. Here are some key quotes:

"This is the cost of talking to white people at all. The cost of your own life, as they suck you dry. There are no good apples out there. White people make my blood boil."

"I had fantasies of unloading a revolver into the head of any white person that got in my way, burying their body, and wiping my bloody hands as I walked away relatively guiltless with a bounce in my step."[14]

"We need to remember that directly talking about race to white people is useless, because they are at the wrong level of conversation. Addressing racism assumes that white people can see and process what we are talking about. They can't. That's why they sound demented. They don't even know they have a mask on. White people think it's their actual face. We need to get to know the mask."

Khilanani stands by her words and claims that her lecture "used provocation as a tool for real engagement." But officials at Yale School of Medicine were so concerned about Khilanani's profane and racially explosive statements that they limited viewing access to the Yale community ("Grand Rounds" lectures are normally open to the public). Yale officials explained, "We weighed our grave concern about the extreme hostility, imagery of violence, and profanity expressed by the speaker against our commitment to freedom of expression." Khilanani says that Yale knew exactly what to expect from her because "they knew the topic, they knew the title, they knew the speaker."[15]

I'm not attacking Aruna Khilanani for her views, which seem to be generalizations based on personal experiences. For example, she says that when she was doing her residency at Weill Cornell Medical Center in New York, a family member of one of her patients physically assaulted her. She has expressed many bizarre ideas, such as her belief that white people don't eat bread. She describes a "white person" as a "demented, violent predator who thinks that they are a saint or a superhero."[16]

As Khilanani herself noted, Yale officials knew the kind of lecturer Khilanani was. The title of her talk—"The Psychopathic Problem of the White Mind"—was printed on Yale's invitation to the event. Yale openly embraces far-left, neo-racist extremism while persecuting mainstream conservatism.

But when Aruna Khilanani delivered a lecture so shocking and offensive that Yale officials knew they had a PR problem, they suppressed it. They got caught trying to hide what they had done.

And what Yale did was cover itself with shame.

Gaslighting at Med School

The University of Virginia was founded in Charlottesville in 1819 by Thomas Jefferson. When Jefferson wrote his epitaph, he listed only three of his many accomplishments: author of the Declaration of American Independence, author of the Statute of Virginia for Religious Freedom, and father of the University of Virginia. If he could return today, he wouldn't be so proud of what his beloved university has become.

Kieran Bhattacharya attended the University of Virginia's medical school. On October 25, 2018, he was in the audience for a panel discussion on microaggressions. During the Q&A session, Bhattacharya raised his hand and addressed a question to assistant dean Beverly Cowell. "Thank you for your presentation," he said. "I had a few questions, just to clarify your definition of microaggressions. Is it a requirement, to be a victim of microaggression, that you are a member of a marginalized group?"[17]

Dean Adams replied that being marginalized was not a requirement for being a victim of a microaggression. Her reply contradicted the most common understanding of the term "microaggression," which is defined as commonplace insults or derogatory attitudes directed at marginalized groups, such as racial minorities, gender minorities, the poor, or the disabled. (The term was invented by Harvard psychiatrist Chester Pierce in the 1970s.[18])

Bhattacharya and Adams politely discussed the meaning of microaggression theory for about five minutes, then the moderator called on another questioner. One of the panel's organizers, assistant professor Nora Kern, took offense at Bhattacharya's questioning of Adams and later filed a "professionalism concern card," claiming that Bhattacharya had violated university policy.

According to Nora Kern's version of events, Bhattacharya had "asked a series of questions that were quite antagonistic toward the panel . . . and stated one faculty member was being contradictory. His level of frustration/anger seemed to escalate until another faculty member defused the situation by calling on another student for questions. I am shocked that a med student would show so little respect toward faculty members. It worries me how he will do on wards." ("On wards" refers to hospital wards; Kern was questioning Bhattacharya's fitness to become a medical professional.)

If not for Kern's "professionalism concern card," the matter would have ended quietly. But the card, with its claim of an escalating "frustration/anger" level set in motion a series of email exchanges and meetings between Bhattacharya and school officials. The Academic Standards and Achievement Committee sent him a written warning that he should "show mutual respect" to faculty and "express yourself appropriately." The committee also encouraged him to seek counseling.

Bhattacharya insisted that he had neither lost his temper nor felt frustrated with the panel—and an audio recording available online seems to support his claim.[19] To Kern's claim that the student had displayed "frustration/anger," Bhattacharya replied that it "was not at all how I felt. I was quite happy that the panel gave me so much time to engage with them about the semantics regarding the comparison of microaggressions and barbs. I have no problems with anyone on the panel; I simply wanted to give them some basic challenges regarding the topic."[20]

On November 26, Bhattacharya received a notice from a school official that the original suggestion that he seek psychological counseling had become mandatory. He would not be allowed to attend classes until he had been evaluated by the university's psychological services.

Bhattacharya asked school officials to explain what he was accused of and under what authority he was ordered to seek counseling. It appeared that his reasonable five-minute discussion of the definition of terms had been blown up into a crisis that left his enrollment in doubt. University officials seemed determined to punish him—but for what? Bhattacharya's situation resembled that of Josef K. in Franz Kafka's *The Trial*—the story of a man arrested and prosecuted by authorities who never tell him what he's accused of.

Days later, Bhattacharya was summoned before the University of Virginia's Academic Standards and Achievement Committee. During the half-hour hearing, which he recorded with the committee's knowledge, he asked the committee members to state exactly what offensive behavior he had committed. The committee members would only speak in generalities, stating that he needed to change his "aggressive, threatening behavior." Several times, he asked the committee to name one example of this behavior. They told him his audio-recording of the meeting constituted "unprofessional behavior."

In the end, the school suspended Bhattacharya for unspecified "aggressive and inappropriate interactions in multiple situations." On December 30, campus police ordered him off university property. The administrators who expelled him from the university never cited a single "aggressive" action he had committed. *Reason* commentator Robby Soave described how the school engaged in "gaslighting" (trying to make Bhattacharya doubt his own perception) and deprived him of his First Amendment rights:

> [The University of Virginia's] administration engaged in
> behavior that can be described as "gaslighting." Administrators
> asserted that Bhattacharya had behaved aggressively when he
> hadn't, and then cited his increasing confusion, frustration,
> and hostility toward the disciplinary process as evidence that
> he was aggressive. And all of this because Bhattacharya asked
> an entirely fair question about microaggressions, a fraught
> subject.

Kieran Bhattacharya went to the United States District Court and filed suit against the University of Virginia, seeking injunctive relief and damages. In March 2021, when the university filed a motion to dismiss, presiding judge Norman K. Moon ruled that the trial should proceed, saying:

> Bhattacharya sufficiently alleges that Defendants retaliated
> against him. Indeed, they issued a Professionalism Concern
> Card against him, suspended him from [the University of
> Virginia] Medical School, required him to undergo counseling
> and obtain "medical clearance" as a prerequisite for remaining
> enrolled, and prevented him from appealing his suspension or
> applying for readmission.[21]

Kieran Bhattacharya deserves to win his case—and the University of Virginia deserves a lesson in how not to bully students who respectfully stand on their First Amendment rights. I hope and pray he wins.

Blacklisted by DePaul

DePaul University is a private Catholic university in Chicago. It is also one of the most politically correct, anti-free-speech institutions in the nation.

Jonathan Cohen, who taught mathematics at DePaul for many years, has called the university "ground zero in the battle to reform academia's corrupted political culture."[22] In a 2016 article titled "Is DePaul America's Worst School for Free Speech?," Chicago attorney Ari Cohn chronicled DePaul's history of hypocrisy and injustice by silencing conservative speech while inviting propagandists for Marxism and other far-left ideologies.[23]

In January 2006, the DePaul Conservative Alliance set up an "Affirmative Action Bake Sale" table in the campus Student Center. It was a creative experiment in satire and free speech. The table offered cupcakes and cookies to students at prices that varied according to race. Black and Hispanic students paid less; white and Asian students paid more. The purpose of the bake sale was not to make money but to provoke a conversation about race in America—the kind of conversation progressives always *say* they want but always avoid. The bake sale drew a crowd and started some spirited conversations.

Before an hour had passed, DePaul's dean of students showed up and shut down the bake sale. University officials claimed the event was shut down because it was not held in an appropriate location. Yet, one week later, DePaul allowed the far-left animal-rights group PETA to set up an information table at that exact location.[24]

DePaul has a history of inviting the worst radical-left guest speakers, including Weather Underground terrorist Bernardine Dohrn (formerly on the FBI's Most Wanted list), Marxist professor Angela Davis (an advocate for political violence and the recipient of the Soviet Union's Lenin Peace Prize), and radical activist Ward Churchill (who famously said that the World Trade Center victims on 9/11 got what they deserved).

In October 2018, Candace Owens and I were scheduled to speak at DePaul University. Because of DePaul's history of suppressing conservative speech, I considered it one of the most important stops on Turning Point USA's 12-event Campus Clash tour. Our advance team was careful to follow every protocol so that DePaul would have no excuse to cancel our event. When DePaul raised a concern that the TPUSA chapter had mistakenly issued tickets to our event before it was approved, we quickly stopped the ticket distribution.

We were not surprised when, less than a week before our scheduled appearance, DePaul's associate VP of student affairs Rico Tyler announced that the university was canceling our event. He cited concerns about "violent language" and "identified populations being singled out in a demeaning fashion." Wait, what? *Who* was he accusing of "violent language" and demeaning people? Me? Or was he talking about leftist protesters who often showed up to start a fight? Tyler cited no examples and declined to clarify.[25]

DePaul has had a troubled history with conservative guest speakers. When outspoken gay conservative Milo Yiannopoulos spoke at DePaul in 2016, Black Lives Matter protesters stormed the stage, physically threatened Yiannopoulos, and shut down his talk. Though DePaul had required the College Republicans to pay for extra security guards at a cost of $1,440, not one of the sixteen security guards the university supplied attempted to intervene. [26]

In a letter to students, university president Dennis Holtschneider blamed Yiannopoulos for the ruckus. He wrote that "speakers of Mr. Yiannopoulos' ilk" are "more entertainers and self-serving provocateurs than the public intellectuals they purport to be."[27]

By blaming the speaker instead of the mob, DePaul surrendered to "the heckler's veto," a situation in which terrified authority figures (such as timid university presidents) surrender to protesters and hecklers, squelching free speech. Surrendering to "the heckler's veto" is a crime against the First Amendment.

What Are They Afraid Of?

When I learned that DePaul had canceled our event, I told the media, "We've been blocked from campus simply because we're conservative. DePaul's plan was to delay, delay, delay, and then claim there was no longer 'enough time.' . . . They never intended to let us speak and they used every bureaucratic tactic in the book to restrict our speech. This is discrimination, plain and simple. . . . They have only emboldened us."

I also took to Twitter, saying, "The left hates the idea there are other ideas. They DENIED us because they say we say 'potentially violent' things. Hey

DePaul, your fascism is showing."

Locked out of the DePaul campus, we held our event a few days later at the J. W. Marriott Hotel in Chicago's South Loop. Police were positioned outside the hotel, expecting trouble, but no demonstrators showed up. After my talk, we did some Q&A, and I invited anyone who disagreed with me to come to the front of the line, take the microphone, and debate me. A few people accepted my offer, and we had some stimulating, polite discussion. It's a shame that such a healthy exchange of ideas couldn't take place on the DePaul campus.

During the Q&A, I said, "What is DePaul so afraid of? Are they afraid of a room full of conservatives peacefully allowing people that disagree with them to come to the front of the line and have calm discussions with ideas? If they're scared of that, they aren't a university. They're an island of totalitarianism."

I know *exactly* what DePaul is afraid of. The university fears that if Charlie Kirk is allowed to speak on campus, DePaul students will hear the truth, they'll be persuaded—and there will be a lot fewer leftists on the DePaul campus. They can't afford to allow intellectual freedom on campus. The moment DePaul students are free to think for themselves, the administration and faculty lose control.

> Universities have redefined "inclusion" to mean exclusion and "diversity" to mean rigid conformity.

I have a nickname for institutions like DePaul, Yale, UT Austin, the University of Virginia, and many other American colleges and universities. I call them "Brainwash U."

A university is supposed to be a place where students are exposed to a smorgasbord of ideas and viewpoints. As William F. Buckley observed, "Though liberals do a great deal of talking about hearing other points of view, it sometimes shocks them to learn that there *are* other points of view."[28] That's why we see these supposed bastions of "inclusion" and "diversity" and "intellectual freedom" suppressing free speech. They have redefined "inclusion" to mean exclusion and "diversity" to mean rigid conformity.

They invite Marxists and anti-American radicals to deliver hateful, inflammatory tirades, and they blame conservative speakers for the actions of leftist protesters. They gaslight, punish, and expel students who dare to ask questions about their radical ideology. They shut down conservative tables on the campus quad. They deny conservative students academic credit. They punish and prohibit conservative student groups. Do you see any hope that this politically corrupt system can be reformed and redeemed?

That's my case for Count 6 of our ten-count indictment of the college industry: *"College indoctrinates students into destructive ideologies."* Four more counts to go.

7

VIOLENCE AND HATE ON CAMPUS

COUNT 7:

Colleges and universities breed violence and hate.

Sproul Plaza is the student activity hub of the University of California at Berkeley. It's the historic site of many student protests, beginning with Mario Savio and the Free Speech protests of 1964. Sproul Plaza was ground zero for the protests against the Vietnam War and it's the place where the California National Guard tear-gassed student protesters in 1969. Today, the plaza is a popular tabling site where student groups advertise their activities.

On February 19, 2019, Hayden Williams, a field representative for the Leadership Institute and Turning Point USA, had set up a recruiting table on Sproul Plaza. The table was laid out with conservative buttons and stickers, a pair of American flags, and signs that read "The Real Free Speech Zone" and "We Support Our President."

While Williams was at the table, a man in his late twenties approached and shouted, calling Williams a "racist" and unleashing the most vile, obscene threats and insults imaginable. Williams remained calm as both he and a bystander recorded video of the unfolding scene. The video shows the aggressor, a non-student named Zachary Greenberg, shoving Williams and screaming just inches from his face—then brutally sucker-punching him in the right eye. Then Greenberg strides away without a backward glance.

Greenberg was arrested for the assault about two weeks later by the University of California Police. Authorities had clear, closeup, identifiable video of Greenberg, so I don't know why it took so long for police to arrest him. But I was relieved when the thug who is seen on the video assaulting our campus representative was finally in custody.

I released a statement that read, "Hopefully, this dark chapter will act as a wake-up call to those concerned about politically motivated hate crimes in America. Berkeley and all college campuses across America should be safe havens for free thought and opinions—especially for a targeted conservative minority."

Hayden Williams also released a statement, saying that he was "disappointed by the U.C. Berkeley Administration, which allowed a culture of intolerance and violence toward conservatives to grow. I hope U.C. Berkeley's leadership will seize on this moment-in-time to take deliberate steps to establish a zero tolerance policy when it comes to violence, and restore Berkeley's legacy as 'Home of the Free Speech Movement.'"[1]

Not long after the vicious attack on Hayden Williams, I received a call from President Donald Trump. He told me he had seen the video of the attack on television and he was appalled. "I can't believe what I saw," he said. "This young man was simply exercising his First Amendment rights on campus—and for that he gets smacked in the face? Charlie, we've got to stand by our people. We've got to do something about this."

And he did. Later that month, at CPAC 2020, President Trump called Hayden Williams to the platform and introduced him to the attendees. The crowd responded with a thunderous standing ovation.

In March 2020, one month after the attack on Hayden Williams, President Trump stood in the East Room of the White House, surrounded by scores of conservative student activists who had also suffered mistreatment on campus. There he signed an executive order designed to promote free speech at colleges and universities across America. Violation of the order would bar an institution from receiving federal research grants.

But what about the assailant? A search of Alameda Superior Court records shows that case number 19-CR-003557 was filed on March 5, 2019. In that filing, Zachary Greenberg was charged with one misdemeanor and four felonies (including assault with "force likely to produce great bodily harm," which the California criminal code classifies as assault with a deadly weapon).[2] Greenberg pled not guilty to all counts. As I write these words, two and a half years have passed since the assault and Zachary Greenberg still has not faced trial for the crime.

Even worse, this violent tale doesn't end with the assault on Hayden Williams.

A Black Eye and a Media Blackout

Fast-forward to Sunday, August 9, 2020, and the seaside village of Princeton-by-the-Sea, near Half Moon Bay. There, two men, a pedestrian and a bicyclist, got into an argument. The pedestrian was angry because the cyclist was riding on the sidewalk. In the course of their altercation, the pedestrian pulled a four-inch folding knife from his pocket, stabbed the bicyclist multiple times, then fled the scene.[3]

The cyclist—the father of two small children, a foster parent, and an emergency room worker—was hospitalized at San Francisco General Hospital. He underwent surgery and survived the attack.[4]

The knife-wielding assailant, according to police, was Zachary Greenberg—still free on bail after his assault on Hayden Williams. Greenberg was arrested minutes after the stabbing. Deputies stopped a car near the scene of the crime and Greenberg was in the passenger seat. Witnesses identified Greenberg as the attacker, and deputies found the knife in the car. Greenberg was charged with assault with a deadly weapon.[5]

Stabbing someone over a sidewalk disagreement is incredibly senseless. But it's no less senseless than assaulting someone over a political disagreement. Political violence is, unfortunately, not uncommon on American campuses today. And most of that violence, by far, is perpetrated by radical leftists like Zachary Greenberg. This violence is an assault on the First Amendment principle of free speech.

And what about the news media? How was the assault of Hayden Williams treated by print and broadcast journalists?

The dramatic video of the Sproul Plaza assault is exactly the kind of graphic, violent imagery the major networks love to lead their newscasts with. "If it bleeds, it leads," they say—but not this time. It was largely left to Fox News to shine a spotlight on this politically motivated attack. To the rest of the media, it simply wasn't news.

The media blackout on the Berkeley attack isn't surprising. The so-called "mainstream media" is not "mainstream" in the sense that it represents the mainstream of American thought. Rather, the "mainstream" of media outlets—from the *New York Times* to ABC, NBC, CBS, and CNN—all lean *way* to the left of the *true* mainstream of American opinion. And there's a reason for this: The journalists who decide what is and isn't news are all products of our colleges and universities.

The leftist "mainstream media" are part of an overall movement bent on tearing down traditional American values—belief in God, the sanctity of the family, belief in hard work and freedom and personal responsibility, and the principles embodied in the Declaration of Independence and the Constitution. These traditional American values are conservative values. They are not the values of the left.

The narrative that grips both academia and the "mainstream media" derives from Marxist ideology. According to this narrative, there are victims and there are oppressors. And the left views traditionalists and conservatives as oppressors, as the enemy. To the mainstream media, Hayden Williams is part of that oppressive system. He's one of the bad guys. Leftists are the good guys.

When Zachary Greenberg was caught on camera assaulting a harmless conservative who is merely exercising his free speech rights, he didn't merely give Hayden Williams a black eye—he gave the political left a black eye. In that video, the leftist is clearly the oppressor and the conservative is the victim. These facts don't fit the media narrative. It creates cognitive dissonance in the minds of leftist journalists—so they pretend it never happened.

One of the few "mainstream media" outlets that *did* report the attack on Hayden Williams was the *Washington Post*. The *Post* noted that Williams's black eye was still visible when he appeared on Fox Business Channel and said, "There is a certain culture that is especially hostile on Berkeley's campus, and across the country, to conservative students. They're willing to use violence if they think you're being too controversial."[6]

The Violent Tendencies of the Left

This brings us to Count 7 of our ten-count indictment of the college industry: *"Colleges and universities breed violence and hate."* Violence against conservative students is commonplace on campus—and leftist school officials routinely side with violent campus radicals instead of protecting the free-speech rights of all students.

A week after the Sproul Plaza attack, I went to the campus to encourage our Berkeley TPUSA leaders and members. During my talk, I asked them what the media response would have been if a conservative activist had punched a leftist on campus? We all knew the answer: it would have made front-page news. The story would have dominated cable news coverage for days. Why? Because that's the false "mainstream media" narrative: conservatives are the oppressors, leftists are heroes and victims. As a rule, the media only covers stories that fit the narrative.

> Violence against conservative students is commonplace on campus—and leftist school officials routinely side with violent campus radicals instead of protecting the free-speech rights of all students.

Another theme in the media narrative is that people on the left are "tolerant" and welcoming of "diversity," whereas people on the right are "racists," "homophobes," "misogynists," and "bigots." But how do leftists define "tolerance" and "diversity"? They refer only to skin color, ethnicity, gender, sexual orientation, economic class, and physical disabilities. They don't believe in tolerance and diversity when it comes to conservative ideas and values. Leftists claim to be "open-minded" but their minds are closed to other viewpoints.

And here's the paradox: most conservatives are every bit as tolerant and welcoming of diversity as those on the left *claim* to be. We hold no prejudice against people of other races or genders or sexual orientations. We want all human beings to have their God-given rights to life, liberty, and the pursuit of happiness. We want all human beings to have their full First Amendment rights to the free exercise of religion, freedom of speech and the press, the freedom to peaceably assemble, and the freedom to petition the government. We want to prevent the American Dream from becoming a socialist American Nightmare.

The left doesn't believe in a free market of ideas and freedom of speech. The left labels any speech it disagrees with as "hate speech." The left labels people with opposing viewpoints as "racists" or "bigots." That's what Zachary Greenberg did to Hayden Williams. He depersonalized Hayden and called him a "racist [expletive]" merely because he represented a different political viewpoint. Then, after *verbally* assaulting him, he *physically* attacked him.

> As a rule, the media only covers stories that fit the narrative.

Not all leftists will go to the extreme of physically punching a conservative in the eye. But most leftists don't hesitate to smear us as "racists" or "white supremacists." Once those on the left have caricatured their ideological opponents as evil people, as the enemy, all bets are off. It becomes an easy thing to move from merely cursing us to physically assaulting us. Zachary Greenberg is the inevitable result of the same hateful mindset that pervades liberalism, progressivism, and radical leftism in America today—and especially on American campuses.

At colleges and universities across America, the violent tendencies of the American left are on full display.

A Bike Lock to the Head

On April 15, 2017, conservative groups held a free speech rally in Civic Center Park in Berkeley, just three blocks from the U.C. campus. Video taken at the rally shows a conservative activist in a red shirt and backpack surrounded by a leftist mob. He is talking to the mob with his hands raised. A companion behind him is holding up a phone and taking video. Two masked women in the mob swat at the young man's upraised arms as others in the crowd taunt and curse him.

Suddenly, a man lunges forward from the back of the crowd. He's dressed all in black like a comic-book supervillain—black mask, shades, hoodie, pants, and gloves. He slams a U-shaped bike lock against the conservative's skull with a sickening thud. The victim puts his hands to his head and staggers away, blood streaming down the side of his face. It's a rough video to watch. [7]

Treated at the scene, the young man was able to walk away from the park.

Police later identified the black-clad assailant as Eric Clanton, a former professor at Diablo Valley College in the East Bay. *Rolling Stone* identified him as "an ethics professor who taught philosophy and critical thinking." According to his OkCupid account, Clanton described himself as a "gender-nonconforming" sapiosexual eager to "precipitate the end of civil society." Raised in a conservative family, Clanton graduated from a private evangelical school, Bakersfield Christian High School, where he said he felt like an "oddball" because of his belief in what he called an "embryonic anti-state communism." He became increasingly radicalized during his undergrad studies at Cal State Bakersfield and post-grad studies at San Francisco State.[8]

Court records show that Clanton assaulted at least seven people at the rally, always aiming for the head. One person required five staples to close the wound. Another person, who wore a helmet, was struck so hard that part of the helmet broke off.

It took more than a month for police to locate and arrest Clanton. Tips from the public were key to his capture. A police search of his San Leandro home turned up evidence linking Clanton to "Anti-Fascists and Anarchy political groups," according to court records. Police pinged his cell phone to locate him at a West Oakland house, where they arrested him and found flags and literature connecting Clanton with Antifa and other anarchist groups. The search also recovered black apparel and bike locks, along with a camera containing selfies of Clanton geared up like the assailant in the videos. Clanton's phone records also placed him at the scene at the time of the attacks.

Clanton eventually struck a deal in which he pled "no contest" to a single misdemeanor battery charge, and the felony charges were dropped. He was placed on three years' probation, which ended August 8, 2021.[9] For a series of brutal assaults, which easily could have resulted in death, this violent "ethics professor" barely received a tap on the wrist.

Whether in the "free speech zone" on Sproul Plaza or at a "free speech rally" at Civic Center Park, leftist radicals aren't interested in anyone's free speech rights. They have no respect for the First Amendment. If they think you stand in the way of their socialist pipe dream, they will throw a fist or swing a bike lock at your head. They will counter your words with violence.

Attack after Attack

These attacks happen more frequently than you might imagine.

At Bentley University in Waltham, Massachusetts, in April 2019, College Republicans president Alex Christoffersen was tabling and collecting signatures to bring Fox News host Tomi Lahren to speak on campus. A male student walked up to Christoffersen's table, told him "You should be scared for your safety," and assaulted him with his fist. When I learned of the incident on July 9, I tweeted the phone video of the assault and wrote "[This] is the new, violent left. Will Democrats condemn this assault on a Republican practicing his first amendment rights?"[10]

In October 2019 at the University of Michigan, a leftist student destroyed a Turning Point USA information table. As he trashed the TPUSA materials and vandalized the table, he shouted at the table workers, accusing them of "hate speech." The students called campus police, and the offender fled the scene.

In November 2019 at the State University of New York at Binghamton, College Republicans and Turning Point USA chapters held a joint table event to advertise a speaking appearance by Arthur Laffer, the brilliant economist who formalized supply-side theory with his famous Laffer Curve. In addition to posters for the event, the tables displayed such items as American flag buttons, "Big Government Sucks" and "Taxation Is Theft" posters, and "Capitalism Cures" stickers.

A video posted online [11] shows a crowd of angry leftist students cursing and yelling at student conservatives, ripping and shoving their materials off the tables, then overturning and kicking the tables. "Pack this [expletive] up and go! Pack it up! Just go!" says one of the female leftists.

Another tells the Republican students, "The fact that ya'll are comfortable to even do this means that we're not doing enough. You are never gonna be able to table again. You're never gonna be able to do this again."

One loud female heckler gets right in the face of the conservative student who is recording the attack. She bizarrely repeats, almost as a chant, "Why are you shaking so? Why are you shaking so? Look at you laugh! Look at you laugh! Steady yourself! Steady yourself! Smile more! Smile more! With teeth! Teeth!" Standing inches from the camera, she rants and curses about having "a right to stand here," then goes back to taunting the videographer, "Stop shaking! Put on your [expletive] jacket!"

Other female leftists join and press in on the videographer, forcing her back, prompting campus police to move in and separate them. The leftists respond by turning against the campus police, chanting, "No justice, no peace, no racist police!"

A Binghamton official later issued a statement blaming the conservatives for the disturbance. The statement claimed the College Republicans had not obtained proper clearances for the tabling event and would face disciplinary action. The leftist protesters, the statement added, "acted in a manner that may have violated University rules" but officials would "not seek to identify or charge any protesters." As usual, the peaceful conservatives were blamed for the destructive violence of the left.[12]

Oh, and one more thing: the lecture by Arthur Laffer was shut down by rioting protesters.[13]

At Chico State College in northern California, College Republicans president Michael Curry was tabling outdoors. The conservative students had every right to be there and were not interfering with any passersby. A group of leftist protesters arrived and heckled the conservatives by playing ear-splitting music near their table. Video of the incident, tweeted by Michael Curry,[14] shows a female heckler taking a position opposite the College Republicans table, holding a sign that reads "Black Trans Lives Matter."

Curry made a sign of his own on a sheet of typing paper: "All Lives Matter." Then he took the sign and walked to a spot about four feet away from the female protester. Without speaking to her or looking at her, Curry held up his sign. (For the record, the female heckler did not appear to be either black or transgender, so Curry was not mocking or taunting her; he was merely counter-protesting, quietly and civilly.)

When the female protester glanced over and saw Curry's sign, she became enraged and snatched it out of his hands, shouting, "Get the [expletive] out of my [expletive] face! Get the [expletive] away from me!" Then she struck him in the face with the paper sign.

With a surprised expression, Curry put his hands in his pockets and calmly stepped away. He had done nothing to provoke such an attack. In a rational time, among rational people, the words "All Lives Matter" would be viewed as a sane, humanitarian statement. Only in a society that has become unhinged by the bullying of the Marxist organization Black Lives Matter would anyone be enraged by the words "All Lives Matter."

The female protester was clearly unhinged. Michael Curry was quietly minding his table when the protester and her friends showed up to create a disruption—yet she acted as if Curry was the aggressor. As Curry walked away, she continued her obscene rant: "You have the nerve to stand this close to me, when you [expletive] sacrificed my [expletive] safety!"

"Yeah, you're making her feel unsafe, back up!" another heckler said. (Universities have taught students to wield the word "unsafe" as a bullying tactic.)

"[Expletive] you!" the female protester continued. "You sacrificed my [expletive] safety, and you're acting like I'm the one spreading lies, and then you have the nerve to stand right next to me?"

Michael Curry was not injured during the incident, but no student should ever strike another student. The female protester and her radical-left cohort are the product of university indoctrination. Her leftist professors have taught her to think and behave irrationally. They have trained her to see herself as the victim even as she is engaging in aggression. They have taught her to view a calm, reasonable young man with an "All Lives Matter" sign as a threat to her safety. The result of that indoctrination is rage and violence.

As Michael Curry said in a statement to *The College Fix*, "Over the last semester myself and the members of the Chico State Republicans have been spat on, battered, assaulted, followed around campus, sexually harassed, and even mobbed by 300 students at once. This is the kind of environment that has been created by the modern day college campus."[15]

"You're Gonna End Up Dead!"

Just after midnight on Saturday morning, March 23, 2019, Jackson Arnold, a twenty-year-old student at Tulane University in Louisiana, heard the fire alarm sound in the hallway of his dormitory. Arnold opened the door of his room and found a sign posted on the door was ablaze. He put the fire out, then evacuated the building with all the other residents of the dormitory. Once outside, Arnold texted his roommate, twenty-year-old Peyton Lofton, who was off-campus with friends.

When Lofton read the text, he was furious. The arson fire of the dorm room door came a few days after Arnold and Lofton had been doxed—their personal information posted publicly on the internet—as revenge for their membership in a libertarian student organization, Young Americans for Liberty, and because Lofton was a Tulane chapter president for Turning Point USA.

"I was originally really angry," Lofton said later. "[I] stormed back to campus and once I got there, reality started setting in. I was a little scared, a little nervous. I could have been sleeping."

Soon after the incident, Tulane campus police arrested two male suspects and one female: Robert Money, 21, David Shelton, 20, and Naima Okami, 20. The three students were charged with aggravated arson—a charge which could result in up to twenty years in prison. Aggravated arson is defined by Louisiana law as intentionally staring a fire which could foreseeably endanger human life.[16]

At Sacramento State University in December 2019, College Republicans president emeritus Floyd Johnson II was engaged in a heated online debate with leftist political science classmate Keaton Hill. The argument began with a hateful comment Hill had posted on the Facebook page of one of Johnson's pro-life friends: "I hope that kid on your page dies of whatever cancer they have." During their online argument, Hill told Johnson to tell him face-to-face anything he had to say.

The next day, during a political science class they shared, Hill passed by Johnson and whispered, "[Expletive] you." Later that morning, Floyd Johnson and a friend, Henry Seufert, confronted Hill about his conduct—exactly as Hill had invited him to. Both Hill and Johnson had their phones out and were video-recording each other during the exchange.

In Johnson's video,[17] Hill holds his phone up and says, "Dude, do you want me to talk to [student conduct administrator] Tom Carroll about it? I'm happy to go get him. Come on."

Johnson replied, "There's nothing wrong with this." (Meaning, there's nothing wrong with Johnson wanting to talk to Hill about his bad behavior.) "What have I done?"

"You're harassing me," Hill said—then, without warning, Hill lunged at Johnson, landing an open-handed blow to Johnson's face.

The video shows blurred motion while Johnson says, "Whoa! That is not okay! That is not okay!"

As Hill hastily exits the building, Johnson and Seufert follow him outside. Johnson says, "You cannot do that! That is battery! That is assault!"

Hill stops, turns, and slaps at Johnson again, cursing him as Seufert moves behind Hill to hold his arms and stop the attack. Johnson points to Hill while telling his friend, "Henry, it's okay! Look at this, look at this!"

In a fit of rage, Keaton Hill snarls, "Mother[expletive]! You're gonna end up [expletive] dead! You're gonna end up [expletive] dead!"

Seufert tries to hold Hill back, but Hill gets loose and attacks Johnson again, knocking the phone out of Johnson's hand. As Johnson retrieves his phone, Hill hurries away and several bystanders step in to calm everybody down.

Keaton Hill was the aggressor at every point in this exchange. It was Hill, the leftist, who posted the hateful remarks on Facebook. When Johnson responded, it was Hill who invited Johnson to meet face-to-face. When Johnson accepted the invitation to talk, Hill responded with violence. Throughout the incident, Johnson never hit back.

"I didn't choose to fight back," Johnson told the *Sacramento Bee*. "I'm 6-foot-5 and he's 5-foot-6 or 5-foot-7 or something. It really would have been unfair. And anyway, the way he was hitting me was open-handed. If he was connecting and actually hurting me, then I would have engaged with him, but in that moment I was more focused on videoing the incident and recording what was going on."[18]

Police and the university student conduct office promised to investigate the incident,[19] but a search of news reports failed to turn up any findings of an investigation. Repeated emails to the Sacrament State University public information office went unanswered. I can find no indication that Keaton Hill was disciplined in any way for his violent assault on Floyd Johnson.

Vehicular Violence

In April 2019, Katie Daviscourt told Breitbart News, "I started a Turning Point USA chapter at South Seattle College to try to bring together like-minded conservatives such as myself in a part of the country where we are shunned and ostracized." She never imagined that peacefully advocating for her views could lead to an attempt on her life.

Two weeks after the founding of the TPUSA chapter, Daviscourt set up a table in a building on campus to recruit more members. "This was only my second day tabling for Turning Point," she recalled. "I was tabling in Olympic Hall and I had another student helping me for much of the morning, but she had to leave at around 11:30. Soon after she left, a male student approached the table, very angry and acting erratically. He began arguing about the 'Big Government Sucks' sign and he vandalized the table. He ripped down some of my signs and walked out of the building with them. I followed him out of the building to get a photo of him. I wanted the picture in case I had a problem with him in the future."

When the student saw Katie taking the photo, he became even angrier. She stood her ground and demanded that he hand over the signs he had taken. He gave them to her and walked away. Katie went back to her table, hoping the incident was over. It wasn't.

Her next class would begin soon, so she packed up her tabling materials and carried them out of the building and hurried toward her car. She recalled, "Because of the way the parking lot is laid out, I had to walk in the middle of the lane to get to the gravel lot where my car was parked. It didn't occur to me that the student who vandalized my table would be waiting for me in his car."

As Katie was in the lane, she heard a car behind her, accelerating quickly. "The car roared past me," she recalled, "missing me by about two feet. He continued driving really fast through the parking lot, making a big circle to come around again. My impression was that he wasn't just trying to scare me—he was trying to hit me."

Why did the driver miss Katie? It happened so fast that she can't be sure if she stepped out of the path of the onrushing car—or if the driver was so full of rage and adrenaline he couldn't drive straight. She recalls that he was driving erratically as he sped through the lot. Only when he turned a corner and she saw his face did she realize that this was the same student who had argued with her at her table.

"He was staring me down with, like, demon eyes. I froze for a moment, then I kept walking, trying to get to the lot where my car was parked. He stopped not far from my car and watched me. I didn't know if he knew which car was mine, or if he was planning to ram my car, or what. But I knew I didn't dare approach my car. My life was really in danger."

For several moments, neither Katie nor the driver moved. The driver was staring straight at her. Did he have a gun? What was this hotheaded young man capable of?

Katie took cover behind a parked car, pulled out her phone, and called 911. "I explained the situation to the dispatcher," she said. "The dispatcher told me I should try to make it back into the building. So I ducked behind cars and tried to get back to Olympic Hall."

The driver saw Katie—and he accelerated toward her. "He was coming down the lane of the parking lot. He was staring me down, not watching where he was going. A car was backing out, and he crashed into it—he completely totaled the other car. Then he sped off—hit and run. He pulled onto the road that led to the exit onto 16th Street, driving in the wrong lane. He was driving out of control and he narrowly missed several cars and pedestrians. A number of people witnessed the incident and called 911."

Seattle police came and took reports. "The officer I talked to was very kind," Katie said, "and he wrote up the incident as a hate crime. That's exactly what it was—an attack on me because of my political speech."

The totaled car was driven by a sixteen-year-old girl. She had only been driving for a week and was traumatized by the incident. "The girl's family had to pay for most of the damage themselves," Katie said. "I don't know why the driver wasn't held liable for what he did."

The violent driver was quickly identified, thanks to Katie's photos and security camera video. But was he arrested? No. According to Katie, no charges were filed. Was he expelled from school? No. The school merely suspended him—and he was welcome to return to campus at the end of his suspension. After attempting to run down and kill a fellow student, he was cleared to return to school. Fortunately, he decided not to return.

Though the police officer wrote the incident up as a hate crime, the college chose to ignore it. Katie explained: "The school essentially dropped the matter because I'm a conservative. In fact, the administration was terrible to me."

Katie bravely returned to tabling for Turning Point USA. Soon afterward, members of a campus club for "equity, diversity, and inclusion" (with the apparent approval of club's faculty advisor) posted flyers around campus that called Katie a "white supremacist." The flyers, Katie said, were printed with funds from student fees. "After this horrible incident happened to me, they printed the flyers that lied about me, paid for with school resources that I contribute to. Teachers even passed out these flyers in classes."

At Katie's college—and at many colleges and universities across America—leftist violence against conservative students is tolerated and excused. Administrators and professors blame conservative students for the criminal actions of violent students. "That's why it's so important that Turning Point USA is on college campuses," Katie says today. "There is no conservative representation on campus. It's an indoctrination camp. Students are not free to think and speak freely on campus without repercussion."

> When students are repeatedly taught to view words and ideas or even ideological neutrality as "violence," then it's inevitable that they will see violence as an appropriate response to opposing viewpoints.

Katie still deals with the after-effects of the incident. "It chokes me up talking about it. I wish I could forget it. I have a protection order, and I purchased my first firearm after the incident. I don't feel safe, because the police in Washington state won't investigate a breach of a protection order unless it involves a violent crime."

Katie works for Turning Point USA, helping students start new campus chapters and teaching them the basics of tabling. "Whenever I'm working with TPUSA volunteers," she said, "I'm always checking my surroundings, watching for someone who might threaten me or my students who are tabling. My paranoia level is up, but it's good to be wary. Never assume you are safe on campus. These are scary times."[20]

Dangerous "Snowflakes"

College used to be a place where young adults gathered to have their thinking challenged by new ideas and their character strengthened by rough-and-tumble debates and the Socratic method. Not anymore. Today, college is a place where students are coddled and insulated against "microaggressions" and protected from great ideas and great literature by "trigger warnings."

A generation of college students has been taught that "words are violence," that "silence is violence," and that *real physical violence* is an acceptable response to words and ideas they don't like. When students are repeatedly taught to view words and ideas or even ideological neutrality as "violence," then it's inevitable that they will see violence as an appropriate response to opposing viewpoints. That's why we are seeing a rise in violence against conservatives on college campuses—violence that ranges from overturning tables to a punch in the eye to a terrifying attempt at vehicular murder.

Turning Point USA has more than 1,000 chapters on campuses across America. Again and again, our TPUSA volunteers have been assaulted by leftist students and even by professors. They have been yelled at, cursed, punched, and pelted with feces and other objects. Why? Simply because they uphold conservative, constitutional values of free speech, freedom of religion, limited government, and respect for the family.

> When angered, "snowflakes" don't melt. They become aggressive and dangerous.

These used to be bedrock, unassailable values that all Americans believed in. Today, colleges and universities teach young people to hate everything America stands for. And they are encouraged to respond with violence.

For years, conservative commentators laughingly referred to emotionally fragile students as "snowflakes." The term comes from a line in Chuck Palahniuk's novel 1996 *Fight Club*: "You are not special. You are not a beautiful and unique snowflake."[21] Universities have coddled and infantilized students, offering them "safe spaces" where they can hide from scary conservative speech and constitutional ideas. Many conservatives found it hilarious that universities provided rooms to pamper and comfort these "snowflakes," rooms with cookies and coloring books, pillows and calm music, and puppies to hug. It seemed amusing that so many students left college so delicate, so easily offended, so narcissistic.

Today, no one is laughing. We've seen these "snowflakes" become a violent avalanche that threatens our civilization. These coddled students who are quick to cry "I feel unsafe!" are not as harmless as we supposed. When angered, "snowflakes" don't melt. They become aggressive and dangerous. They demand their opponents be silenced, shamed, canceled, and fired. And sometimes, they explode with violence.

When the "snowflakes" leave campus and enter the real world, they take their rage and violence with them. That's why, in the summer of 2020, we saw rioting, looting, and murder in the streets of Minneapolis, Portland, Seattle, Chicago, Washington, D.C., and New York. We saw "snowflakes" braving tear gas, lasering cops in the eyes, burning buildings, and pulling down statues. They belonged to Antifa and Black Lives Matter, and they were the product of our finest schools.

They saw themselves as warriors for social justice, and they struck fear in the hearts of mayors and city councils and everyday Americans. They shouted, "Defund the police!" and local governments across the nation surrendered to the mobs, sparking a nationwide crime surge. The "snowflakes" fully believe in their right to loot and assault and burn cities down. They've been taught that whoever is declared the most oppressed victim gets to be the meanest bully.

And they learned it in their college classrooms.

Psychologist Jordan Peterson put it this way: "Why do you think ideological thought is pushed so heavily at the universities? One-third laziness, one-third ignorance, and one-third malevolence. Laziness: it's easier to apply a doctrine to everything at once than to think through complex issues. Ignorance: the less you know about a problem, the easier you think it is to solve. Malevolence: it's great to find the enemy in others so that you have someone against whom to direct your resentment."[22]

It's too late to reform academia. Donors, why are you funding this madness? Parents, why are you sacrificing your young people on the altar of academia? Student, are you ready to reconsider the myths you've been taught about the need for a college education? You don't need to go to college to get your ticket punched. And you certainly don't need to go and get your face punched.

You've seen the evidence for Count 7 of our ten-count indictment of the college industry: *"Colleges and universities breed violence and hate."* We're not ready for a verdict yet. We have three more counts to go.

8

FOREIGN INFLUENCE ON CAMPUS

> COUNT 8:
>
> **Colleges and universities have been infiltrated by subversive foreign groups.**

The COVID-19 pandemic is the worst human-caused catastrophe in recorded history, having killed nearly 5 million people as this book goes to press. The Centre for Risk Studies at the University of Cambridge says the pandemic may cost the world *as much as $82 trillion* over five years.[1] From what we now know, it's almost certain the pandemic originated at China's Wuhan Institute of Virology.[2]

In early 2018, American scientists from the State Department tour the Wuhan lab with the permission of Chinese authorities. The American scientists were so alarmed by conditions at the lab that they cabled Washington, warning *explicitly* of the lab's work on bat coronaviruses and of a potential coronavirus pandemic. Less than two years later, the deadly coronavirus plague spread around the globe—exactly as scientists had predicted.[3]

There is hardly a person on the planet whose life has not been impacted by the coronavirus and the lockdown that followed. Communist China allowed the virus to escape from the lab, then engaged in a massive cover-up, driving up the death toll. And this same country, Communist China, has infiltrated universities and colleges around the world—and probably a campus near you.

Are you a parent? If so, you've invested an enormous amount of time and money raising your children. Think of all the evenings you've shared around the dinner table, faithfully attending church or synagogue, praying with your children at bedtime, teaching them respect for God, for America, for the flag. Then you send them off to college—

And at college they're taught the principles of Communism and a white-washed version of the history of China—a history with no mention of the mass starvation of Mao's "Great Leap Forward," no mention of Tiananmen Square, no mention of Tibet and Taiwan, no mention of the brutal oppression of Hong Kong. Your student graduates fully indoctrinated, courtesy of the Communist Chinese government. Beijing's influence on American academia is a malignancy that threatens our freedom and our way of life.

The Thousand Talents Program

This brings us to Count 8 of our ten-count indictment of the college industry: *"Colleges and universities have been infiltrated by subversive foreign groups."* Here's a case in point:

> Beijing's influence on American academia is a malignancy that threatens our freedom and our way of life.

Harvard's Charles Lieber is one of the most influential scientists of our time. An internationally recognized innovator in the field of nanotechnology, Lieber co-founded two nanotechnology companies, Nanosys and Vista Therapeutics. He was the chair of the Chemistry and Chemical Biology department at Harvard until 2020, when he was arrested on federal charges.

In June 2020, a federal grand jury indicted Lieber, charging him with lying to federal investigators about his involvement in Communist China's Thousand Talents Program. He is accused of covering up his work as a "strategic scientist" with China's Wuhan University of Technology. He awaits trial as this book goes to press.[4]

China's Thousand Talents Program is an effort, sponsored by the Chinese Communist Party, to infiltrate universities, research facilities, and tech companies to recruit Western scientists and engineers to serve Communist China.

The Department of Justice claims the Thousand Talents Program paid Lieber "$50,000 USD per month, living expenses of up to 1,000,000 Chinese Yuan (approximately $158,000 USD at the time) and . . . more than $1.5 million to establish a research lab at [Wuhan University of Technology]," while earning his full salary from Harvard.[5]

Other scientists and academics recently convicted of involvement with the Thousand Talents Program include: NASA scientist Meyya Meyyappan, who had access to sensitive government technology;[6] Song Guo Zheng, a professor at Ohio State and Pennsylvania State University who was caught trying to fly two information-laden laptops, three cell phones, USB drives, and silver bars to China;[7] MIT professor Gang Chen, whose crimes include defrauding U.S. taxpayers out of $19 million in grants to enhance China's nanotechnology research.[8]

Harvard and Yale are currently under federal investigation for allegedly failing to report millions in donations from China and Saudi Arabia. Yale alone may have taken in at least $375 million in unreported foreign money.[9]

In July 2020, the FBI announced a major crackdown on Chinese students in American universities. The crackdown resulted in four individuals being charged with student visa fraud and lying about their membership in China's People's Liberation Army (PLA). The FBI also interviewed thousands of Chinese student visa holders in more than 25 American cities about their possible affiliation with the PLA and the Chinese Communist Party.[10]

Operating in secret, the Thousand Talents Program has quietly infiltrated an unknown number of American universities. But an even more effective infiltration program has been operating for years in plain sight, disguised as a harmless Chinese language-and-culture program at American universities.

These centers of Communist espionage and propaganda are called Confucius Institutes.

Confucian in Name Only

In 2017, Chinese-Canadian filmmaker Doris Liu produced a documentary titled *In the Name of Confucius*. The film exposes Communist China's program of planting Confucius Institutes and Confucius Classrooms in hundreds of universities and K-12 schools around the world. It includes video of Xu Lin, a highly placed official of China's elite State Council, expressing her joy over the many top universities in North America that "work for us" as host campuses for Confucius Institutes. Xu Lin is also shown receiving China's "Influencing the World Award" and telling the audience, "Confucius Institutes are an important part of our soft power. We want to expand China's influence."[11]

According to the East Asia Research Center, the Confucius Institutes are Confucian in name only. They do not teach the philosophy of Confucius, as recorded in his *Analects*. Instead, the Institutes, in the guise of teaching Chinese language and culture, are indoctrination centers dispensing sanitized Chinese history, Communist propaganda, and praise for Communist China's so-called "democracy."[12]

The teachings of the Chinese philosopher Confucius, who lived 500 years before Christ, directly contradict Marxism, Maoism, and Chinese Communism. For example, in *Analects* 2.3 and 13.6, he describes a good leader as one who is morally self-disciplined, who leads by example and instruction, and correct with love and kindness rather than punishment and harshness. The brutal, lying, amoral leaders of Communist China could not be more opposed to the teachings of Confucius.

Confucius Institutes are on the front lines of China's war of subversion against the West. Confucius Institutes are one of the most visible form of "soft power" that Communist China projects around the world at an estimated cost of $10 billion a year.[13] "Soft power" refers to China's effort to peacefully seduce and deceive the world alongside its "hard power" efforts to intimidate, coerce, and bully the world.

In 2018, there were 37 Confucius Institutes on college and university campuses in 23 states:

Alabama: Troy University; Alabama A&M

Arkansas: University of Central Arkansas

California: Stanford University; University of California, Santa Barbara

Colorado: Colorado State University

Georgia: Wesleyan College

Idaho: Northwest Nazarene University

Indiana: University of Indianapolis

Kansas: Kansas State University

Louisiana: Xavier University

Michigan: Western Michigan University

Minnesota: St. Cloud State

Missouri: Webster University

New Jersey: New Jersey City University

New York: Alfred University; Stony Brook University; University at
Albany; State University of New York College of Optometry; State
University of New York; State University of New York Global
Center; Columbia University; University at Buffalo; Binghamton
University

Ohio: Cleveland State University; University of Akron; University of Toledo

Oregon: Portland State University

Rhode Island: Bryant University

South Carolina: Presbyterian College

Texas: University of Texas, Dallas

Utah: University of Utah; Southern Utah University

Washington: University of Washington; Pacific Lutheran University

Wisconsin: University of Wisconsin, Platteville

West Virginia: West Virginia University [14]

There are also Confucius Classrooms on high school campuses across the nation. Turning Point USA maintains an updated list of Confucius Institutes across the United States at ChinaOnCampus.com. I encourage you to check often to see if a school in your area has been added to the list.

Suppressing the Truth

In 2011, a member of the Chinese Communist Politburo in Beijing, Li Changchun, gave a speech that was never intended for Western ears. He said, "The Confucius Institute is an appealing brand for expanding our culture abroad. It has made an important contribution toward improving our soft power. The 'Confucius' brand has a natural attractiveness. Using the excuse of teaching Chinese language, everything looks reasonable and logical."[15]

Confucius Institutes present a Communist-approved version of history in which certain places and events are never mentioned. I call them "the three T's": Taiwan, Tibet, and Tiananmen Square. Mention any of those three T's in China and you're likely to land in prison.

Taiwan is a free and sovereign nation located 100 miles off the Chinese mainland. It's an island democracy with more than 23 million people who have a distinct culture and history. Chinese dictator Xi Jinping claims that Taiwan is a rebellious province of China, and he is determined to conquer Taiwan as part of his so-called "China Dream." Confucius Institutes teach that Taiwan belongs to Communist China.

Tibet is a region controlled by the People's Republic of China. In 1950, a year after the Communists conquered China, the People's Liberation Army marched into Tibet and annexed it, claiming Tibet as a province of China. Tibet's political and spiritual leader, the Dalai Lama, escaped to exile in India in 1959. Most Tibetans people still view the Dalai Lama, not Xi Jinping, as their legitimate head of state. Confucius Institutes teach that Tibet belongs to Communist China, even though the Tibetan people want to be free.

The Tiananmen Square protests of 1989 were student-led demonstrations held in Tiananmen Square, Beijing. The students demanded reforms to the oppressive one-party political system. The protests lasted from April 15 until the

Tiananmen Square Massacre on June 4 when the People's Liberation Army fired on protesters, killing and wounding thousands.

The leaders of Communist China are paranoid and afraid. They don't want the Chinese people to hear about Taiwan, Tibet, and the Tiananmen Square protests. And China is using its clout to cow American citizens and companies into submission.

In May 2021, actor John Cena gave an interview to promote *F9*, the latest movie in Universal's "Fast and the Furious" franchise. Appearing on the Taiwanese broadcast network TVBS, he said that Taiwan would be the first country to see the film. He made the "mistake" of calling Taiwan a "country"—which it is. Soon afterwards, Cena issued a groveling apology on Chinese social media: "I am very sorry for my mistake. I am so sorry, I apologize." My guess is that Chinese officials leaned on Universal, which in turn leaned on John Cena. And Communist China has plenty of sway over Universal because of the company's $20 billion Universal Beijing Resort,[21] which opened in July 2021.

Another company that squirms under the thumb of Communist China is The Walt Disney Company. At the end of the 2020 live-action adventure film *Mulan*, Disney thanked the Xinjiang Public Security Bureau in Turpan, which runs the Uighur slave camps in Xinjiang. At Beijing's insistence, Disney altered the storyline of the script in a subservient bow to Communist ideology.[17]

The company with the biggest China problem of all is Apple Inc. Apple CEO Tim Cook directed the company's entry into Communist China two decades ago. Now Apple manufactures nearly all its products in China—and earns 20 percent of its revenue there. But as the *New York Times* observed, "Just as Mr. Cook figured out how to make China work for Apple, China is making Apple work for the Chinese government."[18]

Chinese workers in Apple factories make between $2 and $3.15 per hour assembling iPhones that sell for $1,000 and up. Chinese factory laborers work about 11 hours per day, six days a week. Many live in factory-owned huts with bunk beds, roughly the same conditions as a prison.[19] (The next time you open your MacBook or check your iPhone, say a prayer for the liberation of the people who assembled it.)

Communist China has penetrated American companies and American campuses. China starts by making partnerships and cultivating relationships. These partnerships and relationships seem mutually beneficial at first. But all that Chinese Communist money comes with strings attached. No, not strings. Chains. And when Chairman Xi yanks your chain, you must obey.

When Will We Rise Up?

In December 2020, the Trump administration proposed a federal rule, to be administered by the Department of Homeland Security, requiring American colleges and universities to disclose any arrangements with Communist China to host Confucius Institutes on their campuses. In a disastrous decision, President Joe Biden rescinded that rule days after his inauguration.[20]

The United States Senate, through the Permanent Subcommittee on Investigations, has repeatedly warned of the malevolent influence of Confucius Institutes and Confucius Classrooms. In a report titled "China's Impact on The U.S. Education System," the Senate subcommittee concluded, "Through Confucius Institutes, the Chinese government is attempting to change the impression in the United States and around the world that China is an economic and security threat. Confucius Institutes' soft power encourages complacency towards China's pervasive, long-term initiatives against both government critics at home and businesses and academic institutions abroad."[21]

Numerous senators have called for the closure of Confucius Institutes across America. Senator Susan Collins of Maine said, "The Chinese Communist Party uses Confucius Institutes as backdoors to spread their propaganda and undermine constitutional freedoms on college campuses as well as in the wider community."[22] And Senator Tom Cotton of Arkansas said, "Confucius Institutes are front groups for the Chinese Communist Party on American campuses. The federal government ought to shut down these regime-run institutes or, at a minimum, require colleges to disclose their secret agreements with them."[23]

Stanford University opened its Confucius Institute, funded by Communist China, in 2009. The university also opened the Stanford Center at Peking University in 2012. While claiming to espouse human rights, free expression, and racial equality, Stanford accepted $58.1 million in gifts and contracts from the oppressive Communist Chinese regime from 2013 to 2020.[24] Stanford, with its world-famous SLAC National Accelerator Laboratory, is a prime target for espionage. Stanford is sitting on a $28.9 billion endowment, so it hardly needs to sell out to Communist China. But as we've seen in previous chapters, greed drives the college scam.

Chinese dictator Xi Jinping is working steadily toward achieving his "China Dream" of replacing America as the world's only superpower. Through the Confucius Institutes, Xi deceives American students about the intentions of the authoritarian Chinese Communist regime. As Xi tightens his grip on China, he worries about a repeat of the Tiananmen Square student protests. He is terrified that his people might rise up to topple the Chinese Communist Party. God willing, his worst nightmare will be realized sometime soon.

I love the wonderful Chinese people, but I hate the authoritarian Communist system that imprisons them. When will the Chinese people rise up against the Communist Party? And more to the point, when will the American people rise up against the Confucius Institutes and the colleges and universities that have invited these Trojan horses inside America's gates?

> I love the wonderful Chinese people, but I hate the authoritarian Communist system that imprisons them.

And China isn't the only nation that has rolled a Trojan horse inside the walls of American academia.

Shaping American Opinion and Policy

From 2012 to 2019, more than $10 billion poured into American university coffers from foreign countries. All of this supposed "generosity" toward American academia serves only one purpose: to shape public opinion and policy in the United States. Those funds come from such countries as Qatar, Saudi Arabia, Russia, and China. Though universities are required to disclose foreign gifts, there are accounting techniques and legal loopholes that enable many schools to take in *unreported* funds. For example, Iran made donations to some thirty U.S. and Canadian universities through a known front organization, so none of these funds are reported as foreign donations.[25]

According to a Clarion Project review of Education Department records, the tiny but wealthy Islamic nation of Qatar (population 2.8 million) provided almost $1.5 billion to twenty-eight American universities and colleges from 2012 to 2019. The Clarion study notes that funding often comes from entities with "known links to subversion, spying, terrorism and extremist ideology" and cited the example of the "terror-linked Qatar Foundation" which donated $33 million to Georgetown University in a single year, 2018.[26]

The Muslim Brotherhood established a front organization, the International Institute of Islamic Thought, to fund and train academics in the U.S. According to the Clarion Project, the organization has been investigated for ties to Hamas, Palestinian Islamic Jihad, and foreign governments. Because it was chartered in the U.S., it is legally considered an American entity, so its donations are not counted as foreign donations.[27]

Here is the Clarion Project's analysis of reported foreign donations to American universities, 2012 to 2019:

1. Qatar	$1.5 billion	28 universities
2. China	$680 million	87 universities
3. Saudi Arabia	$650 million	63 universities
4. United Arab Emirates	$231 million	32 universities
5. Russia	$99 million	13 universities
6. Kuwait	$66 million	17 universities
7. Iraq	$44 million	4 universities
8. Turkey	$38 million	15 universities

Also on the list are Lebanon, Pakistan, Venezuela, Syria, and the Palestinian Authority. Even though these are far from wealthy nations, they considered it a good investment to donate huge sums of money to American universities. The

Palestinian Authority, which constantly pleads poverty, donated more than $1 million to Harvard University (which has a $40.9 billion endowment).[28]

Saudi Arabia funnels money to American colleges and universities largely through Middle Eastern Studies (MES) programs and centers on campus. The Saudis hope to sway the opinions of future American leaders and policymakers. They target universities viewed as "feeder schools" to the State Department and other government agencies. The Saudi government also sponsors thousands of Saudi students at American universities.[29]

A Brookings Institution analysis of foreign students studying in the United States from 2008 to 2012 showed that Saudis comprised 5 percent of foreign students on F-1 student visas, the fifth highest percentage of all nations. China placed first with 25 percent of foreign students—which is not surprising, given China's population. What is surprising is that, on a per capita basis, Saudi Arabia had *more than ten times* as many students studying at American universities as China.[30]

American colleges and universities are being inundated with foreign students, foreign money, and foreign organizations. Lax accountability allows universities to accept billions in foreign money with hardly any transparency. Hostile foreign nations are buying political leverage, stealing America's secrets, spying on their own nationals in America, and indoctrinating American students with their "cultural" propaganda programs.

> Hostile foreign nations are buying political leverage, stealing America's secrets, spying on their own nationals in America, and indoctrinating American students with their "cultural" propaganda programs.

Anti-Semitism, Pure and Simple

In March 2019, I visited Israel as a guest of the Im Tirtzu Zionist organization (whose name is based on the Hebrew saying *Im tirtzu ein zo agadah*, "If you will it, it is no dream"). At a Jerusalem restaurant, my hosts invited me to give a talk to about the cultural and political ties between the United States and Israel. I told the audience about my growing concern about radical Marxism and foreign influences on American campuses.

"Colleges and universities," I said, "are a growing threat to the world, because they are turning out hordes of indoctrinated leftists. An entire generation is being brainwashed into an ideology of destruction that has nothing but hatred for both America and Israel. These young radicals have been fed a Marxist worldview that sees everything as a struggle between victims and oppressors. Because America and Israel are the two greatest success stories in human history, these radicals see America and Israel as oppressors, and they want to tear America and Israel down."

I told them I was dismayed to see the rise of militantly anti-Israel groups on American campuses. One of those groups, Jewish Voice for Peace (JVP) seeks to undermine America's support for Israel. Another, IfNotNow, actively opposes Israel's presence in Gaza and the West Bank. Both groups are anti-Zionist and their message is making inroads on campus.

These Jewish anti-Zionist groups often join forces with pro-Palestinian Islamic groups like Students for Justice in Palestine. I've had many conversations with students in both groups, and I often say, "So you're upset about supposed injustices in Israel. Do you also oppose the oppressive dictatorships in China, Iran, and North Korea?" They say, "No, we just want to undermine Israel." They seek the destruction of Israel—and that's anti-Semitism, pure and simple.

Americans and Israelis face a common foe on American campuses: radical-left, anti-American, anti-Israeli student organizations.

Under the Guise of "Social Justice"

In July 2018, the Israeli Knesset passed the "Nation-State Bill," declaring Israel to be the nation-state of the Jewish people. Half a world away, at Stanford University, twenty-year-old Hamzeh Daoud, a Palestinian Arab raised in Jordan, posted his angry response on Facebook, "I'm gonna physically fight Zionists on campus next year if someone comes at me with their 'Israel is a democracy' bullshit. And after I abolish your ass I'll go ahead and work every day for the rest of my life to abolish your petty ass ethno-supremacist, settler-colonial state."[31]

Daoud was slated to become a resident assistant in the fall. Apparently realizing that it's uncool for RAs to threaten students, Daoud edited his Facebook post, changing "physically fight" to "intellectually fight." He later resigned his RA position and, in a letter to the *Stanford Daily*, apologized for his original post.

Where did his rage and hatred come from? Much of it undoubtedly came from his membership in a radical organization, Students for Justice in Palestine (SJP).[32]

The Zionist Organization of America calls SJP "the largest student anti-Israel group in the country. While the group claims to fight for a positive cause, it in fact aims solely for the annihilation of the only Jewish state. SJP tries to hide under the guise of 'social justice,' when in reality, the group promotes hatred and intolerance."[33]

With 200 campus chapters nationwide, SJP has enormous influence. Many student activists and professors express anti-Semitic ideas, such as equating Zionism (nationalist support for Israel) with racism, Nazism, and white supremacy. The anti-Semitic leanings of the campus left are intensified by "woke" ideology, which reinterprets the nation of Israel as a "colonizer nation." Ignoring the reality that Jews lived in the Holy Land thousands of years before Christians and Muslims, the radical left views Israelis as "European settlers" who are "stealing" land from "indigenous" Palestinians. This false narrative enables leftists to feel justified in their hatred of Jews and Israel.

"DePaul Must Dump Hill!"

Jason D. Hill is a tenured philosophy professor at DePaul University in Chicago. Born in Jamaica, he is black, openly gay, and politically conservative. In April 2020, Dr. Hill filed suit against DePaul University, provost Salma Ghanem, and Faculty Council president Scott Paeth. The suit accuses them of defamation, breach of contract, and economic interference.

Hill claims that DePaul University, Ghanem, and Paeth waged an "unfair campaign of harassment" against him, targeting him because he is black and gay. He also said that university officials were trying to dismiss him from his tenured position.

The controversy began with an April 2019 piece Hill wrote for *The Federalist* titled "The Moral Case for Israel Annexing the West Bank—And Beyond." In that piece, Hill stated, "Israel has the moral right to annex all of the West Bank, for a plethora of reasons. Israel's right to exist is non-negotiable and it has a right to unilaterally apply Israeli law over its nation-state."[34]

It might seem unlikely that a far-left institution like DePaul would attack a professor for being black and gay. But Dr. Hill's court filing explains how the university mistreated him in a way that is both racist and homophobic:

> Dr. Hill has been subject to these discriminatory actions on account of his race and sexual orientation, in that he has departed from opinion defendants have deemed permissible and acceptable for someone of his race and sexual orientation, whom defendants require to espouse prevailing liberal opinion . . . against Israel.
>
> More particularly, defendants have subjected Dr. Hill to unlawful racial discrimination in that as an African-American they expect him to adhere to the opinion that African-Americans, whose ancestors were slaves, must view the Palestinians as an enslaved race and the Israeli government as a slave regime.[35]

According to the filing, the DePaul Faculty Council drew up a formal resolution of censure, drafted by Paeth. The resolution claimed that Hill "expresses positions that are factually inaccurate, advocate war crimes and ethnic cleansing, and give voice to racism with respect to the Palestinian populations." The resolution called Hill's *Federalist* op-ed "an abuse of academic freedom" that failed to "exercise adequate concern for accuracy, restraint, or respect for the opinions of others, as per AAUP guidelines." According to Hill, the claim that he had violated the guidelines of the American Association of University Professors (AAUP) was a pretext for eventually firing him.

That full text of the Faculty Council resolution, with its defamatory accusations, was published online by the student newspaper, *The DePaulia*.[36] Rifqa Falaneh, a board member of Students for Justice in Palestine, celebrated the resolution. "This is a really big win for us and we're not stopping here," she said.[37]

Soon Hill began receiving death threats in his campus email. On April 23, 2019, students staged a "Dump Hill" protest. Signs hanging in the Arts and Letters Hall read "DePaul Must Dump Hill!" and "Palestine Is Not up for Debate!"[38] On April 26, Hill wrote an email to the provost, Salma Ghanem, stating in part:

> Students are still protesting—they just yesterday stormed my department and inundated the floors with 3 different flyers with my picture on it, calling that all sorts of punitive actions still be taken against me. I am still receiving threats. . . .
>
> My concern right now is for my physical safety. Campus security has assessed the situation and decided that I am still in need of escort on campus for at least the next week or so. . . . My home institution [DePaul] feels like a threatening and hostile work environment. . . .
>
> So, I am truly here, asking for your help.[39]

Hill says that Ghanem not only refused to help, but she publicly encouraged those who attacked him. Faculty members urged students to boycott Hill's classes and co-sponsored a dinner for students on May 28 with an invitation that read, "Come Celebrate the Censure of Professor Hill." DePaul permitted students to occupy buildings and distribute leaflets depicting Hill as "a racist, a xenophobe, a sexist," and demanding his termination.[40]

This kind of concerted persecution of a tenured professor seems surreal—but this is the impact that foreign-based organizations are having at DePaul and on campuses across the nation.

The Education and Anti-Semitism Connection

In March 2021, *Tablet*, an American-Jewish online magazine, published a story about a survey conducted by researchers Jay P. Greene, Albert Cheng, and Ian Kingsbury. For years, *Tablet* says American Jews have trusted that education, especially higher education, would be the *remedy* to intolerance and anti-Semitism. However, the survey by Greene, Cheng, and Kingsbury shows that higher education actually *increases* anti-Semitism.

The conventional wisdom states that teaching courses in "diversity, equity, and inclusion" should make students more welcoming of Jews and other minorities. Earlier surveys seemed to confirm this view. But researchers Greene, Cheng, and Kingsbury suspected a flaw in the methodology of previous surveys, which simply asked respondents their opinion of Jews and whether they agree with certain obvious anti-Semitic stereotypes.

Greene, Cheng, and Kingsbury devised a more subtle survey to uncover people's *real* attitudes toward Jews. They explained:

> We developed a new survey measure based on . . . [the] defining feature of anti-Semitism: the double standard. We drafted two versions of the same question, one asking respondents to apply a principle to a Jewish example, and another to apply the same principle to a non-Jewish example. Subjects were randomly assigned to see one version or another so that no respondent would see both versions of the question. . . . Sophisticated respondents would have no way of knowing that we were measuring their sentiment toward Jews, and no cue to game their answers.[41]

For example, the survey asked whether "a person's attachment to another country creates a conflict of interest when advocating in support of certain U.S. foreign policy positions." Some respondents were asked that question with Israel as an example. Others were asked with Mexico as an example. Respondents with more education tended to judge Israel more harshly than Mexico.

The survey was administered to more than 1,800 people and the results were striking. The researchers found that it was education, not ignorance, that produced anti-Semitism. "By preventing subjects from knowing that they were being asked about their feelings toward Jews," wrote the authors, "we discovered that more-highly educated people in the United States tend to have greater antipathy toward Jews than less-educated people do."[42]

Colleges and universities teach young people to hate Israel and be suspicious of Jews. The more education, the greater the anti-Semitism. The researchers found that a bachelor's degree made people 5 percent more likely to hold anti-Semitic views. For people with advanced degrees, that figure rose to 15 percent. People with advanced degrees were 11 percent more likely to oppose in-person Jewish funerals during the COVID-19 pandemic than Black Lives Matter protests.[43]

> Colleges and universities teach young people to hate Israel and be suspicious of Jews. The more education, the greater the anti-Semitism.

Anti-Semitism is alive and well on college campuses because it is being nurtured and taught there. If we want to eliminate xenophobia and anti-Semitism, don't look to higher education as the solution. Higher education is the problem.

Anti-Jewish, Anti-Israel Activism on Campus

Here are a few among many documented instances of anti-Jewish, anti-Israel hate on American campuses:

At Georgetown University, Students for Justice in Palestine held an "Israeli Apartheid Week" in early April 2019. Events included the construction of an "apartheid wall," a showing of the Al Jazeera documentary *The Lobby* (which alleges that pro-Israel lobbyists have too much influence on the U.S. government), and a panel on Boycott, Divestment, and Sanctions (BDS)—the movement to force Israel to its knees through economic blackmail. The campus newspaper *The Hoya* called Israeli Apartheid Week an effort "to raise awareness about the Israeli state policies against Palestinian citizens."[44]

The University of Massachusetts at Amherst conducted panel discussions on Israel in May and November 2019. Both events featured only pro-BDS, anti-Israel speakers. At the November event, radical socialist Cornel West applied the Marxist victim-oppressor narrative to the Palestinian-Israeli conflict. Acknowledging that Jews had been "hated, despised, devalued, oppressed, attacked for 2,000 years," he asserted that Jews are now "in a top dog status and losing sight of their own underdogs, the precious Palestinians."[45]

In April 2019, at the University of Texas at Austin, Hillel (the foundation for Jewish campus life) planned an "Israel Block Party" event. When the campus chapter of IfNotNow learned of the event, its members organized a campus-wide petition calling on students to "denounce" the Hillel block party. The petition claimed that Hillel "ignores the occupation, ignores the existence of Palestinians, glorifies the militarization of Israel, [and] endorses the racist Israeli government."[46]

At California State University at Fullerton, in April 2019 and again in November, radical activists constructed an "apartheid wall" bearing the slogan "Zionism = Racism."[47] At New York University, the campus chapter of Students for Justice in Palestine tweeted, "We are UNITED against racism, sexism, transphobia, homophobia, Zionism, and Islamophobia."[48] At Vassar College in New York, a Facebook post by Students for Justice in Palestine proclaimed, "Zionism is inherently racist," because it "necessitates the displacement and subjugation of the Palestinian people."[49]

In April 2019, the Portland State University chapter of Jewish Voice for Peace held an "Israel Apartheid Week," selling T-shirts emblazoned with the hateful message "Israel is a garbage country that's only loved by garbage people. It was founded on ethnic cleansing, apartheid and settler-colonialism. Its flag is a symbol of white supremacy."[50]

During a November rally in New York's Times Square, a crowd chanted, "From Palestine to Mexico, all the walls have got to go!" A representative from Students for Justice in Palestine told the crowd, "We're gonna have an intifada in every classroom! We're gonna have an intifada on every college campus! We're gonna shut down all the Zionist events!"[51]

The entire campus leftist movement is riddled with anti-Israel hostility and anti-Semitism. The heated rhetoric on campus today raises the specter of hate, lies, and suspicion against Jews that have given us a tragic history of pogroms and the Holocaust.

That's my case for Count 8 of our ten-count indictment of the college industry: *"Colleges and universities have been infiltrated by subversive foreign groups."* So tell me, should we have a "boycott, divestment and sanctions" movement against Israel—or against the Great College Swindle?

9

WOKE AND WEAPONIZED

COUNT 9:

Colleges and universities have unleashed waves of woke,

anti-American radicals.

On August 6, 2018, at around 8:30 in the morning, Candace Owens and I were having a chicken-and-waffles breakfast at the Green Eggs Café in Philadelphia. We saw Antifa patches on the clothing of four people at another table, and we figured they probably wouldn't recognize us.

But they did.

After a while, we heard shouts and chants. We looked out the windows and noticed a crowd on the sidewalk. We could see the restaurant servers and patrons becoming alarmed, so Candace and I got up, paid our bill, and told the servers that we're conservatives and this kind of harassment happens all the time.

I turned to the restaurant patrons, who were staring open-mouthed at the commotion, and said, "Have a wonderful day. Enjoy your capitalist breakfast."

We walked outside to face the protesters. They were almost all young white people, the pampered product of our leftist university system. They encircled us so we couldn't leave, chanting, "One, two, three—f*ck the bourgeoisie! Four, five, six—f*ck the bourgeoisie!"

I hate to be critical, but that's a pathetic chant. "Six" doesn't even rhyme with "bourgeoisie." Plus, the poetic meter was terrible. At least they included "bourgeoisie" to show their Marxist bona fides.

They shouted and waved with one finger. We smiled and waved with all five fingers.

They switched to another chant: "F*ck white su-prem-a-cy!" Again, terrible poetic meter and no rhyme—and since neither Candace nor I are white supremacists, what was the point?

When they got tired of chanting, they switched to an even less rational tactic: they gathered around us, blew whistles, and screamed in our ears. They didn't scream slogans. They just screamed like banshees. Or like Yoko Ono.

It was amusing, and we smiled and recorded the festivities with our phones—until a blonde young woman stepped forward and squeezed a bottle of water at my head and chest.

> They were self-proclaimed "anti-facists" using textbook fascist tactics, and they themselves were the very "bourgeoisie" they were protesting.

I'm always eager to have a conversation with people who disagree with me. But Antifa radicals—these mostly white, indoctrinated trust-fund kids—have no interest in a conversation. Their "conversation" is incoherent screaming, dumping a drink on someone, or in some cases, a bike lock to the head.

Moments after the young woman threw water on me, Philadelphia police stepped in to move the protesters back. The police officers were mostly black and Hispanic, and several were female. The protesters—mostly white—started chanting, "No good cops in a racist system!"

These privileged protesters were completely oblivious to the irony: they were self-proclaimed "anti-facists" using textbook fascist tactics, and they themselves were the very "bourgeoisie" they were protesting. Their parents obviously had money, because these kids had plenty of time to protest and didn't need jobs. Their "bourgeois" parents paid the bills and made the sacrifices to send them to college, where they learned to despise the hand that fed them.

Candace and I went to each of the police officers, shook their hands, and thanked them. Our gratitude to the police prompted a young woman with a bullhorn to bellow, "They're not protecting us! They're not protecting you! They're not protecting anyone! They're protecting money and their salaries and their pensions!"

"This is so bizarre," Candace told a female officer. "These white people are saying 'no racists' and 'no good cops' when every cop here is black or Hispanic. We were just having breakfast. We're just conservatives. That's our crime."

Philly Antifa took credit for the incident. I hope their parents realize what a wise investment they made in sending their little darlings to Indoctrination U.

Terrorists on Campus

This brings us to Count 9 of our ten-count indictment of the college cartel: *"Colleges and universities have unleashed waves of woke, anti-American radicals."* One of the most dangerous waves of radicals the college industry has let loose on America is Antifa—a decentralized radical group engaging in both violent and nonviolent action to achieve its goals.

Powerful Democratic Congressman Jerry Nadler once said that Antifa is a "myth" that is "only being spread in Washington, D.C."[1] But Antifa is real and Antifa is on campus. Antifa thugs commit acts of vandalism, bullying, and violence against people they brand as "fascists." Who is a "fascist," according to Antifa? Literally any mainstream conservative or libertarian speaker, or anyone who attends a conservative event.

> Antifa is real and Antifa is on campus

Some Antifa members are even tenured professors. According to the *Stanford Review*, one Antifa ringleader is Stanford literature professor David Palumbo-Liu, a zealously anti-Israel academic who has written in support of the Boycott, Divestment, and Sanctions movement. On his website, Palumbo-Liu says that his writings have "appeared in The Washington Post, The Nation, The Guardian, Jacobin, Salon, Al Jazeera, The Hill, Buzzfeed, Vox, and other venues."[2]

The *Stanford Review* reports that Palumbo-Liu's Facebook page is full of Antifa propaganda and photos of masked Antifa members viciously assaulting "a peaceful pro-Trump rally" at Berkeley in August 2017. Moreover, the *Review* states, "Palumbo-Liu has a history of encouraging violent and militant leftist tactics, including by his own students. In 2015, Palumbo-Liu congratulated several of his students for taking part in an anti-Israel protest that caused car crashes and blocked traffic on the San Mateo Bridge for an hour, allegedly preventing a 3-year-old child in medical distress from reaching the hospital."[3]

Another Antifa prof is Purdue University's Bill Mullen, whose website describes him as a professor of English and American studies who specializes in "American Literature and Studies, African American Studies, Cultural Studies, Working-Class Studies, Critical Race Theory and Marxist Theory.[4] Mullen joined with David Palumbo-Liu to co-found the Campus Antifascist Network (CAN), which recruits students to the cause of "fighting fascism" on campus.

At Mullens's Campus Antifascist Network webpage, he writes that CAN was founded in the summer of 2017 by forty American academics in response to the "rampant rise of white supremacist and neo-Nazi groups." He adds that there are at least thirteen CAN chapters on campuses in North America and the United Kingdom. The CAN Mission Statement proclaims, "CAN brings together faculty, students, staff, and community members across US campuses to stem the rise of fascism, whether proudly displayed in hateful exclusionary slogans and posters, or disguised as 'free speech.'"[5]

Antifa agitators like David Palumbo-Liu and Bill Mullen empower themselves by peddling hate and paranoia on campus.

Antifa Threatens a Church

In 2021, Roger Archer, senior pastor of Motion Church in Puyallup, Washington, invited me to speak at his church. In addition to preaching the gospel, Motion Church is deeply involved in providing food, shelter, counseling services, addiction recovery programs, and education.

My speaking appearance was scheduled for May 2. As soon as the word went out that I was coming to Puyallup, Antifa terrorists sent anonymous threats to the church and the news media. They vowed not only to burn the church to the ground, but to burn down the neighborhood, assault church members, and run riot through the streets of Puyallup. They threatened arson, assault, murder, and domestic terrorism.

Pastor Archer called me and said that, out of concern for the community, he had to cancel my appearance. He told me that the Puyallup Police Department was supportive of the church's right to have me speak, but the police lacked the resources to contain a terrorist threat that could hit multiple locations at once. I told him I fully understood his decision. Motion Church had made the only decision possible under the circumstances.

The radical terrorists of Antifa have no conscience about burning down a church that actively cares for the people Antifa falsely *claims* to care for—the poor, the marginalized, the lost. To silence one mainstream conservative, they were willing to commit limitless destruction and mayhem.

Some of the blame for the rise of Antifa rests with Washington's far-left governor, Jay Inslee, who has hamstrung the police while making excuses for rioters, looters, and arsonists. Some of the blame rests with Jenny Durkan, the far-left mayor of nearby Seattle. She tolerated the radical takeover of six city blocks and a park by radical activists of the so-called "Capitol Hill Autonomous Zone." The actions—and inaction—of the governor and the mayor led to the resignation of more than 200 Seattle police officers from 2020 to 2021.

> The radical terrorists of Antifa have no conscience about burning down a church that actively cares for the people Antifa falsely claims to care for—the poor, the marginalized, the lost. To silence one mainstream conservative, they were willing to commit limitless destruction and mayhem.

No wonder the Seattle-area branch of Antifa feels it has the power to shut down constitutionally-protected speech. The government has granted them the heckler's veto. As Pastor Archer said in a YouTube video addressing the situation,

"Recent history has taught us that there is an apparent lack of interest at the state level of leadership to protect decent taxpaying citizens. Those terrorist mobs know that there is no consequence for their lawlessness. They have nothing to lose and nothing to fear."[6]

> All of academia is hopelessly riddled with Marxism, radicalism, and the teaching that violence is a justifiable response to opposing opinions.

But most of the blame for the rise of Antifa rests with the universities that breed and indoctrinate these terrorists. Professors like David Palumbo-Liu and Bill Mullen, with their Campus Antifascist Network, are just the visible symptoms of a much more widespread and metastatic cancer in our university system. All of academia is hopelessly riddled with Marxism, radicalism, and the teaching that violence is a justifiable response to opposing opinions.

Academia trains young people to bully people in the name of anti-bullying, to oppress people in the name of freedom, and to commit fascist acts in the name of anti-fascism. One of the defining traits of a fascist is the forcible, violent silencing of opponents and opposing ideas. Antifa may claim to be "anti-fascist," but if it looks like a fascist and it bullies like a fascist and it suppresses speech like a fascist—well, Antifa just might be a bunch of fascists.

The Mob Is Coming for You

Wokeism is a mindset of self-righteous hyper-vigilance against offenses, real or imagined. Woke sanctimony was on full display during the summer of 2020, when radical mobs tore down statue after statute—and not just monuments to Confederate generals. Woke rioters also toppled statues of Jesus, the Virgin Mary, Frederick Douglass, assorted abolitionists, assorted poets, George Washington, Thomas Jefferson, Abraham Lincoln, Ulysses S. Grant, Hiawatha, Mahatma Gandhi, and an elk, to name a few.[7]

There's nobody more woke than Professor Joyce Coleman, vice president of the School of Extended Learning at Santa Barbara City College. During a

Zoom meeting in March 2021, she reportedly told participants, "There is no such thing as not being racist. Either you are anti-racist or racist," echoing the false dichotomy offered by Ibram X. Kendi on page 9 of *How to Be an Antiracist*. She is also quoted as saying, "White folks are all on a journey to realize their own guilt."[8]

On March 23, 2021, she spoke to the college's Equal Opportunity Advisory Committee. The Committee had just formed a new "affinity group" on behalf of Asian Americans and Pacific Islanders. Affinity groups are a big thing in the leftist academia because progressives today aggressively promote racial segregation. Coleman said that "it's about time" that such an affinity group be formed for Asians.

She went on to say that she had always been baffled by Japanese-Americans during World War II who allowed themselves to be shut up in internment camps. While visiting an internment camp, she noticed that the fence was not very high and she wondered why people in the camps "did not just leave" the way Blacks had escaped to freedom via the Underground Railroad.[9]

People in the meeting were aghast and accused Professor Coleman of "victim blaming."[10] Which, of course, she was.

So, as of April 2021, Professor Joyce Coleman is suspended from her position for the crime of offending the Asian-American Pacific Islander community.[11] She has learned a bitter lesson: no matter how woke you think you are, eventually you'll say the wrong thing and the mob will come for you.

The Mission Has Changed

The University of North Carolina at Charlotte's mission is to "develop thoughtful, community-minded and engaged leaders and *citizens of the world.*"[12]

"Fairleigh Dickinson University is a center of academic excellence dedicated to the preparation of *world citizens* . . ."[13]

"Clark University's mission is to educate undergraduate and graduate students to be imaginative and contributing *citizens of the world* . . ."[14]

"The University of Washington educates a diverse student body to become responsible *global citizens*..."[15]

"Cornell's mission is to discover, preserve and disseminate knowledge, to educate the next generation of *global citizens*..."[16]

Look up the mission statement of just about any college or university in America, and it will probably read like the ones above: "Blah blah blah citizens of the world" or "Yadda yadda yadda global citizens." What does that even mean?

There was a time when the mission of the college or university was to prepare students for life by teaching them to pursue truth, defend liberty, and be good *American* citizens. In the process, students would learn the skills they need to have a good career and to contribute to society. There was a commonly held belief that the way to solve the world's problems was for America to set a good example to the world of liberty, personal responsibility, opportunity, and hard work.

> Radical professors are indoctrinating a generation into a nihilistic way of thinking and teaching them to hate America, reject their American citizenship, and become "citizens of the world."

No more. Today, colleges teach students that nothing matters except deconstructing and destroying everything around them. Radical professors are indoctrinating a generation into a nihilistic way of thinking and teaching them to hate America, reject their American citizenship, and become "citizens of the world." In the process, they are unleashing waves of angry young people on the world.

Shortly before Independence Day 2021, *Campus Reform* reporter Ophelie Jacobson went to Washington, D.C., and interviewed young women from Georgetown University. Jacobson's first question: "Are you proud to be an American?"

"No," said a young blonde. "I feel embarrassed to be an American every day. I think a lot of things about this country are really embarrassing. Just like, I mean, racist history, colonization, even currently, just what's going on with politics and the cops."

"Like, partly," said an Asian young lady. "I just think our economy just cares about money and not about humans in general."

"No," said a young black woman. "Be proud of what? What is there to be proud about if you're black and being, like, you know? Because like there's still a lot of stuff that goes on for black people."

Jacobson asked: "Do you think America is the greatest country in the world?" Again and again, the answer was, "No." One said, "I would honestly rather kind of live somewhere else." Jacobson asked the Georgetown girls, "Can you name a better country than the United States?" None of them could—though one young lady hesitantly offered, "Europe?"[17]

These are elite students at one of America's elite universities—yet they are embarrassed to be Americans. Is there any other nation in the world where students are taught to be embarrassed and ashamed of their country? Do you think college students in Communist China or Putin's Russia are taught to despise their own horrifying history?

I'm not suggesting that colleges and universities should cover up America's history of slavery and segregation. But along with those truths, students should learn about the great American heroes who abolished slavery and fought to end segregation. And for context, they should learn that there are nations *today*, such as Communist China, that *still* practice slavery on a shocking scale.

To see just how much the mission of academia has changed, consider this:

In January 2020, the Yale art history department announced it was eliminating one of its most popular courses, "Introduction to Art History: Renaissance to the Present." For decades, this course was *the* quintessential survey course. Its demise made news across the nation.

The public affairs journal *Commentary* responded: "Yale's Art Department Commits Suicide." The *New York Post* declared, "Barbarians at Yale: PC Idiocy Kills Classic Art History Class." The *Wall Street Journal* lamented, "Civilization Is History at Yale."

The original course was created by the world-renowned art historian Vincent Scully, whose lectures were famous for stirring emotions and summoning applause. That course was replaced by a new course created and taught by Tim Barringer, current chairman of Yale's art history department. Barringer cited all the "politically correct," woke reasons for canceling the original course. *The Yale Daily News* reported:

> This change is the latest response to student uneasiness over an idealized Western "canon"—a product of an overwhelmingly white, straight, European and male cadre of artists. . . . The course's instructor Tim Barringer told the *News* that he plans to demonstrate that a class about the history of art does not just mean Western art. Rather, when there are so many other regions, genres and traditions—all "equally deserving of study"—putting European art on a pedestal is "problematic," he said. . . .
>
> The class will also consider art in relation to "questions of gender, class and 'race'" and discuss its involvement with Western capitalism, Barringer wrote. Its relationship with climate change will be a "key theme," he wrote.[18]

> Today, college is a place where your professors tell you there is no truth, beauty, or goodness— such ideas are mere "social constructs," and you shouldn't waste your time searching for them.

Notice how easily Professor Barringer is able to transform an introductory art history course into an indoctrination session on gender, class, race, and "Western capitalism." And how does the history of art intersect with the "key theme" of climate change? Here we see in unmistakable terms how the mission of academia has changed. It has veered sharply away from education and toward indoctrination.

College used to be a place where your professors would introduce you to a world of truth, beauty, and goodness.

They would inspire you and ignite your imagination, and they would tell you that, if you work hard enough and study the great ideas of human history, you could discover what those words mean. Today, college is a place where your professors tell you there is no truth, beauty, or goodness—such ideas are mere "social constructs," and you shouldn't waste your time searching for them. Instead, they say, become an angry activist, join the revolution, and help tear down our civilization.

The old academic model has been swept away. In its place is the new academic model of the university as political indoctrination camp.

Today's campus is where young people go to become woke—and weaponized.

The Origin of Critical Theory—and "Wokeism"

Wokeism is a creation of Critical Theory, which encompasses Critical Legal Theory, Critical Race Theory, Critical Gender Studies, and on and on. Critical Theory had its origins in the ideas of Herbert Marcuse, Paul-Michel Foucault, and other Postmodern thinkers. From Critical Theory in its many forms comes what I call the "Diversity-Industrial Complex."

In his 1961 farewell address, President Eisenhower warned against the "Military-Industrial Complex," an unholy alliance between the military and the defense industry. In much the same way, the "Diversity-Industrial Complex" is an unholy alliance among the woke, "diversity"-obsessed professors, administrators, journalists, leftist politicians, entertainers, and social media entrepreneurs who control the commanding heights of our culture.

The term "woke" can be traced to a colleague of Herbert Marcuse, a Brazilian neo-Marxist named Paulo Freire. In *Pedagogy of the Oppressed*, Freire coined a term in Portuguese: *conscientização*, or "critical consciousness." A person reaches critical consciousness when he or she achieves a Marxist understanding of the world. A person who has reached critical consciousness is ready to join the revolution against the world's oppressive systems. Reaching critical consciousness is like waking from sleep. Once "awakened" to critical consciousness, a person is said to be "woke."

For decades, Black America had been making steady progress, according to the liberal Brookings Institution. In a 1998 study, "Black Progress: How Far We've Come, and How Far We Have to Go," Brookings found that 60 percent of black female employees worked as domestic servants in 1940 versus 2.2 percent in 1998 (in fact, 60 percent of black female employees in 1998 held white-collar jobs). In 1964, the year Congress passed the Civil Rights Act, 18 percent of whites had a black friend versus 86 percent in 1998; also in 1998, 87 percent of blacks claimed to have white friends. Many other statistics told a similar story of steady improvement in race relations. Brookings concluded, "Progress is the largely suppressed story of race and race relations over the past half-century."[19]

But while race relations were improving in society, university and college campuses quietly kept racism on life support, decade after decade. Now we see racism, in the form of Critical Race Theory and wokeness, vomited forth from the deep recesses of academia to be injected into American society.

At the beginning of 2020, hardly any Americans had ever heard of Critical Race Theory (CRT). But after the Black Lives Matter protests of 2020, there are few people who *haven't* heard of CRT. Yet much of the talk about CRT in the media, both right and left, is riddled with misunderstanding, hyperbole, and lies. Most conservatives only know that CRT is a scary idea and we don't want it in our public schools. And most progressives claim (either ignorantly or dishonestly) that CRT is merely a conversation about racism and the legacy of slavery in America. To clear away the misunderstanding, let's see where Critical Theory began.

Critical Theory was founded by Herbert Marcuse and other "Frankfurt School" Marxist theoreticians. Marcuse emigrated from Germany to the United States in 1934. In the 1950s, he taught political science at Columbia University, later at Harvard University, then at Brandeis University in Massachusetts. Marcuse's neo-Marxist writings and speeches at student protests strongly influenced the student movement of the 1960s, earning him the title "Father of the New Left."

In October 1962, during a campus rally protesting the Cuban Missile Crisis, Marcuse met eighteen-year-old Angela Davis. She was a black student studying French at Brandeis. Marcuse invited her to join his philosophy class and encouraged her to become a revolutionary activist. When Marcuse moved to the University of California at San Diego in 1965, Davis moved, too, and Marcuse served as her doctoral advisor. Davis went on to teach at UCLA, San Francisco State University, and UC Santa Cruz.

Angela Davis achieved infamy in 1970 as a fugitive from justice. She was wanted by the FBI for supplying guns used in a Marin County courtroom siege that killed a judge and three gunmen. After a two-month pursuit by the FBI, she was captured, tried, and acquitted (prosecutors couldn't prove she knew the guns would be used in a crime). Davis ran twice for president on the Communist Party USA ticket and has been preaching "abolish the police" and "overthrow the capitalist class" since the 1960s. She continues to teach at UC Santa Cruz and lecture at Yale and elsewhere.

In 1965, Herbert Marcuse released his essay, "Repressive Tolerance." James Lindsay, America's leading expert on Critical Theory and Wokeism, writes:

> The logic of the left today is overwhelmingly rooted in a single essay published in 1965 by the neo-Marxist philosopher Herbert Marcuse. That essay is "Repressive Tolerance." The thesis statement of this essay can be boiled down to "movements from the left must be extended tolerance, even when they are violent, while movements from the right must not be tolerated, including suppressing them by violence." This asymmetric ethic has been the heart and soul of left politics in the West since the 1960s, and we're living in the fruit of that catastrophe now.[20]

(Lindsay has been a guest on my podcast. If you want an in-depth understanding of Critical Theory and Wokeism, take a deep dive into his *New Discourses* podcast and read *Cynical Theories* by James Lindsay and Helen Pluckrose.)

Marcuse's image of a perfect society is that brutally straightforward. He wants the political left to have all the power and privilege, and he wants the right to be silenced and ultimately extinct. Lindsay notes that it's easy to see how Marcuse's argument "has set the stage for the totalitarianism we see today in Wokeism and from Big Tech."[21]

Who gets to decide what is true and what is false? Who gets to decide what ideas are tolerated and what ideas must be suppressed? According to Marcuse, these decisions must be left to the Marxist Critical Theorists. As Lindsay observes:

> In our own time, it is the Woke and the high-powered elites
> in government, media, education, and law who have taken
> up this mantle of being able to decide, in the spirit of Herbert
> Marcuse, what must be tolerated, no matter how bad it is, and
> what must be suppressed, no matter how legitimate it is. The
> parallels to our own time are undeniable. . . . We live in the
> asymmetric and totalitarian logic of "Repressive Tolerance"
> today.[22]

Nowhere is this atmosphere of "repressive tolerance" more shamelessly displayed than on American college campuses.

Replacing "Class Struggle" with "Race Struggle"

Classical Marxism—the economic and social theory of Karl Marx and Friedrich Engels—is a materialist interpretation of history and society. Marx focused on the struggle between two classes—the "proletariat" (the oppressed people who sell their labor and add value to the goods they produce) and the "bourgeoisie" (those who own the means of production and who exploit the proletariat for profit). Marxism is a "good versus evil" fable with a victim and a villain. In the Marxist fable, the proletariat is the noble victim, the bourgeoisie is the wicked and villainous oppressor.

Since the founding of the Soviet Union in 1922, more than two dozen nations have tried a Marxist form of government, from the once-mighty Soviet Union to the tiny Caribbean island of Grenada. Of all the nations that have tried a Marxist government, how many are still Marxist today? Just five: China, Cuba, Laos, Vietnam, and North Korea.

Why did all those other nations abandon Marxism? Because Marxism fails every time it's tried. The five remaining Communist states have had to violate Marxist dogma and adopt market-based reforms to survive. Pure Marxism only works in theory, never in reality. A system that does away with private property ownership, market incentives, and human liberty inevitably leads to poverty, starvation, corruption, and political repression. Yet the Marxists keep trying to impose their failed ideology on us all.

One of the cleverest attempts to rescue Marxism from the ash heap of history is Critical Race Theory. Marx predicted that the proletariat would inevitably rise up and revolt against the oppressors—but Marx's proletarian revolution never materialized.[23] CRT theorists recognized this flaw in classical Marxism, so they adapted Marx's victim/oppressor narrative, replacing "class struggle" with "race struggle."

> Marxism fails every time it's tried.

In neo-Marxist Critical Race Theory, victims are oppressed because of their race, ethnicity, gender, or sexual orientation. In CRT, the oppressive "bourgeoisie" have been replaced by a "white supremacist" power structure. CRT claims that racism is the fundamental organizing force in society, and that all of America's founding documents, laws, education system, economic system, and society are founded on white supremacy.

Critical Race Theory was devised in the mid-1970s by a number of legal scholars, most notably Harvard law professor Derrick Bell and his student Kimberlé Crenshaw. Building on the Critical Theory of Herbert Marcuse, Bell and his colleagues hammered out a framework that viewed white supremacy as a social construct to empower white people while disempowering blacks and other minorities.

Around the time Derrick Bell was laying the foundations for Critical Race Theory, the U.S. Supreme Court heard a case titled *Regents of the University of California v. Bakke*. Allan P. Bakke, a white Vietnam veteran and former NASA engineer in his early thirties, was rejected by the University of California, Davis, medical school, even though less qualified nonwhite applicants were accepted. He filed suit, citing the Equal Protection Clause of the Fourteenth Amendment, and fought the case to the Supreme Court.

The high court announced its decision in June 1978. Justice Lewis F. Powell Jr. wrote the majority opinion, which struck down the U.C. Davis minority admissions plan, and ordered that Bakke be admitted to the medical school. Powell wrote that the "guarantee of equal protection cannot mean one thing when applied to one individual and something else when applied to a person of another color. If both are not accorded the same protection, then it is not equal."[24]

Powell's opinion rejected racial quotas but did not ban using race as a factor in college admissions. While Allan Bakke won the right to enter medical school, the practice of affirmative action—granting advantages to some racial groups by disadvantaging others—continues in college admissions to this day.

One of the dissenting opinions in the Bakke decision became a cornerstone rationale for Critical Race Theory. Justice Harry Blackmun (who famously wrote the majority opinion in *Roe v. Wade*) defended his dissent: "In order to get beyond racism, we must first take account of race. There is no other way. And in order to treat some persons equally, we must treat them differently."[25] Blackmun's looking-glass "logic" has had an enormous impact on Critical Race Theory thinking over the years. Ibram X. Kendi quoted Blackmun's words in *How to Be an Antiracist*, and added this commentary of his own: "The only remedy to racist discrimination is antiracist discrimination. The only remedy to past discrimination is present discrimination. The only remedy to present discrimination is future discrimination."[26] In short, discrimination without end.

The Supreme Court decision in the Bakke case enabled Allan Bakke to overcome an unjust policy at U.C. Davis. But that decision also helped lay the philosophical groundwork for Critical Race Theory, which is tearing our society apart today.

Derrick Bell's Totalitarian Mindset

Thomas Sowell is a black conservative economist and a senior fellow at the Hoover Institution, a conservative think tank at Stanford University. As a college student, Sowell was a committed Marxist. He graduated magna cum laude from Harvard in 1958, and earned a master's at Columbia in 1959. While pursuing his doctorate in economics at the University of Chicago, he was mentored by free-market economist Milton Friedman. There, Sowell questioned—and eventually abandoned—Marxism.

As a former Marxist, Sowell understands Marxism from the inside out. He recalls a long and disturbing conversation he had with Derrick Bell in the 1980s.

"There is this ideological intolerance that Bell has," Sowell told an interviewer. "He really has a sort of totalitarian mindset. . . . He's not a stupid man. But you have to understand, Derrick Bell was put in an impossible position. He was hired as a full professor at Harvard Law School when he himself said [he was not qualified]."[27]

In a 2012 newspaper column—written years before most Americans ever heard of Critical Race Theory—Sowell drew upon his acquaintance with Derrick Bell to explain the origin of the race-based notion that is ripping our society apart today. Sowell describes Bell as a professor whose writings on Critical Race Theory promote "an extremist hostility to white people." But Derrick Bell wasn't always an extremist.

For years, Sowell writes, Bell was "a civil rights lawyer, but not an academic legal scholar of the sort who gets appointed as a full professor at one of the leading law schools." Sowell describes Bell's mindset: "He could not expect to command the respect of either faculty or students at the Harvard law school—or, more important, his own self-respect. Bell himself admitted that he did not have the scholarly credentials that most full professors at the Harvard law school have."

Derrick Bell had two options: he could live in obscurity as a minor legal scholar at Harvard—or, Sowell said, Bell could invent "some wild tangent of his own, and appeal to a radical racial constituency on campus and beyond."

Building on the radical Marxist ideas of Herbert Marcuse, Bell constructed a new interpretation of social structures and power, viewed through the lens of racial grievance. Sowell notes that Bell's previous writings had been those of "a sensible man saying sensible things about civil rights." But once he invented Critical Race Theory, Bell's writings were rife with irrational and incoherent claims, "the main drift of which was that white people were the cause of black people's problems."[28]

Today, the woke violence of Antifa, the woke insurgence of Black Lives Matter, the radicalism in academia, the bullying "racial justice training" sessions at major corporations, and the coercive "anti-racist" agenda of Ibram X. Kendi—all of this corrosive societal idiocy can be traced back to the inferiority feelings of Derrick Bell. His ideas are poisoning our society and threatening to plunge America into a suicidal race war.

The Tenets of Critical Race Theory

Here's a "quick start" summary of the basic tenets and themes of Critical Race Theory:

- CRT claims that racism is present in every aspect of society; therefore, society can only be transformed by a race-conscious approach, not a "colorblind" approach.

- CRT rejects the concept of "equality" (equal opportunity) in favor of a demand for "equity" (equal outcomes). We must take race into account at all times and equalize outcomes for all racial groups.

- CRT rejects evidence and reason in favor of storytelling and speaking one's "lived experience." This silences debate because no one is allowed to question another person's "lived experience."

- CRT disregards science and reason as "white" ways of knowing. Storytelling and "lived experience" are "black" ways of knowing.

- CRT offers a revisionist interpretation of U.S. history, in which civil rights gains for American blacks only happened when it suited the self-interest of the white power structure.

- A key concept in CRT is "intersectionality" (attributed to Kimberlé Crenshaw) which states that your racial identity intersects with your other identities—gender, economic class, physical disability, and so forth—to create complex combinations of "privilege" or disadvantage.

- CRT segregates people into socially constructed groups according to the boxes they check. CRT does not recognize individuals or individual rights.

- CRT seeks to dismantle our free society and replace it with a controlled society. (Guess who's in control.)

- CRT bullies anyone who disagrees with CRT; if you disagree or deny, it's because you're a white supremacist (even if you are black conservative or a black police officer, who is part of the "white" power structure). CRT is essentially totalitarian, demands absolute conformity, and punishes those who think for themselves.

Popularizers of Critical Race Theory include Robin DiAngelo, a white academic who has become extremely wealthy conducting corporate "diversity training" seminars. Her bestselling book *White Fragility: Why It's So Hard for White People to Talk About Racism* is cleverly designed to put white people in a no-win situation, first demanding that they take part in a conversation about racism, then using anything they say against them. Deny being a racist, and it's proof of your "white fragility." DiAngelo doesn't claim to be a CRT theorist, but she has built her "white fragility" argument on a foundation of CRT.

CRT Is Not a Fad

For more than four decades, Critical Race Theory was the subject of academic discussions in elite law schools, completely unnoticed by most Americans. In the leftist media, we heard CRT buzzwords like "equity," "implicit bias," "colonialism," and "white privilege," but these theoretical conversations about race seemed far removed from our lives.

Sure, we all knew that "people of color" faced tougher economic and employment challenges than the average white American. Yes, we all knew that racism was still a reality in twenty-first-century America. But we believed in Dr. King's dream of a colorblind America, in which all people would be judged by the content of their character, not the color of their skin. And for a while, it seemed we were moving toward that goal.

Then came May 2020 and the death of George Floyd. Black Lives Matter and Antifa unleashed waves of protests across the nation. Cities and states were unprepared for the onslaught of protests, riots, murders, and looting of the summer of 2020. Coming amidst the coronavirus pandemic, it seemed we were caught in an insane cultural moment. Soon, everyone was talking about this idea called Critical Race Theory.

Some say CRT is a fad that will eventually burn itself out. Don't believe it. Critical Race Theory is not a fad. Wokeism is not a fad. These ideas, though false and destructive, have staying power. They have been institutionalized as dogmas in academia and are gaining traction in all other institutions of our society. Major corporations, the government, and the military are already implementing "diversity training" programs based on CRT.

Critical Race Theory is a clear and present danger to our American way of life and our Constitution. Don't take my word for it. Take the word of Ibram X. Kendi, director of the Center for Antiracist Research at Boston University.

Kendi has put a serious and troubling proposal on the table: "To fix the original sin of racism, Americans should pass an 'anti-racist amendment' to the U.S. Constitution." Kendi's amendment would make "racial inequity" unconstitutional. It would enshrine as a constitutional principle, "Racial inequity is evidence of racist policy."[29] In other words, if there are any differences in outcomes between any racial groups, that would be conclusive proof that racism is to blame. In Kendi's words, his amendment would:

> Critical Race Theory is a clear and present danger to our American way of life and our Constitution.

... establish and permanently fund the Department of Antiracism (DOA) comprised of formally trained experts on racism and no political appointees. The DOA would be responsible for preclearing all local, state and federal public policies to ensure they won't yield racial inequity, monitor those policies, investigate private racist policies when racial inequity surfaces, and monitor public officials for expressions of racist ideas. The DOA would be empowered with disciplinary tools to wield over and against policymakers and public officials who do not voluntarily change their racist policy and ideas.[30]

In other words, "trained experts on racism" like Ibram X. Kendi himself would have totalitarian power over every public agency, every public official, and every law. That is the ultimate goal of Wokeism in America. And don't take it lightly. Kendi is one of the most influential thinkers in American education today, and local school boards are buying his racist "anti-racism" book to indoctrinate your children in elementary schools and high schools.

Kendi's proposal is a naked plan for seizing power and brutally suppressing all opposition, especially from conservatives. It would dismantle the Bill of Rights, starting with the First Amendment. You might say, "That's ludicrous! It will never happen! Our leaders would never let things get that far."

But look at all the other social changes we once believed would never get this far—a wide-open border, driver's licenses for illegal immigrants, biologically male people destroying women's sports and invading women's restrooms, American social media companies censoring a sitting American president, and on and on. Could you have imagined twenty years ago that America could decline so steeply and so rapidly?

And consider the ultimate goal of Ibram X. Kendi for his "Department of Anti-racism." He once said, "In order to truly be antiracist, you also have to truly be anti-capitalist."[31] Kendi's goal is to impose Marxism on us all, including our children and grandchildren.

How to Take a Stand

How do we stand up against Critical Race Theory and Wokeism?

We start at the source—the university campus. These destructive Marxist ideologies originated on our campuses. Derrick Bell concocted CRT at Harvard Law School. Ibram X. Kendi spreads his poisonous ideas from Boston University. Colleges and universities have been totally taken over by CRT and Wokeism—and they are spreading this ideological cancer throughout our society.

As a result, colleges and universities are bringing back the Jim Crow era for the twenty-first century. A recent survey showed that more than seventy-five American colleges held segregated blacks-only graduation exercises.[32] Columbia University held six separate graduation ceremonies in 2021, all segregated by racial identity and sexual orientation.[33] Many universities—including Cal State Los Angeles, the University of Connecticut, UC Davis and UC Berkeley—offer racially segregated housing on-campus. These trends prompted the late Professor Walter E. Williams of George Mason University to wonder how long it would be before universities offered racially segregated restrooms and drinking fountains.[34]

Critical Race Theory is not leading America into a new utopia of racial harmony and justice. Instead, colleges and universities are taking race relations back to the era of segregation. The woke and weaponized professors and students on our campuses are determined to completely dismantle our civilization.

We cannot wait for academia to come to its senses. We cannot wait for our cowardly political leaders to stand up and do what's right. You and I are the ones who must stand up and be counted. You and I are the ones who must raise our voices in protest against the madness that has seized our campuses. You and I are the ones who must take a stand at this American moment and say, "Stop! No more! The madness stops here and now."

> Critical Race Theory is not leading America into a new utopia of racial harmony and justice.

Speak to your local school board, the Board of Trustees of your local university, the deans and administrators and professors, the students in your home, your neighborhood, in your church. Teach your children to stand up to the woke bullying from their teachers and peers.

You've seen the evidence for Count 9 of our ten-count indictment of the college cartel: *"Colleges and universities have unleashed waves of woke, anti-American radicals."* You may think you're ready to render a verdict—but wait. There's one more count to go.

10

THE PROFESSOR WATCHLIST

COUNT 10:

Many professors are leftist radicals bent on indoctrinating students.

In the spring of 2020, during the early stages of the coronavirus pandemic, many professors transitioned to teaching their courses online. Anthony Bosman, an assistant professor of mathematics at Andrews University, quickly recognized the danger faced by many of his colleagues. In March 2020, on his personal Facebook page, Bosman posted his concern that "all it takes is one zelous [zealous] student and that recording can hit the blogosphere . . ."[1] After controversy erupted over Bosman's Facebook post, he apparently removed his post or took it private.[2]

On March 22, 2020, I tweeted:

> To all college students who have their professors switching to online classes:
>
> Please share any and ALL videos of blatant indoctrination with @TPUSA at http://TPUSA.com/ContactUs
>
> Now is the time to document & expose the radicalism that has been infecting our schools
>
> Transparency!

In response to my tweet, the *Chronicle of Higher Education*, a newspaper aimed at faculty and administrators, published an article titled "A Side Effect of Remote Teaching During Covid-19? Videos That Can Be Weaponized." The *Chronicle* piece began, "The coronavirus-prompted shift to remote teaching was stressful enough for faculty members before Charlie Kirk weaponized online learning. . . . The general thrust of Kirk's call to action was nothing new. Turning Point, Campus Reform, and other groups have created a cottage industry of naming and shaming professors who they say advance what they call the liberal agenda."[3]

First, Turning Point USA is hardly a "cottage industry"—it's a fast-growing nationwide movement whose stated mission is "to educate students about the importance of fiscal responsibility, free markets, and limited government."[4] We are the community organizers of the right.

Second, we don't set out to "shame" anyone. Our Professor Watchlist website uses verified news reports and the professors' own words to accurately describe what they are teaching.

Third, the professors on our Watchlist are not merely advancing a liberal agenda, but are engaging in a radical leftist indoctrination and anti-American activism. The *Chronicle* needs to do its homework and get its facts straight.

The *Chronicle* reported on precautions some professors are taking, apparently to shield their curricula from the public eye. For example, sociology professor Dylan Bugden of Washington State University told the *Chronicle* he had decided not to record his lectures. Instead, he would offer his remote students "post presentation slides," quizzes, activities, an exam, and office hours to answer questions. Is this what students are paying for at Washington State—a prof who won't lecture out of fear of the outside world discovering what he teaches?

Bugden told the *Chronicle*, "I find it difficult to teach without referring to important events and issues in the world. Doing so is a powerful way to help students see that what we learn in class is not just abstract or a mere intellectual exercise, but matters for the things they and their peers care about." Bugden admitted that student evaluations of his course have urged him to leave politics out of his lectures.[5]

I believe in academic freedom. I believe professors should have the freedom to teach as they see fit. I also believe a professor should be willing to stand by his or her words—and that includes any political rants or indoctrination they engage in. They should be proud to have their work openly available to the public.

The Tenth and Final Count

This brings us to Count 10, the conclusion of our ten-count indictment of the college industry: "*Many professors are leftist radicals bent on indoctrinating students.*" Because college professors are overwhelmingly radical progressives, they have created a massively hostile environment for students who do not conform to leftist groupthink.

> Because college professors are overwhelmingly radical progressives, they have created a massively hostile environment for students who do not conform to leftist groupthink.

That's why I founded Turning Point USA. That's why we are on campus, telling students the truth about the American system of liberty and free markets. And that's why we maintain the Professor Watchlist website. The Watchlist is not a blacklist. We're not trying to have anyone fired, harassed, or censored. The Watchlist doesn't deter professors from spouting any poisonous, far-left nonsense they choose. It is simply a student's consumer guide to college professors, so that students can make informed choices.

You'll find the Watchlist at ProfessorWatchlist.org. (If you are in the United Kingdom, our sister organization, Turning Point UK, maintains a website called Education Watch at PointUK.co.uk/education-watch/. The Professor Watchlist is carefully compiled from published news stories and offers guidance to students who are selecting courses and professors.

Predictably, the American Association of University Professors and the *New York Times* complain that Professor Watchlist threatens academic freedom. How can that be? The Watchlist is carefully curated to be factually accurate. Some professors wear their Watchlist entry proudly, like a seal of approval.

Take, for example, Julia Gruber, an associate professor of German at Tennessee Technological University. In April 2021, Professor Gruber, along with her colleague, Professor Andrew Smith, hung flyers around campus condemning the school's Turning Point USA chapter and its faculty advisor, Professor Andrew Donadio. The posters featured a photo of Professor Donadio and read:

> This racist college professor thought it would be a
> great idea to help start a Tennessee Tech chapter for
> this national hate group, where racist students can
> unite to harass, threaten, intimidate, and terrorize
> persons of color, feminists, liberals, and the like,
> especially their teachers. Their organization created a
> national "Professor Watchlist" to harass and intimi-
> date progressive educators, including many women,
> African-American, and Muslim professors.
>
> Professor Donadio and Turning Point USA.
> You are on our list.
>
> Your hate & hypocrisy are not welcome at
> Tennessee Tech.
>
> No Unity With Racists.
>
> Hate Speech Is Not Free Speech.[6]

Professor Gruber and Professor Smith didn't sign their names to these flyers, nor did they offer any proof that Professor Donadio and Turning Point USA are "racist" or had ever harassed or terrorized anyone. This kind of vague, anonymous accusation is a common leftist tactic to bully opponents.

Appearing on *The Rude Pundit* podcast, Julia Gruber admitted to distributing the flyers on campus. Why did she feel justified in denouncing a colleague and TPUSA as "racist" without evidence? Gruber claimed that "it's not bad to call someone a racist," and besides, everyone who grew up in America "grew up being racist."

The Watchlist team emailed Professor Gruber, informing her that we were adding her to the Watchlist and asked if she had any response. She replied, "Please go ahead and add me; I'd be honored to join all the other fabulous scholars on it. Can my husband join too?" And she added the P.S.: "My subversive dog Fauci and my ungovernable cat Mrs. Maisel would like to be featured on a list as well. Does TPUSA also keep a list for liberal pets?"[7]

There's one radical prof who is proud of her actions, proud of her ideology, and proud to be on the Professor Watchlist.

The American Association of University Professors claims that some professors on the Professor Watchlist have received harassing emails. I don't know if that claim is true, but I'll say this to anyone who would harass people on the Watchlist: *please stop or get out of our movement. That's not how we behave.* Turning Point USA is about reasoned discussions of issues. We don't cancel people or seek to harm anyone. The Professor Watchlist is a kind of "Yelp review" of far-left professors, not a tool for stalkers.

To see if your professor is on our Watchlist, go to ProfessorWatchlist.org and search the database. Here's a selection of professors from the Watchlist:

Professors Out of Control

In a video you can view on YouTube,[8] Penn State sociology professor **Sam Richards** shames two white, male students because of the color of their skin, telling them they are oppressive, arrogant, and "dumb" because they are white (Richards is also white). The video was livestreamed on March 4, 2021, and captured by *Campus Reform* before Professor Richards made it private and unavailable.[9]

The video opens with Richards praising the Coca-Cola Company's neo-racist "diversity training" program, and posting a quote from the Coca-Cola indoctrination materials: "To be less white is to: be less *oppressive*, be less *arrogant*, be less *certain*, be less *defensive*, be less *ignorant*, be more humble, listen, believe, break with party, break with white solidarity."[10]

This is a nearly 800-student Zoom class, "SOC119: Race and Ethnic Relations," which Richards claims is "the largest race and cultural relations course in the United States."[11] Richards puts two white male students on-screen, Brian and James, and he cross-examines them on their impression of the Coca-Cola indoctrination statement. "Let me just ask you this, Brian—what white people would find that offensive?"

"Umm," Brian says cautiously, "conservatives, I guess?"

"What would they find offensive about it? . . . What's the point that it's trying to say?"

"I dunno. I don't want to get canceled so I'm trying to be careful what I say."

Richards is amused. "Dude, whatever you do, don't get canceled, don't get canceled." After a few minutes of interaction, Richards asks, "Who have you guys oppressed today?"

Brian replies, "I haven't oppressed anyone today."

"Are you sure of that, dude? You're breathing. Have you left your house today?"

"Yes."

"Okay, so you may have oppressed somebody. And in what ways today have you demonstrated your ignorance about being white? . . . It's organic to you being white men, that you're ignorant."

You tell me: Is that teaching—or indoctrination? Watch the video, and you'll see a student, Brian, who responds like a victim of Stockholm Syndrome: "I dunno. I don't want to get canceled."[12] Is Professor Richards teaching a course on race relations—or is he indoctrinating his students into the religion of Critical Race Theory?

In an in-person lecture titled "White Discomfort," Professor Richards calls a white student and a black student in front of the class. He states as fact that there is no racial equality in America, and he predicts that on graduation day, the black student's prospects will be bleak due to societal prejudice and discrimination. Then he stands behind the two students and announces to the class, "You're going to be at graduation and you're going to assume that these two guys are equal—*and they're f*cking not equal.*"[13]

In an in-person class titled "Christian Sharia," Richards lectures on the threat Christians pose to America. He puts up a slide of a Muslim man holding a sign: "Behead Those Who Insult Islam!!!" Then Richards holds up a copy of the Qur'an and says, "Where do you get that? It's not in here! It's not in here!" Richards is claiming that the Qur'an contains no commands to behead infidels. He is apparently unaware that Qur'an 8:12 says, "I will cast terror into the hearts of those who disbelieve. Therefore strike off their heads . . ."[14]

Next, Richards holds up a Bible and makes the baseless claim that he can find beheading commanded to Christians in the Bible: "You know what? I bet I could find it in here! I *know* I could find it in here. It's in here! It doesn't take much. You just go and put a couple of things together and you'll get someone to be like, 'Hey! Go behead people who insult Jesus, who insult God! Kill them! They should be killed!'"[15]

There's *nothing* in the Bible that *remotely* suggests that Christians should behead people for insulting Jesus. There are *accounts* of beheadings in the Bible, as when Herod beheads John the Baptist. But there are no commands to Christians to "strike off their heads," as in the Qur'an. Richards is filling his students' minds with misinformation and anti-Christian prejudice. This is educational ignorance.

Professors Who Censor Speech

Academia used to be a forum for free expression. Today, free speech is ruthlessly suppressed on campus. Brandeis University periodically updates its "Oppressive Language List," a catalogue of words students and faculty may not speak. In 2021, Brandeis banned "policeman" (use "police officer" instead) and "that's crazy" (use "that's bananas"). Brandeis even banned words that were invented by progressives, such as "trigger warning" ("trigger" might trigger people) and "African-American" (coined by Jesse Jackson in the 1980s;[16] use "Black" instead). Even "people of color" is banned at Brandeis; use "BIPOC" ("Black, Indigenous, and People Of Color").

Free speech on campus? Forget it. There is no place in America more repressive and tyrannical than a college campus. Here, from the Professor Watchlist, are a few of the most flagrant campus censors:

Alvin Lee Jr., is a human resources training specialist at Purdue. In a Management 301 class, Lee gave a presentation titled "Diversity Issues in the World of Work" in which he banned these perfectly innocent statements:

"There is only one race, the human race."

"Everyone can succeed in society if they work hard enough."

"I believe the most qualified person should get the job."

"America is a melting pot."[17]

What's wrong with these statements? Lee claimed they promote "the myth of meritocracy" and suggest that "race or gender does not play a role in life successes." A class handout states that when white people claim to be racially "colorblind," it means that "a white person does not want to or need to acknowledge race."[18]

And what about Professor Lee's objection to the term "melting pot"? We found another professor, **Pamela Brekka**, who also hates the term. She teaches art appreciation at the University of Florida, and her course materials warn (in all caps): "DO NOT EVER USE THE PHRASE 'MELTING POT' IN THE CLASS. IN THIS CLASS WE CELEBRATE DIVERSITY, NOT SAMENESS." She banned "melting pot" because it "signals a Euro-White Colonial standard, point blank, period." Despite explicitly banning the use of a widely accepted term from her class, she nevertheless claims, "I welcome open debate in all my classes."[19]

Professors Lee and Brekka don't seem to grasp what a beautiful metaphor the "melting pot" is. It was coined by the London-born Jewish playwright Israel Zangwill in his 1908 play *The Melting Pot*. A character in the play talks about the many ethnicities in this land and shouts, "Into the Crucible with you all!

God is making the American."[20] As Americans, we appreciate the richness of other cultures and we see each other not as hyphenated Americans, but simply as Americans. A professor who *truly* celebrates diversity does not censor speech.

In 2017, literature professor **Ulrich Baer** of New York University penned an op-ed for the *New York Times* titled "What 'Snowflakes' Get Right About Free Speech." He wrote, "The idea of freedom of speech does not mean a blanket permission to say anything anybody thinks. It means balancing the inherent value of a given view with the obligation to ensure that other members of a given community can participate in discourse as fully recognized members of that community."[21] Wrong, Professor Baer. The First Amendment says that freedom of speech is *precisely* "blanket permission to say anything anybody thinks."

Next, meet **Nadiya Fink**, statistics lecturer at the University of Michigan-Ann Arbor. In 2016, the university announced a new "pronoun policy" allowing students to input their chosen gender pronouns into a university database. The computer system would add the pronouns to the student biographies sent out to teachers.

One student, Grant Stroble, entered his chosen pronoun into the database: "His Majesty." In an interview, Stroble said, "It is respectful to make a reasonable effort to refer to students in the way that they prefer. . . . So, I henceforth shall be referred to as: His Majesty, Grant Stroble. I encourage all U-M students to . . . insert the identity of their dreams."[22]

Professor Nadiya Fink called Stroble's actions "disrespectful" and warned her class, "People who do what that kid did will be punished."[23] Because U-M is a public university, under the authority of the state of Michigan, Fink violated her students' First Amendment rights to free speech.

Professors Who Hate America

One of the most common traits among American academics is hatred for their own country combined with enthusiasm for Communist and Islamofascist regimes. Their desire to indoctrinate students with hatred for America is so strong that even professors of science, religion, and the arts devise ways to weave anti-Americanism into unrelated lectures. Some examples:

Then there's **Rudy Busto**, an associate professor in the Department of Religious Studies at UC Santa Barbara. In 2020, during a class on Asian-American religion, Busto went on a lengthy rant attacking "American exceptionalism." He told his students that the idea of "American exceptionalism" was invented so that the "dominant class" could "maintain control." The idea, he said, is an "error" disproven by history.

As evidence of America's lack of exceptionalism, Busto cited America's loss in Vietnam, the failure to prevent 9/11, the "ongoing, unwinnable wars in the Middle East," and America's high coronavirus death rate. Busto compared Americans who now believe in "American exceptionalism" to those in the past who accepted slavery as normal.

A freshman student who endured Busto's lecture told *Campus Reform* he couldn't understand what a "litany of the wrongdoings of America" had to do with Asian-American religions, adding that Busto seemed to want an excuse "to bash America and push Marxist propaganda."[24]

At the University of Colorado at Colorado Springs, lecturer **Jared Benson** and sociology instructor **Nicholas Lee** co-teach a class called "Resistance and Revolution." They present a revisionist history of the American Revolution, portraying the Founding Fathers as hypocrites, terrorists, and greedy tycoons who stirred up the early Americans to revolt against England merely to line their own pockets. Benson and Lee also offer a fractured version of more recent history, such as the end of the Cold War. In defiance of logic, they claim that Mikhail Gorbachev, not Ronald Reagan, engineered the collapse of the Soviet Union. But why would a lifelong Communist who has risen to the highest position in the Communist Party want to humiliate and dismantle his own country?[25]

Nicholas De Genova is an anthropology professor and current Chair of the Department of Comparative Cultural Studies at the University of Houston. He advocates abolishing national borders and allowing people to migrate freely without restrictions. He asserts that borders between nations are the most "violent" divisions ever constructed.[26]

From 2000 to 2009, De Genova was an assistant professor of anthropology and Latino studies at Columbia University. In early 2003, as American forces were in the early stages of the war in Iraq, De Genova helped lead a Columbia faculty "teach-in" against the war. During the "teach-in," he said he wished for "a million Mogadishus,"[27] a reference to a disastrous American-led operation in Mogadishu, Somalia, in October 1993 that left nineteen Americans dead and seventy-three wounded.

In a letter to the *Columbia Daily Spectator*, De Genova defended his outrageous statement and added that he "stressed the necessity of repudiating all forms of U.S. patriotism," and he called on American soldiers to "refuse to fight and contribute toward the defeat of the U.S. war machine."[28]

Professors Who Advocate Rioting, Anarchy, or Genocide

American university and college professors regularly advocate outrageous, racist notions without fear of repercussion. A few examples:

George Ciccariello-Maher is a visiting scholar of "decolonizing humanities" at the College of William & Mary in Virginia. He previously taught history at Drexel University in Philadelphia. On Christmas Eve 2016, while teaching at Drexel, he tweeted to his 10,000 followers, "All I Want for Christmas is White Genocide."

When the *Philadelphia Inquirer* asked him to explain the tweet, Ciccariello-Maher hid behind the claim that he was engaging in "satire." He stated, "On Christmas Eve, I sent a satirical tweet about an imaginary concept, 'white genocide.' For those who haven't bothered to do their research, 'white genocide' is an idea invented by white supremacists. . . . It is a figment of the racist imagination, it should be mocked, and I'm glad to have mocked it."[29]

Drexel officials issued a statement condemning Ciccariello-Maher's tweets: "While the University recognizes the right of its faculty to freely express their thoughts and opinions in public debate, Professor Ciccariello-Maher's comments are utterly reprehensible, deeply disturbing, and do not in any way reflect the values of the University."[30]

In a 2015 op-ed piece for *Salon*, Ciccariello-Maher applauded rioters and looters in Baltimore, writing, "Riots work. But despite the obviousness of the point, an entire chorus of media, police, and self-appointed community leaders continue to try to convince us otherwise, hammering into our heads a narrative of a nonviolence that has never worked on its own, based on a mythical understanding of the Civil Rights Movement."[31]

From calling for genocide to cheering on political violence, George Ciccariello-Maher epitomizes the worst impulses of far-left academia.

Nathan J. Jun is a philosophy professor at Midwestern State University in Wichita Falls, Texas. According to his faculty bio, he teaches "Philosophy of Race and Racism," "Multicultural Philosophy," "Philosophy of Horror and Macabre," and other courses. In a 2020 Facebook post, he stated, "I want the entire world to burn until the last cop is strangled with the intestines of the last capitalist, who is strangled in turn with the intestines of the last politician."[32]

Setting aside for a moment the sheer malevolence of Jun's rant, it's worth noting that he wasn't even original. In the early 1700s, anarchist-heretic priest Jean Meslier wrote, "I would like to see the last king strangled with the guts of the last priest."[33]

According to *The Wichitan*, the campus newspaper, Nathan Jun is a member of the violent extremist group Antifa.[34]

Professors Who Promote Marxism

"Higher education" is riddled with Marxism through and through. Here are just a few of the countless Marxist professors indoctrinating students across America:

Patrisse Cullors is the faculty director of the MFA degree program in social and environmental arts practice at Prescott College in Arizona. Her faculty bio says, "Artist, organizer, educator, and popular public speaker, Patrisse Cullors, is a Los Angeles native and Co-Founder of Black Lives Matter Global Network . . ."[35]

That's right, Black Lives Matter is yet another destructive movement to come out of academia. Patrisse Cullors cofounded Black Lives Matter in 2013 with Alicia Garza and Opal Tometi. Of course, the phrase "black lives matter" is an idea every decent human being supports. We all want to end the gang violence that kills so many black youth. We want young black people to learn how to access the limitless opportunities of America. But that's not what the *organization* called Black Lives Matter (BLM) is all about.

BLM is dedicated to the abolition of the police and prisons, and cutting off aid to Israel. BLM was overwhelmingly involved in the nationwide protests and riots that followed the death of George Floyd in May 2020. BLM is also committed to disrupting and deconstructing the American nuclear family.

On its "What We Believe" webpage, Black Lives Matter stated: "We disrupt the Western-prescribed nuclear family structure . . ." The organization scrubbed that page off its website in September 2020, after conservative media began reporting on the *real* beliefs of BLM.[36]

The disruption of the family structure is an idea that comes straight from Karl Marx. In Part Two of *The Communist Manifesto*, Marx wrote:

> Abolition of the family! Even the most radical flare up at this infamous proposal of the Communists.
>
> On what foundation is the present family, the bourgeois family, based? On capital, on private gain. In its completely developed form, this family exists only among the bourgeoisie.
> . . .
> The bourgeois family will vanish as a matter of course when its complement vanishes, and both will vanish with the vanishing of capital.[37]

For more than a decade, Patrisse Cullors was mentored in political organizing and radical Marxist ideology by Eric Mann—a hard-left radical who has worked for a long list of militant leftist organizations, including the Weather Underground domestic terrorist group.[38]

Patrisse Cullors was interviewed in 2015 by Jared Ball of the Real News Network, and she boasted that she and her fellow cofounders of BLM had been trained in Marxist ideology. "We actually do have an ideological frame," she said. "Myself and Alicia in particular are trained organizers. We are trained Marxists. We are super-versed on, sort of, ideological theories. And I think that what we really tried to do is build a movement that could be utilized by many, many black folk."[39]

Anthony Zenkus teaches at both the Columbia University School of Social Work and Adelphi University Graduate School of Social Work. His official bio describes him as an "activist" who was an organizer for Occupy Wall Street and was "trained by former Vice President Al Gore as a presenter in the Climate Reality Project."[40]

> Capitalism doesn't start wars. Capitalism creates prosperity, provides jobs, and lifts people out of poverty.

During exchanges on Twitter, Zenkus blamed capitalism for Naziism, slavery, genocide, and two World Wars. Zenkus tweeted on January 15, 2018, "Odd how you forget the millions who died under #capitalism. The two world wars, centuries of slavery and the genocide of native americans."[41] In another tweet the same day, Zenkus wrote, "Hitler was a capitalist. Good friends with Henry Ford."[4]

Zenkus demonstrates a tenuous grasp of history. World War II was started by Adolf Hitler and the Nazi Party (short for National Socialist Workers' Party). Hitler was a National Socialist, not a capitalist. Being friends with a capitalist does not make you a capitalist any more than Ellen DeGeneres's friendship with George W. Bush makes her a Republican.

Anthony Zenkus blames capitalism for all the world's woes. But capitalism is simply a system in which people compete in the free market, set their own prices, and voluntarily exchange goods and services. Capitalism doesn't start wars. Capitalism creates prosperity, provides jobs, and lifts people out of poverty. Capitalism created the $11.26 billion endowment that enables Columbia University to pay Zenkus's salary so he can spout his anti-capitalist B.S.

On October 16, 2020, Zenkus tweeted, "The American Flag is a symbol of genocide."[43] But to those who understand American history, the American flag is a symbol of freedom. Where is genocide taking place today? Under Communist China's hammer and sickle. But Zenkus prefers hatred of his own country over the harsh truth of Communist genocide.

Asatar Bair, an associate professor of economics at Riverside City College, California, is a self-proclaimed Communist who praises Marx, Stalin, and Mao. In a thread on Twitter, Bair wrote: "People say I 'idolize' Stalin. Not true, I hold a fair and balanced view. The man was neither savior nor saint, but he was, at once, a very successful revolutionary, a great contributor to Marxist theory, and said to be a great listener and collaborator during discussions. . . . I would certainly conclude that he is one of the great leaders of the 20th [century]."[44]

Professor Bair would do well to read historian Norman Naimark's book, *Stalin's Genocides*. Stalin murdered an entire social class, the land-owning peasant farmers called the *kulaks*. Stalin deliberately engineered the Holodomor (or Terror-Famine) that killed millions of Soviet Ukrainians in 1932 and 1933. He issued NKVD Order No. 00447 which called for the mass execution of so-called "socially harmful elements" of the population. He was a mass murderer on a scale that far exceeded Hitler.[45]

Bair's Twitter feed frequently praises Communist China. He denies the existence of the Uighur genocide, calling it "the supposed 'Uyghur genocide' in Xinjiang, China,"[46] or "the 'Uyghur genocide' myth."[47]

Professor Bair also tweeted, "I'm a huge fan of Mao LOL. One of the greatest revolutionary leaders of all time."[48] LOL? I'm not sure what's so "LOL" about Mao Zedong, whose regime killed 65 million Chinese people, including an estimated 40 million who starved to death in his labor camps.

John Bellamy Foster is a psychology professor at the University of Oregon. He also edits the Marxist magazine *Monthly Review* and advocates a "red-green" (Marxist-environmentalist) alliance to abolish capitalism.

Foster admires Soviet Communism and claims that the 1991 collapse of the Soviet Union was a bitter setback for human progress. In the March 2005 issue of *Monthly Review*, he wrote, "Beginning in the 1990s, the world witnessed an even more dramatic shift toward naked capitalism, heartless both in its treatment of workers and its domination of those countries at the bottom of the global hierarchy. Both class struggle from above and imperialism were intensified in the wake of capitalism's triumph in the Cold War."[49]

Norman Markowitz is a history professor at Rutgers University. He is also an active member of the Communist Party USA and teaches about Communism from a Marxist, pro-Communist perspective.

Markowitz claims that the Communist spies, Julius and Ethel Rosenberg, were innocent. The Rosenbergs were executed in 1953 for passing top-secret information about nuclear weapons designs to the Soviets. At the time, the United States was the world's only nuclear-armed nation; the Rosenbergs enabled the Soviets to build atomic weapons. After the fall of the Soviet Union, a collection of declassified Soviet documents, code-named Venona, conclusively proved the Rosenbergs' guilt, yet Markowitz steadfastly proclaims their innocence.[50]

Professors Who Brawl with Students

I could go on for pages. I've just scratched the surface of the Professors Watchlist—a website I hope you'll take advantage of and share with your friends and family. There you'll find well-documented accounts of professors who hate and slander Christians, Jews, Israel, and conservatives; professors who support and defend Islamist terrorism; professors who mock and humiliate their students; professors who call for violence and assassination; professors who defend pedophiles and sexual predators; and much more.

Many, if not most, of the professors on the Professors Watchlist promote "woke" Critical Race Theory and other forms of Critical Theory. At least two professors on the Professor Watchlist, Bill Ayers and Bernardine Dohrn, founded an organization which the FBI considered a terror group, and were involved in bombings and other violent acts as leaders of the Weather Underground. You'll even find professors who have committed acts of *violence* against students—and, incredibly, they're *still employed*.

Take, for example, **Eric Canin**, a cultural anthropology lecturer at California State University at Fullerton. In 2017, the campus chapter of Students for Justice in Palestine staged a protest of President Trump's immigration policies. The Fullerton College Republicans held a counter-protest. Eric Canin angrily confronted the College Republicans—a violation of university policy against harassing speakers on campus.[51] During the argument, Canin tripped over a bike rack and fell—and the College Republicans laughed.

Enraged and out of control, Canin lunged at the College Republicans and tried to rip away a sign held by one of the group, Jared Lopez—a violation of Lopez's First Amendment rights by a state employee. Another College Republican, Bryce Ingalls, attempted to separate the professor from Lopez. At that point, according to news accounts, Canin struck Ingalls in the face, knocking the student to the ground.[52]

College Republicans president Christopher Boyle came up behind Canin and restrained him. Boyle recalls, "I saw a man who had told us he was a professor attacking Bryce Ingalls, and immediately intervened to physically restrain him until police arrived to apprehended him."[53]

After an internal investigation of the incident by Cal State Fullerton officials, the university terminated Eric Canin. The bad-tempered prof appealed the decision, and the California Faculty Association defended him, claiming he was a "victim of harassment" by the College Republicans[54]—even though they didn't confront him, *he confronted them* in violation of university policy.

Starting a brawl with students ought to be a career-ending episode. But the arbitrator concluded that Cal State Fullerton should reinstate Eric Canin after a two-month suspension. Canin still teaches there today.[55]

So that's Count 10 of our ten-count indictment of the college industry: *"Many professors are leftist radicals bent on indoctrinating students."* And for some of these professors, indoctrination isn't even the worst of their outrageous behavior.

You are the jury. You've seen the evidence against the college scam. What is your verdict?

11

ONLY IN AMERICA

> You don't need college to succeed in this land
> of freedom and opportunity.

The world has been shaped and changed for the better by people who never went to college or who dropped out of college. The list of people who impacted the world without obtaining a college degree is long and distinguished:

Leaders in broadcast and print media: talk show host Rush Limbaugh, investigative journalist Carl Bernstein, media mogul Oprah Winfrey, and television entrepreneur Ted Turner.

Entertainment leaders: actor-director Clint Eastwood, filmmaker James Cameron, actor-director George Clooney, actress Julia Roberts, and filmmaker Steven Spielberg. (Spielberg dropped out of college in the late 1960s, enjoyed a hugely successful career directing films ranging from *Jaws* to *Schindler's List*, then returned to Cal State Long Beach in 2002 to complete a BA in film and electronic media—merely to have a college degree on his résumé.)

Business leaders: Virgin Group founder Richard Branson, TV producer Mark Burnett, Whole Foods cofounder John Mackey, Hobby Lobby founder David Green, entertainment magnate David Geffen, fashion magnate Ralph Lauren, Vogue and Condé Nast editor Anna Wintour, and media mogul Barry Diller.

Tech leaders: Apple cofounder Steve Jobs, Microsoft cofounders Bill Gates and Paul Allen, Twitter cofounder Jack Dorsey, Facebook cofounders Mark Zuckerberg and, Oracle cofounder Larry Ellison, and Dell Computers founder

Michael Dell.

There is a saying that has been attributed to both George Bernard Shaw and Steve Jobs. I can't say whether either of them actually said it, but the essence of this statement is true: "To follow the path that others have laid before you is a reasonable course of action; therefore all progress is made by unreasonable people."

People will tell you that in order to succeed in life, you must go to college. Our culture considers this a reasonable course of action. But when you look at the lives of mega-successful, mega-impactful lives, you see again and again that the real difference-makers in this world have been people who avoided college or dropped out of college to pursue their dreams.

Such stories happen all the time in America. Thanks to our American freedoms, we can start out with nothing and achieve great things through hard work and ingenuity alone. Nothing you can dream is beyond your reach because America is the land where dreams come true.

Take, for example, the success story of television producer Mark Burnett. Born in London in 1960, Burnett was the son of middle-class factory worker parents. He served in the British Army, saw action in the Falklands War, then emigrated to the United States in 1982. With few job prospects, he hired out as a combination babysitter and security guard for a family in Beverly Hills. He later performed similar duties for a family in Malibu—and the father of that family hired him to do additional work in his insurance office. On weekends, Burnett went to Venice Beach and sold T-shirts at a fence space he rented. Soon, he made so much money selling T-shirts at the beach that he quit his insurance job. When his landlord saw how much business he was doing, he said, "Only in America, Mark. Only in America."[1]

Mark Burnett and his friends took part in the Raid Gauloises, a New Zealand adventure competition. Burnett was so thrilled with his experience that he lined up investors, purchased the rights, and founded a similar competition in America, *Eco-Challenge: The Expedition Race*. The competition involved an adventure race over multiple days, pitting teams of four or five people against each other—trekking, kayaking, rafting, parachuting, and more. *Eco-Challenge* aired on television from 1995 to 2002 and launched Burnett's successful television career.[2]

Trading Nobility for Mobility

One of the reasons America is a land of opportunity can be found in Article I, Section 9, Clause 8 of the U.S. Constitution: "No Title of Nobility shall be granted by the United States."[3] With those few words, the framers of the Constitution abolished centuries of European class distinctions. According to English tradition, people were born to a specific social class and were expected to know their place and to remain there for life. But America rejected that notion. When the founding fathers abolished the concept of "nobility," they invented a new American concept of "mobility." You could be born poor, but a combination of freedom and hard work could enable you to move up the economic ladder.

For many years, college was seen as an ally of American social mobility. A poor young person could obtain a quality education and become a highly respected and prosperous doctor, lawyer, engineer, architect, or similar professional. But somewhere along the line, a myth infected our culture, stating that *everyone* who wants to be successful and prosperous *must* have a college degree. According to this cultural myth, anyone without a degree was doomed to a life of failure and unhappiness. We created a new class distinction: the college-educated and the non-college-educated. And the college-educated became the new American "nobility."

> When the founding fathers abolished the concept of "nobility," they invented a new American concept of "mobility."

But as we have seen again and again, the high cost of college and crushing burden of student loan debt are destroying countless lives today. Thousands of young people have been robbed of their future because they bought the myth and invested in the failed promise of a college education. Imagine what they might have achieved if they had dropped out of college or avoided college altogether and pursued their life goals.

In 2010, Bloomberg ranked the CEOs of the Standard & Poor 500 companies according to their undergraduate alma maters. Bloomberg found that two schools were tied for having produced the most CEOs on the list. Those two schools were the University of California, which produced twelve of the 500 CEOs, and "the school of hard knocks," which also produced twelve. "The school of hard knocks," of course, means that those CEOs had no college degree.

> According to this cultural myth, anyone without a degree was doomed to a life of failure and un-happiness. We created a new class distinction: the college-educated and the non-college-educated. And the college-educated became the new American "nobility."

For most people, it's still possible to reach the pinnacle of a profession without a college degree. You can start out selling T-shirts at the beach and become a world-renowned TV producer. Why? Because this is America—and America means freedom and opportunity.

We need to tell today's generation of high school students: "You *can* succeed if you are focused on your goals, passionate about your success, and unafraid of risk-taking and hard work. You don't need a college degree to succeed in America."

"To Me, It Was Never Work"

> You can succeed if you are focused on your goals, passionate about your success, and unafraid of risk-taking and hard work. You don't need a college degree to succeed in America."

I recently sought out the insights of two accomplished businessmen and diplomats. First, let me introduce Lee Rizzuto, who served as the U.S. Consul General in Hamilton, Bermuda. Lee is the son of Leandro Rizzuto, founder of the Conair Corporation. He studied marketing at Arizona State University from 1980 to 1982, leaving school to work in the family business. In fact, Lee has been working in the family business almost his entire life.

"From the time I was five years old," he says, "I was going into the Brooklyn, New York, factory and office with my parents and they would let me perform different functions. To me, it was never work. It was always enjoyment and passion. Fortunately, it was before the child labor laws or I wouldn't have been able to have that experience. At a very young age, I was helping to manufacture and package the product.

"Our company's first product was hair rollers. We made a wire mesh hair roller with brush bristles inside the roller—essentially, a spring with a nylon mesh wrapped around the spring and a brush inserted inside of it. I was literally putting the hair rollers together and then placing twelve rollers in the paper tray and feeding the tray into a shrink-wrap machine. For a boy that age, that was pretty exciting and enjoyable. And that's how I got started in the family business."

Lee believes colleges could do a better job preparing young people for a real-world career by offering work experience. "Throughout my academic years," he says, "I always worked on the side every chance I got and was able to apply my work experience to my academic experience and vice versa. So I encourage students who choose to go to college to seek out colleges in which students can go into work-related programs between semesters. I believe all colleges should have programs that link classroom work with real-world experience, and that give students credit for their work-related participation.

> "I believe all colleges should have programs that link classroom work with real-world experience, and that give students credit for their work-related participation."
>
> —LEE RIZZUTO

"Unfortunately, not enough colleges offer that kind of balance between classroom instruction and real-world experience. Classroom instruction—learning from books—is going to give you various perspectives, but nothing will give you a greater perspective than actually doing the job."

Lee Rizzuto strongly believes in academic freedom and the First Amendment, but he is concerned about the violent radicalism emerging from our campuses. "Any movement that wants to voice a political position or advocate for a political cause is fine with me—as long as it's done in a peaceful manner. But the radical actions we are seeing today are extreme and violent. Innocent people have lost their lives. Businesses have been burnt to the ground. That's not the way we advocate for causes in America."

Should parents and students be concerned about the indoctrination on campuses today? "Absolutely," he says. "When parents and students are selecting a college, are they careful to select a college that aligns with their beliefs? Parents and students should ask: Does this school educate—or indoctrinate? Does this school prepare young people to be engaged in American society—or does it radicalize young people and turn them against America?

"College isn't for everybody, but for those who choose to go, both parents and students should investigate the school very closely. Ask a lot of questions. If everything checks out and the school supports your values, fine. But if the school undermines everything your family believes in, why send your student there to be brainwashed? Why would you support that institution with your money?

> So we need to have a conversation, not merely within our own circle of like-minded friends, but with reasonable people across the political and ideological divide.

"It's amazing that many parents and many students don't really look into what is being taught. Parents often send their kids to a school because it has a big name, an elite reputation. They'll donate to a school because it has an impressive reputation or it's their alma mater—but the school has changed since they attended there. People aren't doing their due diligence by looking into the faculty and administration of that school."[4]

A Bias against Profit

Lee shares a personal story that underscores the political bias that permeates American academia. He recalls, "One of my daughters studied for two years at the American University of Rome. She earned an associate degree. Then she returned stateside and earned a bachelor's degree at Cabrini University in Pennsylvania. Prior to graduating, she was very excited and enthusiastic. She kept telling us about this particular professor that she really enjoyed, and she was looking forward to introducing us to her.

"On graduation day, after the ceremony, they held a reception and we got to meet this professor. My daughter introduced us and she said to the professor, 'Oh, I didn't get a chance to tell you before, but my dad got me an internship with [multinational financial services company] UBS over the summer.'

"The professor, with contempt in his voice, said, 'Adriana! We discussed working in the nonprofit sector!' She was actually barking at my daughter, rebuking her for taking an internship with a profit-making company. That's the orientation of so many academics today: profit is evil, capitalism is evil, and the only worthwhile jobs are in the nonprofit sector.

"I said to the professor, 'Adriana shared with me about your conversation about the nonprofit sector. And I explained to Adriana how wonderful working in a nonprofit organization could be. But I also told her how fantastic it would be if she got a paying job. Then she could donate the value of her time—not just for one person, but enough money to equal the volunteer work done by ten people or a hundred people or more. By making an income, you can donate more than just one day's labor volunteering at a nonprofit organization.'

> "In my company, when I'm looking at résumés, no matter what position we're hiring for, I always look for computer skills and language skills."
>
> —LEE RIZZUTO

"The professor was speechless. She had no comeback for that. I said, 'Come on, Adriana, let's meet some of your other professors.' And we walked away.

"It broke my heart that the professor had said that to my daughter. Here she was, not twenty minutes after receiving her diploma, and she was so excited for us to meet her, so eager to go out and work. But the professor treated her enthusiasm with contempt."

Lee is concerned that many professors present a biased view of the world to their students. "They teach their students a one-sided perspective," he says, "and they won't show their students the other side of the equation, as I shared with this professor. Do you want to help a particular cause? There are lots of ways of helping that cause. As wonderful as it might be to volunteer in a soup kitchen and ladle soup for homeless people, you might be even more effective by earning a lot of money to buy the food and supplies for that soup kitchen.

"That doesn't take anything away from that compassionate person who volunteers time to ladle the soup. Those volunteers are an essential part of the process. But if you can do more by earning more and donating more, why should you feel bad for that? Why should a college professor make you feel guilty, as if you made a bad choice? Why should you be criticized for having a paying job?"

What advice does Lee Rizzuto have for students who decide to go to college? "Learn a language," he says. "In my company, when I'm looking at résumés, no matter what position we're hiring for, I always look for computer skills and language skills. We might be hiring for a job in the mailroom, but we always look for extra skills, especially language skills. I created a database of all our employees and their language skills. If we need to communicate with a customer in Pakistan, we can quickly find out if we have an employee who speaks Pashto." Learn a language and hone your computer skills—that's excellent advice for young people, whether they are headed for college or not.

"Do the Simple Math"

Lee is concerned about the greed that seems to permeate the entire university system—and he offers an innovative solution. "From the first day of school," he says, "the student and parents are bombarded with phone calls and emails begging for contributions. And so many of these schools are sitting on huge endowments. Harvard has a $41 billion endowment. Yale has a $30 billion endowment. The endowments of the top ten schools total more than $200 billion. These schools have all this money tax-free, yet the tuitions continue to skyrocket. They put all this money into private investments that have nothing to do with higher education. So we have to ask ourselves a few questions:

"First, why should these wealthy universities have all this money tax-free? They don't use the majority of the money to educate young people. In fact, they have so much money that it would be impossible to spend it all on education.

"Second, in Major League Baseball, they have something called revenue-sharing. This is designed to keep the teams as close as possible to competing on a level playing field. If player salaries exceed a certain amount, a team must contribute a certain percentage to the revenue-sharing program. That money goes to the less profitable teams to keep the teams competitive. What if the schools that have a crazy amount of endowment money were required to share endowments with the poorer schools? Why don't we as a society demand that?

"Third, we hear a lot these days about student loan forgiveness. What if we said to the universities, 'We're going to tax your endowment and use those taxes for student loan repayment'? Instead of making the taxpayer pay for debt forgiveness, why don't we tax the huge endowments of these universities? Shouldn't we tax the institutions that have gotten rich from burdening their students with debt? It only makes sense.

"Do the simple math: What is 1 percent of Harvard's $41 billion endowment? It's $410 million. And 5 percent is $2.05 billion. A tax on Harvard's endowment could pay for a lot of student loans. If we taxed these rich universities, the proceeds could help schools that don't have money, schools that are helping poor students.

> "Instead of making the taxpayer pay for debt forgiveness, why don't we tax the huge endowments of these universities? Shouldn't we tax the institutions that have gotten rich from burdening their students with debt?"
>
> —LEE RIZZUTO

"The interest alone on Harvard's endowment would pay for the tuition of their entire student body—perpetually. There are so many rich schools with huge endowments. Let them help the smaller schools that are struggling. Let them help all these kids who are struggling with a crippling burden of student loans. There are so many ways this money could be put to good use.

"Fourth, we have to ask why schools with huge endowments always have their hands out, asking for donations. If you recall Harvard even took COVID-19 PPP money. No matter how big their endowment, they continually beg for more. Why, then, should we contribute to a school that is already rich, that may not share our values, and that is actively undermining our beliefs? Whether you are liberal or conservative, whether you are giving money or sending your kids, make sure the school you are supporting needs and deserves your support."[5]

Those are wise words—and I hope Lee's words help to spark a "tax the endowments" movement. After all, the left is always saying we have to "make the rich pay their fair share." This is a "tax the rich" idea that both liberals and conservatives should be able to support.

"These Degrees Will Get Them Nowhere"

Next, let me introduce Ambassador David Fischer, the 41st United States Ambassador to Morocco. Ambassador Fischer graduated from Parsons College, a private liberal arts college in Iowa. Until recently, Ambassador Fischer was chairman and CEO of The Suburban Collection, a Michigan auto sales company with thirty-four dealerships and sales of nearly $3 billion a year. He began his career by working in his father's Oldsmobile dealership, writing service orders. He bought the dealership from his father in 1978 and expanded the business to its present size—a true "only in America" story. He stepped down from his role in the company upon his confirmation by the Senate in December 2019.

Ambassador Fischer shared his thoughts with me on the state of higher education today—especially schools run by for-profit companies (the kind that advertise on your local TV station about the ease of obtaining a degree): "I'm especially concerned about these for-profit companies that are really hurting young people. Some of the so-called 'advisors' at these schools are little more than finance managers. They talk these young kids into taking on enormous debt or going after federal grant money. Students come out of school with degrees that are truly useless. They may have worked hard, but these degrees will get them nowhere.

"I was on the board of a pair of schools. One was the state university here in Michigan. It had a good reputation, a medical school, a law school, and some

20,000 students. Even though I felt the degrees that students earned there were worthwhile, I worried because the school kept raising tuition—it never went down.

"There are a lot of young people who shouldn't be in college. They should be in vocational training. In our automobile sales and service business, we took many kids straight out of high school and trained them to work in our service department. We have two schools that we call 'TechCellence Academies.' It was about trying to teach a skill through mentoring and apprenticeship. There was no charge for the school.

"They were mostly poor kids, and we would provide at least one meal a day. Upon graduation, they would receive two certifications in light service work, and we would give them a job that paid $18 an hour in their first job, which was good entry-level pay at that time. We also gave them their own set of tools. Each graduate of our Academy would make $600 or $700 a week and have a foundation for earning additional certifications to advance in their career. We had many technicians who eventually made between $80,000 and $200,000 a year—and they came out of our school with no debts.

"So I have a hard time understanding why so many kids take these expensive courses and incur so much debt. I'm very concerned that many students will never be able to pay their loans back. They'll never be able to make a living. We need to make it clear: Not everybody needs to go to college."

Wise Advice

Does Ambassador Fischer see a problem with our social attitudes toward those without a college degree? "Yes," he replies. "I think America has an unhealthy obsession with the term 'college-educated.' There's a joke that illustrates the problem with this attitude.

"A doctor has an urgent problem with his plumbing. It's Sunday and most plumbers are closed. Finally, he calls one plumber who is open on Sunday. The plumber comes out and says, 'I can fix it, but it will cost $600.' The doctor says, 'Are you kidding me? I'm a doctor, and I don't charge $600 to treat a patient!'

And the plumber says, 'I didn't charge $600 when I was a doctor either.'

"The point is that, in our society, there's a tendency to look down on the plumbing profession and similar professions. Plumbers perform a critical service—and it's a good-paying profession. Many people say, 'Oh, no, I don't want my kid to go to trade school.' But that's the wrong attitude. We need to stop being dismissive of trade school careers. Trade school graduates keep our society running.

"I went to a pretty good private school, Cranbrook Kingswood in Michigan. When I was in seventh grade at the school, I took shop class. I learned to do rudimentary design work. They taught us metalworking and woodworking skills.

> Whether you choose to go to college or a trade school, whether you start your own business or join the workforce, make a plan for your life—then make consistent, daily progress on your life plan.

"But how many schools still teach these skills today? Shop classes have disappeared from schools without anyone noticing. The result of getting rid of shop classes is that we are telling a whole generation of young people that these skills have no value. We are telling them that a career working with your hands is a bad thing. I worry about these kids who haven't been taught any skills, who think they can do nothing with their lives.

"There are many young people who shouldn't be in college, but could learn the skills they need to make a good living and contribute to society. They could make $150,000 a year as a service mechanic, for example. That's a good job. Not everyone in the field will earn that much, but many do make six figures."

How do we turn this cultural attitude around? How do we counteract the false idea that everyone needs to go to college? Ambassador Fischer replies, "As a culture, we need to get back to celebrating skills, including manual skills. We need to find a way of getting these skills back into the schools through metal shop and wood shop. It's important that we teach these basic skill sets. We need to expose young people to the feeling of working with their hands and the sense of accomplishment that comes from that.

"We also need to recognize that people who are capable and skilled with their hands should be considered valued members of society. You don't need a college education, and the debt that goes with it, to acquire these valuable skills."

What advice does Ambassador Fischer offer young people for living a successful and rewarding life? "When I speak to young audiences, I always tell them, 'Keep your eye on where you want to go and be very proactive about your future. Don't be afraid to work hard—but don't forget to enjoy yourself. Above all, you must have a plan. Don't just let life happen to you—make plans and set goals, then focus every day on achieving those goals."

This is wise advice. Whether you choose to go to college or a trade school, whether you start your own business or join the workforce, make a plan for your life—then make consistent, daily progress on your life plan. You don't have to conform to other people's expectations. You don't have to go to college and take on a crushing burden of debt just because your friends are doing so.

Set a courageous course for your life. Live boldly and succeed on your own terms. Someday, you'll look back on your accomplishments with satisfaction and say, "Only in America!"

12

HOW TO SUCCEED WITHOUT A DEGREE

> **Skip college, save your money, and have a great life.**

Winnetka and Kenilworth are villages about fifteen miles north of Chicago. These North Shore suburbs are the wealthiest communities in the Midwest, and among the wealthiest in America—the Beverly Hills of Chicago. In 2019, I went to Winnetka-Kenilworth and spoke to a gathering of about 200 Republicans.

At one point, I asked the audience, "Who here would want their kid to become a plumber?"

The audience laughed, as if I had made some hilarious joke.

I said, "Exactly. None of you here in North Shore Chicago would want your kids to become plumbers. Because you think 'plumber' equals 'stupid.'"

The room went deathly silent.

I said, "You just proved my point. You're all sending your kids to elite universities. Did it ever occur to you that your son or daughter might be better suited to a career as a plumber, carpenter, welder, or electrician—a career that doesn't require a college degree?

> A lot of Americans—good people who think they are not prejudiced against anyone—are prejudiced against what I call the "muscular class."

"A lot of Americans—good people who think they are not prejudiced against anyone—are prejudiced against what I call the 'muscular class.' They have a disdain for people who work with their hands and get dirt under their fingernails. They think that such people are 'stupid' or 'less than.' They think, '*My* kid's not going to become a blue-collar worker. *My* kid will go to Harvard or Yale and join the elite class.'

"You know what happens to kids who go to Harvard or Yale? All too often, they come out as radicals, atheists, and woke progressives. Let me ask you this: Would you rather have your kid become a plumber—or an atheist radical who hates everything you stand for?"

"And consider this: if your kid becomes Joe the Plumber, he will probably earn $90 an hour and he'll be able to feed his family, live in a nice home, and not have any debts."[1]

I didn't get much applause for those statements, but I gave the audience something to think about.

First, let's tear down the assumption that everyone must go to college in order to succeed in life. Second, let's dismantle the attitude which says that those who don't go to college are somehow less intelligent and less wise than those who do.

It's time we demolished two harmful assumptions in our culture. First, let's tear down the assumption that everyone must go to college in order to succeed in life. Second, let's dismantle the attitude which says that those who don't go to college are somehow less intelligent and less wise than those who do.

What is wise about shouldering a mountain of debt to undergo four years of indoctrination? And what is ignorant and stupid about going directly into the workforce, learning a lucrative trade, and living the rest of your life debt-free? What's wrong with a technical school or trade school? Why shouldn't people be proud of a well-paid career as a welder or an electrician?

I have a friend who needed an electrician to replace the outlets in his house. The electrician was so busy that my friend had to make an appointment three weeks in advance. The electrician charged $90 an hour for six hours' work—a total of $540. If that electrician bills only six hours per day (and my guess is he's billing quite a bit more than that), he's making more than *$15,000 a month*, without a college education.

A lot of lawyers wish they made that kind of bank.

Don't Let Them Shame You

George W. Bush was inaugurated as president of the United States in January 2001. Four months later, in May, he addressed the 2001 graduating class of Yale University, his alma mater. He said, "Congratulations to the class of 2001. To those of you who received honors, awards, and distinctions, I say, well done. And to the C students—I say, you, too, can be President of the United States. A Yale degree is worth a lot, as I often remind Dick Cheney—who studied here, but left a little early. So now we know—if you graduate from Yale, you become President. If you drop out, you get to be Vice President."[2]

For President Bush, there was no shame in being a C student—and for Vice President Cheney, there was no shame in dropping out. And there should also be no shame in not going to college at all.

I once had lunch in Palm Beach with three men who had graduated from Ivy League schools. As we talked, I learned that their alma maters were a huge part of their identity. Ivy Leaguers have a special knack for working their school into the conversation.

Finally, one of them turned to me and said, "So, Charlie, where did you go to school?"

I said, "I didn't go to college and I really recommend not going to college."

One said, "What do you mean, you didn't go?"

Another said, "And what do you mean, you *recommend* not going?"

They all looked at me wide-eyed and slack-jawed, as if I had two heads. They couldn't imagine deliberately *choosing* not to go to college.

So they quizzed me, and I laid out my reasons. I told them that college would have been a four-year roadblock to my goals—plus it would have driven me deep into debt. I told them about other people I knew who had become hugely successful by avoiding the college trap.

By the end of our lunch, they were agreeing with me that most students really shouldn't be in college at all. And I wonder if they didn't look at their Ivy League diplomas a bit differently after our conversation.

I've had similar conversations countless times. Because I'm a debater and an outspoken advocate for my beliefs, people often assume I acquired my communication skills in college. Again and again, people ask, "Where did you go to college?"

People have been asking this since I was nineteen or twenty—and the question used to embarrass me. I would answer as if I were ashamed: "Well, you see, I actually didn't, um, go to college." But I haven't been ashamed of that answer in years. Now, I say boldly, "I didn't go to college."

And the number one response I hear from people is "Good for you! That's awesome!" People cheer that answer. I think many recognize the harm the college cartel is inflicting on students and society. People are happy to meet someone who has completely rejected the corrupt culture of academia. Far from being ashamed of not going to college, I own it. It's my badge of honor, a mark of differentiation from the false cultural norms that surround us.

Public opinion is turning against the college industry. This is a recent phenomenon. When I started Turning Point in 2012, attitudes were a lot different. The notion that everyone goes to college was an unquestioned assumption. Today, the college industry is falling out of favor with the American public—and I think I know why.

Almost every American adult has a horror story to share about college. It might be their personal experience, or the experience of a family member or someone they know, but people increasingly have bad college experiences to complain about. There is a pent-up disgust with so-called "higher education" that has been growing over a decade or more. And that disgust is reaching critical mass.

The "Skype-Zoom Class" and the Muscular Class

I can already hear the critics of this book. In fact, I could write the reviews for them: "Charlie Kirk's latest book is an exercise in anti-intellectualism. He attacks higher education, claiming that it's smart to be stupid and stupid to be smart." Well, if you've read this far, you know that's not what I'm saying. I'm not advocating anti-intellectualism. I'm not attacking *real* education. And I acknowledge that there are some professions where you do, in fact, need a college degree and even an advanced degree.

But I will say this clearly: it's the height of stupidity to go deep into debt and have nothing to show for it but a diploma and a brainwashed mind.

Jordan Peterson, a brilliant Canadian psychologist who has taught at Harvard and the University of Toronto, has been a guest on my podcast. During a recent appearance on another podcast, *The Joe Rogan Experience*, Peterson said, "I think you can make a reasonable case that the universities do more harm than good now. . . . The only thing the universities have now that people can't get elsewhere is accreditation. But they're doing everything they can as fast as possible to make their accreditation valueless anyway. . . .

"One of the things that's happened over the last thirty years is that the proportion of university expenditures that's gone to the administration has massively, massively increased. And at the same time, the student loan burden has increased. So what's happened is that, in a weird sense, the administrators have conspired to steal the future earnings of their students. And [students] can't declare bankruptcy, so to me it's indentured servitude. . . .

"It's not particularly useful to burden your citizenry with massive debt as soon as they graduate, at a time when they are most likely to take entrepreneur-

> I'm not advocating anti-intellectualism. I'm not attacking real education. There are some professions where you do need a college degree and even an advanced degree. . . . But it's the height of stupidity to go deep into debt and have nothing to show for it but a diploma and a brainwashed mind.

ial risks. You're not going to take entrepreneurial risks if you're so burdened with debt that you can't get off the ground."[3]

Those are wise words from someone who knows academia inside and out. For most young people today, the college model is obsolete. Students are being deceived and exploited. They are doubly exploited if they major in the humanities or the soft sciences like psychology and sociology. They are triply exploited if they attend an "elite" university like Stanford or Harvard.

There's a growing trend among employers to see Ivy League graduates as a liability, not an asset. Senator Rand Paul, for example, receives hundreds of applications every year for unpaid internships. He can only accommodate a small percentage of applicants. He generally turns down applicants from Ivy League schools in favor of those from less "prestigious" schools. Why? Because Ivy League schools are so rife with radicalism, cancel culture, safe spaces, and coddled "snowflakes" that Ivy League grads are dysfunctional. They can't handle the real world.

Justice Clarence Thomas also avoids Ivy League grads when hiring his clerks. Almost all other Supreme Court justices hire clerks from Yale, Harvard, or occasionally Stanford. But Justice Thomas hires from less "elite" schools around the country. I don't know what his reasoning is, but I have a theory. I think he knows that Ivy Leaguers have an arrogant bias: "If you're not an Ivy Leaguer like us, you're second-class." Justice Thomas has an egalitarian outlook—and he hates snobbery.

I also think Justice Thomas is looking at the big legal picture. He knows his clerks are destined for judgeships or public service. He believes it's good for the nation if its judges are not captives to the Harvard-Yale axis. And he believes he can have a positive influence on young legal minds who will go back to their communities and interpret the law according to sound constitutional principles. So he hires clerks who have been educated, not indoctrinated.

Midway through the coronavirus pandemic, I watched a Fox News interview with historian Victor Davis Hanson. He talked about the division he saw in America today—a division that was starkly revealed by the 2020 pandemic. It wasn't a division over race, as our leftist media would have us believe. It's a division between two social classes—the ruling class and the working class.

Hanson dubbed the ruling class the "Skype-Zoom class"—those on the highest educational and economic rungs of society. They pull the strings and wield the power. He calls them the "Skype-Zoom" class because, during the pandemic, they made bank by sitting safely in front of their MacBooks. They were the corporate executives, stock traders, market analysts, and hedge fund managers who made a six-figure living (or more) in the "brain-power" professions. They are the ambitious class that Tom Wolfe called "the Masters of the Universe."

On the opposite side of the divide, out in the real world, lives the working class, the "muscular class," as I call them. They didn't have the luxury of making their living from their couch and computer keyboard. They were out in the community, braving the virus in their blue masks, working in grocery stores, installing HVAC units, unclogging pipes, repairing appliances, delivering meals for DoorDash, leaving packages for Amazon, and taking risks so the "Skype-Zoom" class could remain safe behind their computer screens.

The divide between the "Skype-Zoom" class and the muscular class goes way back. In cultures where slavery was commonplace—ancient Egypt, China, Babylonia, Persia, Greece, India, the Roman Empire, the Islamic Caliphate, and pre-Columbian America—the powerful upper class *owned* the muscular class. During the Barbary slave trade of the eighteenth and nineteenth century, North African pirates captured and enslaved more than a million Christian Europeans. Slavery was widely practiced during the European colonization of the Americas.

In those cultures, the rich, powerful, well-educated elites *owned* the powerless, uneducated, but physically strong underclass. The upper class has always felt entitled to exploit the production of the underclass. When slavery was abolished in the United States by the Thirteenth Amendment in 1865, the upper class could no longer *own* the muscular class. So the upper class began to *rent* the muscular class by paying wages—and by keeping those wages as low as possible.

But America invented something that enables the muscular class today to thrive and achieve great wealth. America invented the free market system, which is the basis of the American dream. Every American has the opportunity to build his or her own business, be his or her own boss, put hard work and capital at risk, and (with luck and good timing) reap great rewards.

And even if you're not an entrepreneur, America is still a land of limitless opportunity for those who wisely choose to skip college and get on with their lives. Later in this chapter, I'll give you a slate of ideas on how to succeed without a college degree.

Erasing the No-Diploma Stigma

I often tell audiences that it's time we stop treating non-college-educated people as uninformed on the issues, as ignorant, as "less-than." It's time to erase the No-Diploma Stigma. When I tell audiences that, I always get a huge standing ovation.

A 2018 story in *The Atlantic* was headlined, "America Is Divided by Education." The subtitle added, "The gulf between the party identification of white voters with college degrees and those without is growing rapidly." The piece begins:

> It's time we stop treating non-college-educated people as uninformed on the issues, as ignorant, as "less-than." It's time to erase the No-Diploma Stigma.

One of the most striking patterns in yesterday's election was years in the making: a major partisan divide between white voters with a college degree and those without one. According to exit polls, 61 percent of non-college-educated white voters cast their ballots for Republicans while just 45 percent of college-educated white voters did so. Meanwhile 53 percent of college-educated white voters cast their votes for Democrats compared with 37 percent of those without a degree.[5]

This is Progressive diploma-shaming of Republicans. The conclusion we're supposed to draw is that the Democratic Party is the "smart-people party" and the GOP is the party of knuckle-dragging rubes who never went to college.

We see this attitude in political polling all the time. Poll results are frequently broken into "college educated" and "non-college-educated" categories. What the pollsters are really saying is, "Here's what the smart people think and here's what the dumb people think." They don't say that out loud. But it's a subtext: "If you didn't go to college, then you clearly don't know what's going on. You aren't informed on the issues so we can ignore your views."

This attitude underlies the smugness of many on the left who are so well-educated, they think they are smarter than anybody else. Yet they've never run a business, they don't know how the economy works, they don't understand incentives and unforeseen consequences, and they totally lack wisdom. Many non-college-educated people have a basic common sense that has been educated and indoctrinated out of college graduates. Non-college-educated people also have a humility that many college-educated people lack. Unlike so many people with degrees and credentials, non-college-educated people know they don't know everything, so they often have an open-mindedness that is rare in the educated class.

> We need to stop assuming that wisdom comes only from those with a diploma on the wall.

Truly intelligent thinkers understand that academia often trains bright young people to be fools. "Higher education" teaches students to ignore obvious truth and seek convoluted rationalizations for bad ideas. Bertrand Russell put it this way in *My Philosophical Development* (1959): "This is one of those views which are so absurd that only very learned men could possibly adopt them." Similarly, George Orwell wrote in *Notes on Nationalism* (1945): "One has to belong to the intelligentsia to believe things like that: no ordinary man could be such a fool."

So we need to change some attitudes in our culture. We need to stop assuming that wisdom comes only from those with a diploma on the wall. When we encounter people who chose not to go to college, our response should not be "Why didn't you go?" but "Good for you!"

Let's show some respect for the wisdom and common sense of those who work with their hands and muscles and practical skills. They benefit our lives and our society every bit as much as physicians and physicists. They are making good wages and living debt-free. It's time we did away with the snobbery and bias so often displayed toward the "muscular class." It's time to erase the No-Diploma Stigma.

How to Succeed without a College Degree

Here's an array of practical, workable ideas to help you skip college and go straight to a successful, rewarding life. Most of these ideas are in no particular order, but you should absolutely implement idea No. 1 immediately, before you attempt any other ideas in this section. Here we go:

1. Formulate Your Life Plan. Take time to reflect on what kind of life you want to have—then write it down. What kind of life do you want to have over the next three to five years? What do you hope to accomplish? Would you like to start a business? Would you rather work for an employer? Do you want to be involved in service or ministry to others? Do you want to be married? Most people drift through their lives without any plans, goals, or sense of control over their destiny. If you want to live an exciting and rewarding life, you need a written plan.

Jordan Peterson is a strong proponent of sitting down by yourself and formulating your life plan. He said, "People's careers basically have to be self-determined, but that's never part of the education system." Young people, Peterson said, need to design their own lives and articulate their own life plan. "You actually neurologically rewire people by having them formulate their own thoughts. That's why your school teachers used to say, 'Put it in your own words.' . . . If you have to conjure up the thoughts and you have to articulate them, then they change you."

Peterson has created a low-cost set of programs he calls the Self Authoring Suite (SelfAuthoring.com) . The Suite includes the Future Self Authoring Program which helps you write out a plan for your life.

He explains, "[Future Self Authoring Program] asks you some questions about six dimensions of your life—your health (mental and physical), your use of drugs and alcohol, your wishes three to five years down the road for your relationships, family, career, education, and so on. It asks you, what could your life be like three to five years down the road if you set it up as if you were someone you were taking care of? Then it asks you to write for 15 minutes about your vision for your life. . . .

"It also asks you to write for 15 minutes about what your life would be like three to five years down the road if you let your bad habits and your idiocies and your foolishnesses and your weaknesses take the upper hand and augur you into the ground. It's like you get to design a little heaven to strive for and a little hell to avoid. Then you turn that into an implementable plan."[6]

Whether you decide to write out a life plan on your own or use Jordan Peterson's Future Self Authoring Program, I recommend you start by looking within and looking to the future. Formulate and articulate a plan. Then put that plan in writing and refer to it every day.

2. Build Your Skills. Unless you enter college with a strong concentration (pre-med, pre-law, or a similar focus), you'll undoubtedly waste time on courses that are useless to your career. If you bypass college and go straight to building a specific set of practical skills, you can become a specialist in your field. Your mastery of that field will make you more valuable to yourself and your customers (if you choose to be self-employed), or to a potential employer. Here are some ways to build your skills:

Online colleges. Online college courses are far less expensive than a traditional campus-based education. You can focus on a specialization, take only the classes you need to achieve your goals, and complete a degree in months instead of years—and do accomplish it all in your pajamas. Online college courses vary greatly in cost and value, so do your homework before signing on. Check out online reviews. Ask around. Choose an online college that will help you reach your goals.

Massive Open Online Courses (MOOCs). MOOCs are free and open to anyone. You can study any subject imaginable through MOOCs—computer science, communication technology, business and management, languages, and on and on. Put away your Nintendo Switch, unplug your Netflix, and get serious about leveling up your skill set. Get a world-class education (minus the indoctrination), free of charge.

- Learn software development at CodeAcademy.
- Get an Ivy League education for free at Harvard Extension.
- Study subjects ranging from art appreciation to SAT prep to AP Chemistry at Khan Academy.
- Take a wide range of courses offered by such institutions as Duke, Johns Hopkins, Michigan, Penn, Princeton, and Stanford via Coursera.
- Choose from nearly a thousand courses from Caltech, Cornell, Dartmouth, Georgetown, Harvard, and MIT through EdX.
- Learn any subject—business, design, engineering, math, science, you name it—and search for subjects by university name at Academic Earth.
- Study a vast array of subjects, at your own pace and on any device, on Udemy. This platform contains both free and paid content (free content has a green "Free" symbol).
- Explore thousands of free courses from universities around the world on OpenCulture.
- ALISON is a free online learning platform with more than a thousand courses available. Unlike most MOOCs, ALISON offers certification (for a fee) and is accredited for continuing professional development by CPD UK.
- The Carnegie Mellon Open Learning Initiative offers courses with built-in feedback, to make sure you really understand the lesson material.
- Apple's iTunes U offers a library of university courses you can browse by institution and subject. Watch on your iPhone, iPad, or iPod.
- A number of universities offer their own online learning platforms, where you can audit their courses on a vast array of subjects: Stanford Online, Open Yale Courses, UC Berkeley Class Central, MIT OpenCourseWare, and University of Oxford Podcasts.

Jordan Peterson said, "Where is the university? The university is wherever anyone wants to learn about their culture and where anyone wants to expand the domain of human competence. And a lot of that is happening online now."[7]

Invest the time, save your money. Discipline yourself to focus intensely and use your time wisely. The whole world of learning is open to you for free.

Work College. Work colleges allow you to work your way through college without accumulating debt. These four-year colleges also integrate your college learning experience with your work experience. Work colleges are public or private non-profit degree-granting institution, focused on community service. Because you are working hand attending college at the same time, you get the best of both worlds. You are studying a career-related discipline, you are learning responsibility, and you are earning a living.

There are nine work colleges in the U.S. that are recognized and supervised by the U.S. Department of Education: Alice Lloyd College (Pippa Passes, Kentucky), Berea College (Berea, Kentucky), Bethany Global University (Bloomington, Minnesota), Blackburn College (Carlinville, Illinois), College of the Ozarks (Point Lookout, Missouri), Kuyper College (Grand Rapids, Michigan), Paul Quinn College (Dallas, Texas), Sterling College (Craftsbury Common, Vermont), and Warren Wilson College (Asheville, North Carolina).[8]

Vocational Training. There are two kinds of vocational schools—technical colleges and trade schools. Technical colleges are vocational schools with a strong classroom focus related to your chosen career (nursing, the hospitality industry, healthcare, business and finance, corrections and security, drafting, internet tech, and so forth). Trade schools are focused on hands-on training, and can prepare you for a career as an electrician, plumber, welder, machinist, cosmetologist, and so forth.

Job Corps. If you are low-income, between the ages of sixteen and twenty-four, have a good behavior record and you're drug free, you can obtain a free education and job training through Job Corps, a program administered by the United States Department of Labor. For more information, visit JobCorps.gov.

Apprenticeship. An apprenticeship is a method for training practitioners of a trade or profession through a combination of classroom study and on-the-job training. Apprenticeships enable people to become licensed for a regulated occupation after they have demonstrated measurable competencies. In exchange for their training, apprentices agree to work for the employer for a given period of time. For more information, visit Apprenticeship.gov.

3. Join the Military. Military service offers training and discipline, a chance to serve your community and your country, travel, plus education and retirement benefits. A military career will also help you get in top physical shape as you measure yourself against real-world challenges.

4. Find a Mentor. Mentors are experienced advisors who guide you in gaining experience, competence, and confidence in your chosen field. They offer advice, answer questions, and hold you accountable for your progress. I had many mentors as I was building Turning Point USA, and this organization would not exist without their wisdom and advice to guide me at every step. If you want to succeed in your chosen field, I recommend you find a mentor.

Seek out someone who is successful in your field and who exhibits attributes of good character and competence. A mentor will give you honest feedback on your strengths and weaknesses, point you to helpful resources, help you make professional connections, prepare you for your job search or starting your own business, and will provide you with a letter of recommendation, if needed.

To find a mentor, identify your goals for a mentoring relationship. What are you looking for in a mentor, and what do you hope to achieve? Next, research people in your field and make a list of possible mentors. Consider people in your extended family, workplace, or local business and volunteer organizations. Seek out people who are positive and inspiring. Before you approach a person, prepare an "elevator pitch," a succinct presentation of your request. (If you are looking for a mentor to help you start a small business, visit Score.org.)

Once you have selected a potential mentor, schedule a meeting. Offer to buy coffee or lunch. Be considerate of his or her time and attention. Explain why you selected that person. Avoid empty flattery, but state clearly that you value that person's experience and expertise. Don't feel you have to offer gifts or payment—you'd be amazed at how many people are willing to be mentors without expecting anything in return. A good mentoring relationship is rewarding for both mentor and mentee.

5. Volunteer. Find a cause you care about, then get involved. Apply to a ministry or service organization that meets local or global needs. Volunteer experience will enhance your résumé and build your skills. Some organizations will send you out to churches or community organizations to raise support (donations) for your living expenses while you are actively serving others.

6. Start a Business. Starting a business is not for the faint-hearted. You need leadership skills, communication skills, delegation skills, and a high tolerance for risk and stress. You'll need start-up capital, which usually comes from someone who loves you or from a venture capitalist in exchange for a percentage of your business. Do your homework, find a business mentor through Score.org, and learn everything you can about business and finance and the specific challenges of your field. Don't go into business overconfident and undercapitalized. But if you are thoroughly prepared for the adventure of entrepreneurship, if you are ready to sacrifice and work long hours to achieve success, then go for it.

7. Get on a Payroll. Get an entry-level job. Don't be too finicky. If you can't find a great job, settle for a good job. If you can't find a good job, settle for a lousy job. Just get on a payroll. As long as a job is honest, moral, and legal, it's respectable labor. Remember the words of Dr. King: "If a man is called to be a street sweeper, he should sweep streets even as Michelangelo painted or Beethoven composed music or Shakespeare wrote poetry. He should sweep streets so well that all the hosts of heaven and earth will pause to say, 'Here lived a great street sweeper who did his job well.'"

8. Apply for an Internship. Internships may be paid (very little) or unpaid, but they are a good way to gain experience and enrich your résumé. An internship is much like an entry level job, but usually has a limited term, from several weeks to several months. Internships provide invaluable work experience and often lead to a full-time job offer. They are also excellent networking opportunities that can open career doors for the future.

9. *Join a Startup Accelerator.* A startup accelerator (or seed accelerator) is a fixed-term program in which you become part of a "cohort" of would-be entrepreneurs. The program provides education and mentoring, usually for three months, with the goal of enabling you to make a successful "pitch" to venture capitalists on "demo day." The application process is open to anyone, but the field of applicants is highly competitive. Startup accelerators like TechStars, the Thiel Fellowship, Echoing Green, and Y Combinator usually accept between 1 percent and 3 percent of applicants. They prefer entrepreneurial teams over individual applicants. If you have a startup idea you're passionate about, consider applying to a startup accelerator.

10. *Move.* If there are no opportunities in your hometown, consider moving. Get out from under the expectations of family and friends, and start fresh in a new location where there is greater opportunity. Get out of your comfort zone, explore other parts of the country (or the world), and gain a new perspective on your future.

11. *Live on the Cheap.* Make a written budget and stick to it. Cancel your cable and streaming services. Buy used stuff instead of new. Eat in instead of out. Buy bargain clothes. Stop impulse buying. Use the library instead of buying books. Carpool, bike, walk, or use public transportation. Why own a car when there's Uber and Lyft? Cut down on expensive gifts, especially at Christmas time. Stop drinking, smoking, and other expensive habits. Drink tap water instead of bottled water. Hide your credit cards (the interest is murder).

And the best way of all to live on the cheap: *Don't go to college!*

EPILOGUE

TAKE ACTION!

> **Get involved and make a difference.**

Though the radical left seems to dominate an overwhelming majority of American campuses, Turning Point USA is present, we are active, and we are fully engaged in the battle to defend America from the menace that is academia. I know you want to join the battle as well. So, in the closing pages of this book, I want to give you an action agenda so you can begin *right now* to effect positive change:

1. Share the Message

Take what you have learned from this book and share it with others—with students and their parents, with your neighbors and fellow students, with your friends at church or synagogue or mosque, and with elected representatives. Talk about this message with your friends on social media. What is the thesis of this book? College is a scam and a net-negative for students and society—and we need to end it. Let's review.

In chapter 1, we saw that profit has replaced education as the mission of today's universities. Colleges are best described as hedge funds with universities attached. Parents, teachers, and guidance counselors need to change the way they talk to young people about their future. They need to stop asking "Where are you going to college?" and start asking "Why are you going to college?"

In chapter 2, we examined that the claim that a college education increases your lifetime earnings—and *we proved it's a lie*. We saw that student loan debt is crushing the American dream. Lobbyists for universities and the lending industry have rigged the system so that student loans can't be discharged through bankruptcy. As a result, 360,000 Americans have been locked out of homeownership by student loan debt. The college cartel is corrupt and unfixable—and needs to be shut down.

In chapter 3, we saw that *most* so-called "higher education" is fraudulent. After two years of college, 45 percent of students showed no improvement in writing ability, critical thinking, and complex reasoning. Over four years at our "most prestigious flagship universities," according to the *Wall Street Journal*, "the average graduate shows little or no improvement in critical thinking." Half of employers report the college grads are not prepared for the workplace. Our so-called "elite" universities aren't training young people to be leaders. They're just scamming them.

In chapter 4, we saw that a college campus is where inquiring young minds go to be welded shut. Academics talk constantly about "inclusivity" and "diversity," yet they want nothing to do with a *true* diversity of viewpoints. Students who think for themselves are routinely punished, bullied, and doxed. Conservative students rarely speak their minds out of fear of being attacked. In this chapter, we saw example after example of speech being suppressed by the faculty and administration.

In chapter 5, we witnessed the spectacle of leftist hate and violence at colleges and universities across America. It is not just students who commit acts of violence. Sometimes professors pick up a bike lock and commit mayhem themselves. Other professors openly recruit students into Antifa, a violent anti-capitalist hate group. We also saw that when radical leftist students become violent, university administrators blame their conservative victims.

> Colleges are best described as hedge funds with universities attached.

In chapter 6, we looked at foreign influence on American campuses. We saw that groups such as Students for Justice in Palestine, Jewish Voice for Peace, and IfNotNow aggressively undermine American support for Israel, suppress and persecute supporters of Israel, and often engage in outright anti-Semitism. We also saw Communist China's malignant influence on our campuses through the Confucius Institutes.

In chapters 7 and 8, we saw how students become woke and weaponized. University mission statements claim they are turning out "citizens of the world." Translation: radical university professors are teaching a generation to hate America. Universities used to prepare students for life by teaching them to pursue truth, defend liberty, and be good American citizens. In the process, students acquired the skills to have a rewarding career and contribute to society. Today, universities are unleashing waves of angry, violent young radicals on the world.

In chapter 9, we examined an array of ideas for skipping college, avoiding student loan debt, and setting out on the adventure of adulthood at age eighteen instead of twenty-two. Not only is it *possible* to have a successful life without a college degree, but you vastly improve your odds of success if you avoid the trap of the Great College Scam.

2. Talk to Your Kids

As a parent or grandparent, you have a duty to the next generation to make them aware of the state of academia today. Students entering college are walking into a buzzsaw. It would be bad enough if college was super-affordable and everyone came out after four years fully prepared to hold down a job. But college turns out young people who are perpetually in debt, and who have been indoctrinated as ungrateful Marxists. They then feel entitled to have their student loans paid for by the taxpayer.

I've been asked many times why progressives seem to dominate college campuses, and I think I know the answer. Progressivism is a seductive, attractive ideology—especially among college students who have very little real-world experience. Progressivism makes two very appealing claims.

First, progressivism claims that human beings are basically good. People only behave badly because our immoral capitalist society has a corrupting influence on human nature. If we could eliminate the social cancers of private property, capitalism, Judeo-Christian religion, and Western culture, society could progress to a state of justice and equity—just as Karl Marx predicted.

Second, progressivism claims that a utopia—a literal heaven on earth—is attainable. Human nature is perfectible, and we can create a society in which humanity lives in perfect harmony with nature, a world without pollution or global warming, a land without borders or police or religion. That's why John Lennon's sappy "Imagine" is performed at so many progressive events.

One of the most important—and least appreciated—accomplishments of the founding fathers was that they designed a clear-eyed, realistic form of government. Our Constitution is based on the recognition that an earthly utopia is an impossibility—and that human nature cannot be perfected on earth. It's the realism of our Constitution that has led many utopian-minded progressives to reject the founding fathers and our founding principles in favor of unworkable, dangerous, Marxist progressivism.

The appeal of progressivism also has a lot to do with personality and temperament. What kind of people become college professors? What kind of people love the academic lifestyle and can't get enough of college life?

> Not only is it possible to have a successful life without a college degree, but you vastly improve your odds of success if you avoid the trap of the Great College Scam.

Answer: people who are communal and thought-oriented, who have a passion for sitting around, endlessly discussing ideas and theories. They enjoy living in the realm of the mind, with no real-world responsibilities. When they read the theories of Marx and Marcuse, it all makes sense to them because they never have to test these theories against reality. This is the kind of person who meanders around the halls of academia for a decade or so, gets a doctorate degree, and often goes on to a career as a professor. What kind of person am I describing? A leftist, of course.

Campus conservatives tend to have very different personalities. Ask any of them in our TPUSA chapters: "If you could get your degree right now and leave this campus two or three years early, would you do it?" They'd say, "I'd be out of here in a heartbeat! I'm just here to get that piece of paper! I can't wait to get on with my life!"

Progressives have academia in their DNA. They become professors and administrators. Conservatives prefer to do things, build things, not theorize endlessly. That's why you find few conservatives in the structure of a university. Conservatives see the university as a period of their lives that must be endured on their way to a career. You'll find them out in the real world, running a business or working their way up the corporate ladder.

So, as a parent or grandparent, you should have a conversation with the young people in your life. Make sure they understand what colleges and universities have become today. Make sure they understand that they have alternatives and can succeed in life without a college degree. Encourage them to keep their options open. Odds are, they will have a much better life if they sidestep the college scam and leap right into the real world.

Many young people go through a phase of rebellion. That's not always a bad thing. In fact, my message to young people today is this: "If you really want to be a rebel, don't go to college. If you want to accomplish something significant, don't go to college. You'll have no debt, tons of freedom, plenty of opportunity, and you'll stand out in the crowd."

I firmly believe that America cannot be saved unless we cut the college population by half. So it's up to you, parent, and it's up to you, student, to join in this effort to cut off the flow of people and money to these far-left indoctrination centers.

There is hope that we can still reverse America's decline. That hope lies in declining university enrollment. It's that simple. Let's raise up a new generation of independent, responsible young people who think for themselves.

3. Take a Stand for Freedom

Wokeism and radical leftism began on our campuses and has infected every aspect of American society: the bureaucracy, the education establishment, the legal profession, the judiciary, the military, corporations (especially tech companies), the news media, the entertainment media, and on and on. All of the radical left insanity that is creating chaos in our culture can be traced to colleges and universities.

Marxism is epidemic in our society because Karl Marx is alive and well on campus. The growing popularity of Marxism and socialism in academia poses an existential threat to America. A June 2021 *Axios* poll found that Americans are increasingly more favorable toward socialism. Though 52 percent of Americans still oppose socialism, the percentage of adults who are favorable toward socialism grew from 39 percent in 2019 to 41 percent in 2021. *Axios* concluded, "Socialism's appeal in the U.S. continues to grow, driven by Black Americans and women. . . . Socialism is getting more popular, and capitalism is fading."[1]

The growing embrace of socialism by many Americans threatens our freedom, our economy, and our way of life. It threatens the future of our children and generations to come. There is a real possibility that America could become Venezuela or Cuba within our lifetime. As someone once said, you can vote your way into a socialist system, but you have to shoot your way out.

Flying the socialist banner, radical leftists have emerged from our campuses and fanned out into our communities. They are on a mission to eradicate everything that doesn't conform to their far-left worldview. They are blinded by the failed socialist ideology that has oppressed and impoverished people around the world.

We need to stand for the principle of "one nation, under God, indivisible, with liberty and justice for all." We need to stand for America and Western civilization—and against the spread of socialism in our culture. The best way to make that stand is to strike at the source of socialist propaganda in our society. We have to actively, aggressively dismantle the college system.

4. Defend Yourself against Woke Persecution

If you are employed by a major corporation or a student or faculty member at a university, there is a good chance you will face an ordeal called "diversity training" or "equity training." These training sessions frequently require their victims to read Robin DiAngelo's *White Fragility*, a bestseller that has become the standard textbook of the "diversity" industry. Liberal journalist Matt Taibbi has rightly condemned DiAngelo's destructive book as "Hitlerian race theory." He writes:

A core principle of the academic movement that shot through elite schools in America since the early nineties was the view that individual rights, humanism, and the democratic process are all just stalking-horses for white supremacy. The concept, as articulated in [*White Fragility*] . . . reduces everything, even the smallest and most innocent human interactions, to racial power contests. . . .

White Fragility has a simple message: there is no such thing as a universal human experience, and we are defined not by our individual personalities or moral choices, but only by our racial category. If your category is "white," bad news: you have no identity apart from your participation in white supremacy ("Anti-blackness is foundational to our very identities… Whiteness has always been predicated on blackness"), which naturally means "a positive white identity is an impossible goal."[2]

> There is hope that we can still reverse America's decline. That hope lies in declining university enrollment. It's that simple. Let's raise up a new generation of independent, responsible young people who think for themselves.

Please understand this: if you're in a toxic, abusive environment at your workplace or on your campus because of your race or color—regardless of whether you are African American, Asian American, European American ("white"), or any other race or ethnicity—your civil rights are being trampled. Under Title VI and Title VII of the Civil Rights Act of 1964, it's a serious violation for any employer or college administration to shame you, accuse you, or try to impose an ideology on you because of your race.

Sometimes abusive treatment is obvious and extreme. The woke radicals may try to smear you, destroy your reputation, end your career, dox you, and terminate your social media accounts. The gatekeepers of leftist society in academia have assumed the right to decide who is in and who is out. They can't punish you legally for your views and beliefs, so they punish you socially by canceling you and ostracizing you. Such abusive behavior may give you grounds for a lawsuit.

At other times, the abusive treatment will take the form of a humiliating "diversity exercises." For example, there's the "privilege walk" exercise in which participants stand in a line with their eyes closed while a facilitator calls out certain characteristics that constitute "privilege." You take a step forward if a characteristic applies to you. At the end of this blatantly racist exercise, everybody opens their eyes to see who in the group are "privileged" and who are "oppressed."

Another example is "affinity groups" which are multiplying on college campuses. You might have little in common with the other people in your "affinity group." You're only in that group because some "dean of diversity and inclusion" has assigned you there.

For example: in June 2021, two Jewish mental health professionals at Stanford University filed federal complaints of workplace discrimination for what they call "severe and persistent" anti-Jewish harassment by colleagues. Over their objections, Stanford's Diversity, Equity and Inclusion program assigned them to a "whiteness affinity group" where they were accused of "white privilege," even though Jews were historically *oppressed* by white racism. The complaint alleges violations of the law, notably Title VII of the Civil Rights Act.[3]

Here are some resources to help you fight back when your rights have been violated:

CounterweightSupport.com. British ethicist Helen Pluckrose, the editor-in-chief of *Areo* Magazine, created this website for people who face abusive "diversity training" in the workplace. The website provides resources, including templates to help you compose a letter to your employer. The sample letters provide a respectfully-worded, well-reasoned argument for being excused from offensive "diversity" sessions. Resources on the Counterweight website promote viewpoint diversity and individual human rights.

GoldwaterInstitute.org. The Goldwater Institute is committed to defending our constitutional freedoms. The litigation arm of the Goldwater Institute is the Scharf-Norton Center for Constitutional Litigation, whose attorneys "defend individual rights and protect those who cannot protect themselves." At the website, you can fill out a form and submit your case for consideration. If you are an attorney committed to defending liberty and the Constitution, you can apply to join the Goldwater Institute's nationwide attorney network.

CriticalRace.org is a website created by law professor William Jacobson of Cornell University. The website operates a free database of more than 200 colleges and universities. It's designed to inform and empower "parents and students concerned about the negative impact Critical Race Training has on education." The website also offers information on The 1619 Project, CRT in grades K-12, plus a page where you can submit information on indoctrination in your school.

5. Take a Bold Stand for the Truth

On the campus of Chicago's Northeastern Illinois University, there is a building bearing a plaque that reads, "This building is dedicated to public service honoring the memory of Abraham Lincoln—Democrat." Lincoln, of course, was not a Democrat. He was, in fact, the first Republican president— the leader of the party founded to abolish slavery and oppose the pro-slavery Democratic party.

Why would a university in Abraham Lincoln's home state install a plaque misidentifying his political affiliation? The plaque was installed in 1905. University officials claim the word "Democrat" was added because Lincoln was "an advocate for democracy." Nonsense. When historians write about Lincoln, there are many appellations they apply to him, and "Democrat" is not one of them. The Great Emancipator, The Liberator, The Rail-Splitter, Honest Abe, The 16th President, Savior of the Union—but "Democrat"? Never.

I went to the Northeastern Illinois campus and called for the plaque to be corrected. I pointed out that it is miseducating students who pass by that building. The administration refuses to correct the plaque. I can only assume that university officials are perfectly content to mislead their student body and promote the outrageous notion that Lincoln, our first Republican president and arguably our greatest president, was a pro-slavery Democrat.

The Lincoln plaque—and the administration's refusal to correct it—are emblematic of the kind of "education" (i.e., indoctrination) that is dispensed at our universities. By calling attention to the deceptive plaque at Northeastern Illinois University, I hope to educate students at that institution about who Abraham Lincoln really was and why his legacy matters.

I urge you to join me in taking a stand for the truth. Wherever you see leftist deceit, whether in the mainstream media or social media or on a plaque on a university wall, call it out. Be respectful, be reasonable, be sure you have your facts straight, then be bold. Start a conversation. Have a reasonable, fact-based debate.

You may have noticed that I haven't used the word "liberal" very often in this book. I generally referred to our opponents on the far left as "progressives" or "radicals," and their ideology as "wokeism." I make a distinction between "liberals" and "progressives."

I have liberal friends, and we can disagree about many issues and still be friends. But I don't have any radical friends. That's not my choice—it's their choice. By my definition, what makes them "radical" is their unwillingness to engage in a reasoned conversation about our different views.

I can talk to a liberal. No one can talk to a radical. Radicals will shout you down. They are completely intolerant. They have no respect for the First Amendment. They will even try to get you banned from campus.

But liberals are reasonable people. For example, I consider Harvard Law professor Alan Dershowitz a genuine liberal. I don't agree with him on many social or political issues. But I can have a respectful conversation with him, and there are many points where he and I can find common ground. For example, I have a deep respect for his defense of constitutional principles, including free speech, and for his defense of the nation of Israel.

So we need to have a conversation, not merely within our own circle of like-minded friends, but with reasonable people across the political and ideological divide. And one of the issues we must discuss is the destructive effect the university system is having on America.

6. Support Divest U

Every year, well-intentioned Americans proudly send checks to support their alma maters. But as we all know, the road to hell is paved with "good intentions." Radical anti-American leftists have hijacked our universities. Those who donate to "higher education" are subsidizing the ideological indoctrination of our children and grandchildren. Their "good intentions" are sending America to hell.

DivestU is Turning Point USA's aggressive effort to make a meaningful difference by attacking the university menace where it's most vulnerable: the bank account. Multibillion dollar endowments are funding the ideological poisoning of our students on campus. The eight- or nine-figure donations of alumni are financing our destruction. It needs to stop.

I urge you to watch our videos which explain how DivestU works. You can find them at our Turning Point USA website (https://www.tpusa.com/divestu) and at Dennis Prager's PragerU website (https://www.prageru.com/video/divestu/).

Turning Point USA has been very successful in persuading donors to stop giving to universities. We know that more than $60 million have been divested so far, but we are just getting started. Our goal is to divest $1 billion from universities over the next few years. I want to start a major movement of donors who will redirect their charitable giving away from "higher education" and toward causes that do honorable work.

7. Support the Professor Watchlist

Professor Watchlist is a Turning Point USA project that reports on college professors who discriminate against conservative students and teach leftist propaganda in the classroom. The Professor Watchlist is carefully compiled from published news stories and offers guidance to students who are selecting courses and professors. You'll find the Watchlist at ProfessorWatchlist.org/. (If you are in the United Kingdom, our sister organization, Turning Point UK, maintains a website called Education Watch. You'll find that site at PointUK.co.uk/education-watch/.)

While you're online, visit ChinaOnCampus.com and learn more about the subversive activities of Communist China's Confucius Institutes.

> I can talk to a liberal. No one can talk to a radical. Radicals will shout you down. They are completely intolerant.

We Have to Act Now

On June 10, 2020, as mobs of vandals attacked statues across America, one group of radicals attacked the Christopher Columbus statue at the Minnesota State Capitol. A university professor in New York, Erin L. Thompson, tweeted a message to the rioters: "I'm a professor who studies the deliberate destruction of cultural heritage and I just have to say. . . use chain instead of rope and it'll go faster."[4]

Professor Thompson teaches at City University of New York (CUNY). On her website, she describes herself this way: "I am America's only full-time professor of art crime. I study a variety of relations between art and crime, including the looting of antiquities, museum theft, art made by detainees at Guantánamo Bay, and the legalities and ethics of digital reproductions of cultural heritage. I have discussed these topics for the *New York Times*, CNN, NPR, and the *Freakonomics* podcast, among many others."

You'd think a "professor of art crime" would be *opposed* to art crime, not in favor of it—but no. This is the abysmal state of academia today. Our professors are cheering on the end of civilization.

Turning Point USA has been battling campus indoctrination since its founding in 2012. The violence in our streets, the oppressive actions of government at various levels, and the autocratic behavior of our corporations, tech industry, and mainstream media are the direct result of decades of Marxist and anti-American ideas being proclaimed on campus as dogma. Students are emerging from our colleges and universities convinced that America is a systemically evil and oppressive nation.

In 1967, German student activist Rudi Dutschke coined a term to describe his strategy for engendering a Communist revolution: "the long march through the institutions." His goal was to gradually undermine society by infiltrating our institutions (including colleges and universities) with Marxist activists. Herbert Marcuse, the neo-Marxist father of Critical Theory, heard that term and wrote an enthusiastic letter to Dutschke, saying, "I regard your notion of the 'long march through the institutions' as the only effective way to teach at all levels of education . . ."[5]

Today, America's campuses are ground zero for the Marxists' march to revolution. The long march is approaching its destination. Marxists have captured the education system and they now control the pipeline to the credentialed class. To be credentialed to enter an "elite" class, such as government, the media, or "higher education," you must pass through the credentialing pipeline. You must undergo indoctrination and prove yourself to be ideologically pure.[6]

To disrupt that pipeline and break the radical leftist stranglehold on our institutions, we need to urge our elected representatives to enact legislation removing federal guarantees for student loans and revoking tax-exempt status for colleges and universities. We need to urge donors to divest from colleges and universities, and to divert their charitable contributions to organizations and causes that build America up instead of tearing her down.

I'm not alone in calling for the defunding and dismantling of our colleges and universities. Remember Jason D. Hill, the black tenured professor of philosophy at DePaul University who was viciously persecuted by university officials because of his defense of Israel. In July 2018, almost a year *before* his persecution at DePaul began, Professor Hill wrote an op-ed for America's largest independent political news site, *The Hill*. It was headlined, "A Professor's Call to Shut Down Our Nation's Universities."

He wrote from his heart and soul, drawing on years of observations as a professor and visiting lecturer. He recalled that when he entered college more than three decades earlier, "left-wing ideologies dominated American universities, and especially the humanities and social sciences." But there was a different, more tolerant atmosphere in those days. "Free speech was alive on college campuses. . . . Hearing perspectives different from your own was considered essential to your education."

Today, however, the "core principles and foundations that keep the United States intact, that provide our citizens with their civic personalities and national identities, are being annihilated. The gravest internal threat to this country is not illegal aliens; it is leftist professors who are waging a war against America and teaching our young people to hate this country."

He lamented the fact that, among leftist academics, the term "Western civilization" has become synonymous with racism, cultural chauvinism, and oppression. Great philosophers such as John Locke and John Stuart Mill have been labeled "white supremacists," and have been canceled by radical scholars. Hill noted that the cultural relativists on campus had even sought to abolish "reason, rational argument, . . . and belief in an objective reality."

"One cannot argue with such people," Hill adds. "The only alternative is to shut them down." How does he propose to shut down the far left propagandists of academia? He explains: "Educational systems that have become such propaganda machines should not be funded by taxpaying Americans. . . . Withdraw your support and leave them to fund themselves."

Amen and amen.

The first universities were founded more than 800 years ago with a mission of preparing students to love God, to serve humanity, and to contribute to civilization. The University of Bologna, Italy, was probably the first, founded around AD 1088. Oxford University began preparing students to live faithful, constructive lives in about 1096. The early history of *genuine* higher learning is a noble one.

But that spirit of service to humanity, Professor Hill concludes, "no longer exists in our universities. It lies elsewhere, in a philosophic system waiting to be discovered or created."

Those are true words. The old system of colleges and universities is hopelessly corrupt. It's obsolete. It's destructive to our nation and our students.

Let's end it before it's too late.

ACKNOWLEDGMENTS

To my wife Erika, thank you so much for your unending love and support.
You inspire me every day.

To all the incredible staff and supporters at Turning Point USA – this book
would not be possible without you! A special thanks to Bill Montgomery
and Foster Friess, two men whose support has helped make
Turning Point's vision a reality.

Thank you to everyone at Winning Team Publishing, especially Sergio,
Don Jr., Amanda, Connor, Justin, Todd, Melissa, and Kris. I am incredibly
grateful for all of your work getting *The College Scam* published and
in the hands of the American people.

To all the PATRIOTS across America, you are the reason I get up and
fight every day. I hope this book inspires you to stand up for America!

ABOUT THE AUTHOR

Charlie Kirk is the Founder and President of Turning Point USA, a national student movement dedicated to empowering young people to promote the principles of free markets and limited government. With representation on more than 1,500 high school and college campuses and more than 150 full-time staff, Turning Point USA is the largest and fastest-growing conservative youth activist organization in America.

In 2012, while a high school senior, Kirk wrote an essay for Breitbart News on liberal bias in high school textbooks. This led to an appearance on Fox Business Network. Since then, he has appeared on CNBC, Fox News, and Fox Business News more than 800 times. He has also penned columns for *Newsweek* and *The Hill*, and was named to the Forbes "30 under 30" list. Charlie Kirk was the youngest speaker at the 2016 Republican National Convention, and he is the Chairman of Students for Trump, which seeks to engage a million conservative 2020 voters on college campuses in battleground states.

Charlie Kirk is the author of three previous books: *Time for a Turning Point: Setting a Course Toward Free Markets and Limited Government for Future Generations* (2016), *Campus Battlefield: How Conservatives Can WIN the Battle on Campus and Why It Matters* (2018), and *The MAGA Doctrine: The Only Ideas That Will Win the Future* (2020).

His social media reaches more than 100 million people per month and (according to Axios) his is one of the "Top 10 Most Engaged" Twitter accounts in the world, behind only President Trump among conservatives. His podcast, *The Charlie Kirk Show*, regularly ranks among the top 15 news shows on Apple podcast charts. On his show, he combines in-depth political and cultural analysis, plus conversations with some of the most influential newsmakers of our time.

NOTES

Introduction: Laying Out the Case

[1] Elizabeth Redden, "41% of Recent Grads Work in Jobs Not Requiring a Degree," Inside Higher Ed, February 18, 2020, https://www.insidehighered.com/quicktakes/2020/02/18/41-recent-grads-work-jobs-not-requiring-degree.

Chapter 1: The Game Is Rigged against You

[1] Sarah Rose Attman, "I Learned Nothing in College," Huff Post, July 25, 2014, https://www.huffpost.com/entry/i-learned-nothing-in-coll_b_5606640.

[2] National Center for Education Statistics, "Fast Facts: Graduation Rates" (Source: U.S. Department of Education, National Center for Education Statistics, 2020, The Condition of Education 2020, NCES 2020-144, Undergraduate Retention and Graduation Rates), https://nces.ed.gov/FastFacts/display.asp?id=40.

[3] Melanie Hanson, "College Dropout Rates," Education.org, September 14, 2021, https://educationdata.org/college-dropout-rates/.

[4] Jenna A. Robinson, "Does the Bennett Hypothesis Still Matter?," James G. Martin Center for Academic Renewal, December 27, 2017, https://www.jamesgmartin.center/2017/12/bennett-hypothesis-still-matter/.

[5] Press Release, "Rubio Introduces Bill to Eliminate Interest for Federal Student Loans," Rubio.Senate.gov, May 2, 2019, https://www.rubio.senate.gov/public/index.cfm/2019/5/rubio-introduces-student-bill-to-eliminate-interest-in-federal-student-loans.

[6] Sareen S. Gropper, Karla P. Simmons, Lenda Jo Connell, Pamela V. Ulrich, "Changes in Body Weight, Composition, and Shape: A Four-Year Study of College Students," PubMed.gov, September 17, 2012, https://pubmed.ncbi.nlm.nih.gov/22978391/.

[7] Jason Kessler, "Alumna Sues College Because She Hasn't Found a Job," CNN.com, August 3, 2009, https://www.cnn.com/2009/US/08/03/new.york.jobless.graduate/; Tina Cherisse Thompson against Monroe College, Ex Parte and Urgent Motion, Filed July 24, 2009, Bronx County Clerk,

http://i.cdn.turner.com/cnn/2009/images/08/03/thompson.pdf; Bob
Kraft, "5 Most Bizarre Court Cases in US History," PISSD.com, July 5,
2018, https://www.pissd.com/2018/07/5-most-bizarre-court-cases-in-us-
history/.

Chapter 2: The Obscene Cost of a Diploma
[1] AnnaMaria Andriotis, "Over 60, and Crushed by Student Loan Debt,"
Wall Street Journal, February 2, 2019, https://www.wsj.com/articles/over-
60-and-crushed-by-student-loan-debt-11549083631.
[2] Open Secrets, "Student Loan Companies: Lobbying, 2020,"
OpenSecrets.org, March 2021, https://www.opensecrets.org/industries/
lobbying.php?cycle=2020&ind=F1410.
[3] Erin Arvedlund and Bob Fernandez, "Your Student Loan Servicers—
Navient, Nelnet, And Fedloan—Pay Big Bucks to CEOs and Lobbyists,"
Philadelphia Inquirer, July 1, 2019, https://www.inquirer.com/business/
student-loans-navient-fedloan-great-lakes-nelnet-mohela-slsa-scott-
buchanan-doe-20190805.html.
[4] Michelle Singletary, "Your Friend Has No Place to Live and $150,000
in Student Loans. Should You Let Her Move in with You?," Washington
Post, July 3, 2019, https://www.washingtonpost.com/business/economy/
your-friend-has-no-place-to-live-and-150000-in-student-loans-should-
you-let-her-move-in-with-you/2019/07/03/beb8179a-9cfe-11e9-9ed4-
c9089972ad5a_story.html.
[5] George Washington University, Student Accounts, Finance Division,
"Undergraduate Tuition," GWU.edu, accessed June 7, 2021, https://
studentaccounts.gwu.edu/undergraduate-tuition.
[6] Melissa Korn and Andrea Fuller, "'Financially Hobbled for Life': The
Elite Master's Degrees That Don't Pay Off," Wall Street Journal, July 8,
2021, https://www.wsj.com/articles/financially-hobbled-for-life-the-elite-
masters-degrees-that-dont-pay-off-11625752773.
[7] Hillary Hoffower, "Nearly Half of Millennials Say College Wasn't
Worth Student-Loan," Business Insider, April 11, 2019, https://www.
businessinsider.com/personal-finance/millennials-college-not-worth-
student-loan-debt-2019-4.

8 Shahien Nasiripour, "Student Debt Is a Major Reason Millennials Aren't Buying Homes," Bloomberg, July 17, 2017, https://www.bloomberg.com/news/articles/2017-07-17/student-debt-is-hurting-millennial-homeownership.

9 Jessica Silver-Greenberg, Stacy Cowley and Natalie Kitroeff, "When Unpaid Student Loan Bills Mean You Can No Longer Work," New York Times, November 18, 2017, https://www.nytimes.com/2017/11/18/business/student-loans-licenses.html.

10 Christy Rakoczy, "Got Unpaid Student Loans? You Could Lose Your License in These States," Student Loan Hero, September 18, 2019, https://studentloanhero.com/featured/unpaid-student-loans-facing-default-lose-license-states/.

11 Michael Stratford, "Warren Unveils Details of Plan to Cancel $640 B in Student Loan Debt," Politico, July 23, 2019, https://www.politico.com/story/2019/07/23/elizabeth-warren-cancel-student-loan-debt-1611374.

12 Morgan Phillips, "Elizabeth Warren Confronted by Iowa Dad over Student Loan Plan, Saying People Paying for Tuition Would Get 'Screwed,'" FoxNews.com, January 23, 2020, https://www.foxnews.com/politics/warren-confronted-iowa-dad#; Fox News, "Will Warren's Voter Confrontation on Student Loan Debt Hurt Her Campaign?," FoxNews.com, January 26, 2020, https://video.foxnews.com/v/6126569289001#sp=show-clips.

13 Darragh Roche, "Joe Biden Can't Cancel Federal Student Debt, Nancy Pelosi Says," Newsweek, July 29, 2021, https://www.newsweek.com/joe-biden-cancel-federal-student-debt-nancy-pelosi-1614210.

14 Jonathan Turley, "Temple University Reaches Settlement on Alleged Fraud Related to U.S. News and World Report Rankings," JonathanTurley.org, December 22, 2020, https://jonathanturley.org/2020/12/22/temple-university-reaches-settlement-on-alleged-fraud-related-to-u-s-news-and-world-report-rankings/.

15 Staff, "What's Wrong with Most College Rankings," LiberalArtsColleges.com, 2015, https://www.liberalartscolleges.com/whats-wrong-with-most-college-rankings/.

16 Lynn O'Shaughnessy, "Why U.S. News' College Rankings Hurt Students," CBS News Moneywatch, September 10, 2013, https://www.

cbsnews.com/news/why-us-news-college-rankings-hurt-students/.

[17] Jaden Urbi, "This is How College Got So Expensive in America," CNBC, February 2, 2019, https://www.cnbc.com/2019/02/02/higher-education-big-business-college-expensive-student-loan-debt-america.html.

Chapter 3: Where Does All the Money Go?

[1] Jack Shafer @jackshafer, tweet: "Harvard is the new . . ." Twitter.com, July 6, 2020, https://twitter.com/jackshafer/status/128017194554433536 0?lang=en.

[2] Caitlin Flanagan, @CaitlinPacific, tweet: "Harvard suckers customers . . ." Twitter.com, July 6, 2020, https://twitter.com/caitlinpacific/status/1280188137013080065.

[3] Jessica Dickler, "These Colleges Went to Remote Learning but Hiked Tuition Anyway," CNBC, January 22, 2021, https://www.cnbc.com/2021/01/22/these-colleges-went-remote-but-raised-tuition-during-covid-pandemic.html.

[4] Daniel Kurt, "Student Loan Debt: 2020 Statistics and Outlook," Investopedia.com, March 16, 2021, https://www.investopedia.com/student-loan-debt-2019-statistics-and-outlook-4772007.

[5] Josh Moody, "10 Universities with the Biggest Endowments," U.S. News & World Report, September 21, 2021, https://www.usnews.com/education/best-colleges/the-short-list-college/articles/10-universities-with-the-biggest-endowments.

[6] "GDP Ranked by Country 2021," https://worldpopulationreview.com/countries/countries-by-gdp.

[7] Astra Taylor, "Universities Are Becoming Billion-Dollar Hedge Funds with Schools Attached," The Nation, March 8, 2016, https://www.thenation.com/article/archive/universities-are-becoming-billion-dollar-hedge-funds-with-schools-attached/.

[8] Amanda Ripley, "Why Is College in America So Expensive?," The Atlantic, September 11, 2018, https://www.theatlantic.com/education/archive/2018/09/why-is-college-so-expensive-in-america/569884/.

[9] Ripley, "Why Is College in America So Expensive?"

[10] David H. Hubel, "A Top-Heavy Administration?," Harvard Crimson, January 31, 2012, https://www.thecrimson.com/article/2012/1/31/david-

hubel-harvard-administration-deans-medical/.

[11] Farran Powell, Emma Kerr, and Sarah Wood, "See the Average College Tuition in 2021–2022," U.S. News & World Report, September 13, 2021, https://www.usnews.com/education/best-colleges/paying-for-college/articles/paying-for-college-infographic.

[12] Michael Arceneaux, "My Student Loan Payments Are Impossible to Keep Up With. Which Was Kind of the Point," NBC News, April 7, 2020, excerpted from I Don't Want to Die Poor published by Atria Books, https://www.nbcnews.com/think/opinion/my-student-loan-payments-are-impossible-keep-which-was-kind-ncna1178336.

Chapter 4: Colleges Don't Educate Anymore

[1] Phyllis Schlafly, "The Dumbing Down of America's Colleges," OurCivilisation.com, April 1996, http://www.ourcivilisation.com/dumb/dumb2.htm; "How Long Is a College Semester? [2021 Guide], " https://www.mydegreeguide.com/how-long-is-a-college-semester/.

[2] George Leef, "The Roots of Our Educational Failure," NationalReview.com, August 21, 2019, https://www.nationalreview.com/corner/the-roots-of-our-educational-failure/.

[3] Glenn Harlan Reynolds, "Higher Education, Lower Standards: Column," USA Today, January 14, 2014, https://www.usatoday.com/story/opinion/2014/01/13/higher-education-college-university-column/4440369/.

[4] Ibid.

[5] CBS News, "Study: College Students Not Learning Much," January 18, 2011, https://www.cbsnews.com/news/study-college-students-not-learning-much/.

[6] Douglas Belkin, "Exclusive Test Data: Many Colleges Fail to Improve Critical-Thinking Skills," Wall Street Journal, June 5, 2017, https://www.wsj.com/articles/exclusive-test-data-many-colleges-fail-to-improve-critical-thinking-skills-1496686662.

[7] Ibid.

[8] Ibid.

[9] Ibid.

[10] Hamilton Nolan, "Study Reveals: College Kids Learn Nothing,"

Gawker.com, January 18, 2011, https://gawker.com/5736875/study-reveals-college-kids-learn-nothing.

[11] Amanda Ripley, "Why Is College In America So Expensive?," The Atlantic, September 11, 2018, https://www.theatlantic.com/education/archive/2018/09/why-is-college-so-expensive-in-america/569884/.

[12] U.S. Census Bureau, "The Big Payoff: Educational Attainment and Work-Life Earnings," https://www.census.gov/library/publications/2002/demo/p23-210.html.

[13] U.S. Bureau of Labor Statistics, "Employment Projections: Education Pays," BLS.gov, April 21, 2021, https://www.bls.gov/emp/chart-unemployment-earnings-education.htm.

[14] Brad Plumer, "Only 27 Percent of College Grads Have a Job Related to Their Major," Washington Post, May 20, 2013, https://www.washingtonpost.com/news/wonk/wp/2013/05/20/only-27-percent-of-college-grads-have-a-job-related-to-their-major/.

[15] Alex Shashkevich, "Computer Science College Seniors in U.S. Outperform Peers in China, India and Russia, New Research Says," Phys.org, March 19, 2019, https://phys.org/news/2019-03-science-college-seniors-outperform-peers.html.

[16] National Research University Higher School of Economics, "Supertest Evaluates Performance Of Engineering Students in Russia, U.S., India, China," Phys.org, March 2, 2021, https://phys.org/news/2021-03-supertest-students-russia-india-china.html.

[17] Chrissy Clark, "UC San Diego Requires New Assistant Chemistry Professors To Complete Research That Advances 'Anti-Racism,' Anti-Oppression,'" The Daily Wire, July 7, 2021, https://www.dailywire.com/news/uc-san-diego-requires-new-assistant-chemistry-professors-to-complete-research-that-advances-anti-racism-anti-oppression; listing verified by the author at "Assistant Professor (Tenure Track) in Chemistry & Biochemistry, Job #JPF02736," CHEMISTRY & BIOCHEMISTRY / Physical Sciences / UC San Diego / Open date: July 1, 2021, https://apol-recruit.ucsd.edu/JPF02736?emid=3640, accessed July 14, 2021.

[18] NCES, "Fast Facts: Back to School Statistics," National Center for Education Statistics, 2020, https://nces.ed.gov/fastfacts/display.asp?id=372; NCES, "Status and Trends in the Education of Racial and

Ethnic Groups: Indicator 26: STEM Degrees," National Center for Education Statistics, February 2019, https://nces.ed.gov/programs/raceindicators/indicator_reg.asp.

[19] EAB (Education Advisory Board), "Who Works in STEM? 7 Fast Facts," EAB.com, January 23, 2018, https://eab.com/insights/daily-briefing/workplace/who-works-in-stem-7-fast-facts/.

[20] Elizabeth Redden, "National Science Board Report Finds US Dominance in Science Is Slipping," InsideHigherEd.com, January 16, 2020, https://www.insidehighered.com/news/2020/01/16/national-science-board-report-finds-us-dominance-science-slipping.

[21] R. R. Reno, "Why I Stopped Hiring Ivy League Graduates," Wall Street Journal, June 7, 2021, https://www.wsj.com/articles/why-i-stopped-hiring-ivy-league-graduates-11623103004.

[22] Ibid.

Chapter 5: The Lunacy of College

[1] Jon Levine, "Harvard Lecturer Blasted for Defending Existence of Biological Sex," New York Post, July 31, 2021, https://nypost.com/2021/07/31/harvard-lecturer-blasted-for-defending-existence-of-biological-sex/; Meimei Xu, "Biology Lecturer's Comments on Biological Sex Draw Backlash" Harvard Crimson, August 12, 2021, https://www.thecrimson.com/article/2021/8/11/biology-lecturer-gender-comments-backlash/.

[2] Jillian Kay Melchior, "Fake News Comes to Academia," Wall Street Journal, October 5, 2018, https://www.wsj.com/articles/fake-news-comes-to-academia-1538520950.

[3] Yascha Mounk, "What an Audacious Hoax Reveals about Academia," The Atlantic, October 5, 2018, https://www.theatlantic.com/ideas/archive/2018/10/new-sokal-hoax/572212/.

[4] Mikael Nilsson, "Opinion—'Mein Kampf' and the 'Feminazis': What Three Academics' Hitler Hoax Really Reveals About 'Wokeness,'" Haaretz, March 21, 2021, https://www.haaretz.com/us-news/.premium-hitler-hoax-academic-wokeness-culture-war-1.9629759.

[5] James Lindsay, Peter Boghossian, and Helen Pluckrose, "Academic Grievance Studies and the Corruption of Scholarship," Areo, October 2,

2018, https://areomagazine.com/2018/10/02/academic-grievance-studies-and-the-corruption-of-scholarship/; Yascha Mounk, "What an Audacious Hoax Reveals about Academia," The Atlantic, October 5, 2018, https://www.theatlantic.com/ideas/archive/2018/10/new-sokal-hoax/572212/.
6 Katie Herzog, "Med Schools Are Now Denying Biological Sex," Common Sense with Bari Weiss, Substack.com, July 27, 2021, https://bariweiss.substack.com/p/med-schools-are-now-denying-biological.
7 Holly M. Barker, "SpongeBob's Bikini Bottom Is Based on a Real-Life Test Site for Nuclear Weapons," The Conversation, June 1, 2018, https://theconversation.com/spongebobs-bikini-bottom-is-based-on-a-real-life-test-site-for-nuclear-weapons-96687; Celine Ryan Ciccio, "Prof: SpongeBob Perpetuates 'Violent, Racist' Acts against Indigenous People," Campus Reform, October 10, 2019, https://campusreform.org/?ID=13844; Rob Shimshock, "Prof Calls SpongeBob 'Racist' in 10,000-Word Essay," Campus Unmasked, October 16, 2019, https://campusunmasked.com/2019/10/16/prof-calls-spongebob-racist-in-10000-word-essay/.
8 Raj Patel, "Food Injustice Has Deep Roots: Let's Start with America's Apple Pie," The Guardian, May 1, 2021, https://www.theguardian.com/environment/2021/may/01/food-injustice-has-deep-roots-lets-start-with-americas-apple-pie.
9 Ibid.
10 Jon Miltimore, "5 Things Marx Wanted to Abolish (Besides Private Property)," Foundation for Economic Freedom, October 31, 2017, https://fee.org/articles/5-things-marx-wanted-to-abolish-besides-private-property/.
11 Bill Cook, "Johnny Appleseed and His Bench," Glendale New Church, 2017, https://www.glendalenewchurch.org/johnny-appleseed/.
12 Raj Patel, "Food Injustice Has Deep Roots . . . "
13 Troy Worden, "Novak Awards Recognize Outstanding Young Journalists," The Daily Signal, October 9, 2018, https://www.dailysignal.com/2018/10/09/novak-awards-recognize-outstanding-young-journalists/; TFAS, "About," The Fund for American Studies, no date, https://tfas.org/about/.
14 Christine Emba, "Is It Time to Limit Personal Wealth?,"

Washington Post, June 12, 2021, https://www.washingtonpost.com/opinions/2021/06/12/is-it-time-limit-personal-wealth/.

[15] Ibid.

[16] Harvard University, "Languaging and the Latinx identities | Immigration Initiative at Harvard," Harvard.edu, Fall 2021, https://immigrationinitiative.harvard.edu/links/immigration-and-american-society; Harvard University, "AAAS E-119 Chocolate, Culture, and the Politics of Food | CRN 25963," Harvard Extension Course Catalog, Spring 2022, https://extension.harvard.edu/course-catalog/courses/chocolate-culture-and-the-politics-of-food/25963; Harvard University, "WOMGEN 1413: Friendship as Way of Life | Harvard University | History Department," Harvard.edu, Spring 2022, https://history.fas.harvard.edu/classes/womgen-1413-friendship-way-life.

[17] Anita Hamilton, "Not Too Cool for School: Tufts Offers Class on Hipsters," Time, August 21, 2014, https://time.com/3153922/tufts-hipster-culture-course/.

[18] Gil Kaufman, "Lady Gaga Now Subject of College Course," MTV.com, October 29, 2010, http://www.mtv.com/news/1651116/lady-gaga-now-subject-of-college-course/.

[19] UCSB, "Undergraduate Program—Department of History," UC Santa Barbara, Spring 2009, https://www.history.ucsb.edu/news/news/undergraduate-program/.

[20] Sydney Fogel, "The Most Absurd College Courses You Can Actually Take," Livingly, January 22, 2021, https://www.livingly.com/The+Most+Absurd+College+Courses.

[21] UC Santa Cruz, "LING 80K Invented Languages, from Elvish to Esperanto," UCSC General Catalog, Spring-Summer 2022, https://catalog.ucsc.edu/Current/General-Catalog/Courses/LING-Linguistics.

[22] Charlotte Allen, "I got an A in Phallus 101," Los Angeles Times, January 7, 2007, https://www.latimes.com/news/la-op-allen7jan07-story.html; Occidental College, "CTSJ—Critical Theory and Social Justice," SmartCatalogIQ.com, Fall 2020, http://oxy.smartcatalogiq.com/2020-2021/Catalog/Course-Descriptions/CTSJ-Critical-TheorySocial-Justice.

[23] Occidental College, "CTSJ—Critical Theory and Social Justice," SmartCatalogIQ.com, Fall 2020, http://oxy.smartcatalogiq.com/2020-

2021/Catalog/Course-Descriptions/CTSJ-Critical-TheorySocial-Justice.

[24] Sam Schuman, "Extra Credit," Oberlin.edu, February 22, 2019, https://www.oberlin.edu/blogs/extra-credit.

[25] Evergreen State College, "Somatic Studies," Evergreen.edu, Fall 2021, https://www.evergreen.edu/studies/somatic-studies.

[26] UConn, "Puppet Arts | UConn Dramatic Arts," Drama.Uconn.edu, Fall 2021, https://drama.uconn.edu/programs/puppet-arts/.

[27] Santa Clara University, "Department of Physics," SCU.edu, Fall 2021, https://www.scu.edu/bulletin/undergraduate/2018-19/chapter-3/Physics.html.

[28] Glenn R. Stutzky, Christopher F. Irvin, and Keesa V. Johnson, "Surviving the Coming Zombie Apocalypse | Disasters, Catastrophes, and Human Behavior," MSU.edu, Fall 2021, https://zombie.msu.edu/.

[29] UPenn, "Department of English—Wasting Time on the Internet," University of Pennsylvania, Spring 2015, https://www.english.upenn.edu/courses/undergraduate/2015/spring/engl111.301.

[30] UC Santa Cruz, "Trajectories of Justice: Standing Rock, Climate Change, and Trump's Potential Impeachment," 2021–22 UCSC General Catalog, https://catalog.ucsc.edu/en/Current/General-Catalog/Courses/COWL-Cowell-College/Upper-Division/COWL-126.

[31] UC Santa Cruz, "UCSC General Catalog—FMST—Feminist Studies," 2021–22 UCSC General Catalog, https://catalog.ucsc.edu/Current/General-Catalog/Courses/FMST-Feminist-Studies.

[32] TBS Staff, "25 Unique (Possibly Even Crazy) Courses of Study," TheBestSchools.org, November 12, 2015, https://thebestschools.org/magazine/crazy-courses-of-study-part-1/.

[33] Stacy Conradt, "22 Fascinating and Bizarre Classes Offered This Semester," Mental Floss, August 28, 2011, https://www.mentalfloss.com/article/28626/22-fascinating-and-bizarre-classes-offered-semester.

[34] Woodrow Wilson, "The Study of Administration," Hillsdale College: The U.S. Constitution: A Reader, CDN.ConstitutionReader.com, no date, page 664, http://cdn.constitutionreader.com/files/pdf/constitution/ch111.pdf.

[35] Ronald J. Pestritto, "Woodrow Wilson and the Rejection of the Founders' Principles," Hillsdale College, no date, https://constitution.

hillsdale.edu/document.doc?id=313.

[36] Ibid.

Chapter 6: How They Try to Shut Us Up

[1] GOP War Room, "Sen. Kamala Harris Compares ICE to the KKK," YouTube.com, November 15, 2018, https://www.youtube.com/ watch?v=KM-4PROZkUM&t=197s.

[2] Lara Bazelon, "Kamala Harris Was Not a 'Progressive Prosecutor,'" New York Times, January 17, 2019, https://www.nytimes.com/2019/01/17/ opinion/kamala-harris-criminal-justice.html.

[3] Eric Boehm, "The Washington Post Tried to Memory-Hole Kamala Harris' Bad Joke About Inmates Begging for Food and Water," Reason, January 22, 2021, https://reason.com/2021/01/22/the-washington-post-memory-holed-kamala-harris-bad-joke-about-inmates-begging-for-food-and-water/.

[4] Maddison Meeks, "I Tried to Debate a Campus Socialist. He Told Me to 'F***off,'" The College Fix, September 13, 2018, https://www. thecollegefix.com/i-tried-to-debate-a-campus-socialist-he-told-me-to-f-off/.

[5] Maddison Meeks, "At CPAC, Most Students Were Talking about How They're Mistreated on Campus," The College Fix, March 8, 2019, https:// www.thecollegefix.com/at-cpac-most-students-were-talking-about-how-theyre-mistreated-on-campus/.

[6] Ryan Lovelace, "Students Told to Disavow 'American-ness, Maleness, Whiteness, Heterosexuality,'" The College Fix, November 27, 2012, https://www.thecollegefix.com/students-told-to-disavow-american-ness-maleness-whiteness-heterosexuality/; Nathan Harden, "Butler Univ. Criticizes Student Who Exposed Attack on 'American-ness, Maleness, Whiteness, Heterosexuality,'" The College Fix, December 4, 2012, https:// www.thecollegefix.com/butler-u-attacks-student-who-complained-of-anti-white-anti-male-professor/.

[7] Ryan Lovelace, "Students Told to Disavow 'American-ness, Maleness, Whiteness, Heterosexuality . . .'"

[8] Ryan Lovelace, "A Conservative Student Went to College and This Is What Happened," The College Fix, June 6, 2014, https://www.

thecollegefix.com/a-conservative-student-went-to-college-and-this-is-what-happened/.

9 William F. Buckley, God and Man at Yale: The Superstitions of "Academic Freedom" (Chicago: Regnery, 1951), xvi.

10 Ibid., 107.

11 Noah Kim, "Callout Culture: When Controversial Actions Have Online Repercussions," Yale Daily News, January 22, 2016, https://yaledailynews.com/blog/2016/01/22/callout-culture-when-controversial-actions-have-online-repercussions/; Jennifer Kabbany, "Conservative Student at Yale Called 'Bigot,' Pressured to Leave Campus by Peers," The College Fix, September 18, 2015, https://www.thecollegefix.com/conservative-student-at-yale-called-bigot-pressured-to-leave-campus-by-peers/.

12 Tina Nguyen, "'How Is This Okay?': At Yale, Campus Debate Turns into a Social Media 'Cesspool,'" Vanity Fair, December 27, 2017, https://www.vanityfair.com/news/2017/12/yale-campus-debate-reform-the-savages.

13 Ibid.

14 Bari Weiss, "'The Psychopathic Problem of the White Mind'—Common Sense with Bari Weiss," Substack.com, June 4, 2021, https://bariweiss.substack.com/p/the-psychopathic-problem-of-the-white.

15 Michael Levinson (New York Times), "Psychiatrist Spoke at Yale of Fantasies of Shooting Whites," Chicago Tribune, June 7, 2021, https://www.chicagotribune.com/nation-world/ct-aud-nw-nyt-yale-psychiatrist-shooting-white-people-20210607-6bu54qqttze6bgn3wtgb6vncpq-story.html.

16 Bari Weiss, "'The Psychopathic Problem of the White Mind' . . ."; Michael Levinson, "Psychiatrist Spoke at Yale of Fantasies of Shooting Whites . . ."

17 This wording is verbatim, according to an audio recording available online at: Medgate, "Microaggressions (Presented By AMWA)," SoundCloud.com, 2019, embedded audio, https://soundcloud.com/user-381804527/microaggressions-presented-by-amwa.

18 Elizabeth Hopper, "What Is a Microaggression? Everyday Insults with Harmful Effects," ThoughtCo., July 03, 2019, https://www.thoughtco.

com/microaggression-definition-examples-4171853.

[19] Medgate, "Microaggressions (Presented By AMWA) . . ."

[20] Robby Soave, "A Medical Student Questioned Microaggressions. UVA Branded Him a Threat and Banished Him from Campus," Reason, April 7, 2021, https://reason.com/2021/04/07/microaggressions-uva-student-kieran-bhattacharya-threat/.

[21] Casetext: Smarter Legal Research, "Bhattacharya v. Murray, Opinion, Case No. 3:19-cv-00054," Casetext.com, March 31, 2021, https://casetext.com/case/bhattacharya-v-murray.

[22] Jonathan Cohen, "Weaponizing the University: The Case of DePaul," American Thinker, February 1, 2006, https://www.americanthinker.com/articles/2006/02/weaponizing_the_university_the.html.

[23] Ari Cohn, "Is DePaul America's Worst School for Free Speech?," TheFIRE.org, September 9, 2016, https://www.thefire.org/is-depaul-americas-worst-school-for-free-speech/.

[24] Foundation for Individual Rights in Education (FIRE), "DePaul University Calls Affirmative Action Protest 'Harassment,'" TheFIRE. org, January 30, 2006, https://www.thefire.org/depaul-university-calls-affirmative-action-protest-harassment/.

[25] Alana Mastrangelo, "5 Ridiculous Reasons Campus Events Were Canceled in 2018," Breitbart, January 1, 2019, https://www.breitbart.com/tech/2019/01/01/5-ridiculous-reasons-campus-events-were-canceled-in-2018/.

[26] Anthony Gockowski, "Security Guards Fiddle While @Nero Event Burns," CampusReform.org, May 25, 2016, https://www.campusreform.org/?ID=7620.

[27] John Dodge, "DePaul President Apologizes After Conservative Forum Disrupted by Protesters," Chicago.CBSLocal.com, May 25, 2016, https://web.archive.org/web/20160526102748/http://chicago.cbslocal.com/2016/05/25/depaul-president-apologizes-after-conservative-forum-disrupted-by-protesters/.

[28] David Harsanyi, The People Have Spoken (and They Are Wrong): The Case Against Democracy (Washington, DC: Regnery, 2014), 135.

Chapter 7: Violence and Hate on Campus

[1] College Fix Staff, "Suspect Who Punched Conservative at UC Berkeley Finally Arrested," The College Fix, March 2, 2019, https://www.thecollegefix.com/suspect-who-punched-conservative-at-uc-berkeley-finally-arrested/.

[2] Alameda Superior Court—Online Records Search, "Case Information: 19-CR-003557 | The People of the State of California vs. GREENBERG, ZACHARY," Case Number 19-CR-003557, Filed March 5, 2019, Case Type: Felony, Case Status: Active, retrieved at https://publicportal.alameda.courts.ca.gov/publicportal/Home/WorkspaceMode?p=0 on June 24, 2021; Katie Mettler, "Police Have Arrested the Man They Say Punched a Conservative Activist at UC Berkeley," Washington Post, March 1, 2019, https://www.washingtonpost.com/education/2019/02/27/conservative-activist-was-punched-face-uc-berkeley-response-enraged-right/.

[3] Clay Lambert, "Suspect Arrested in Princeton Stabbing," Half Moon Bay Review, August 10, 2020, https://www.HMBReview.com/news/suspect-arrested-in-princeton-stabbing/article_5e0bedec-db58-11ea-b723-f76bc8ce6342.html.

[4] Maureen Kelly, "Suspect Who Allegedly Attacked Activist at UC Berkeley Last Year Arrested Again for Stabbing a Man," KRON 4, August 11, 2020, https://www.kron4.com/news/bay-area/suspect-who-attacked-activist-at-uc-berkeley-last-year-arrested-again-for-stabbing-a-man/.

[5] Jenna Curren, "Man Accused of Punching Conservative Activist in the Face at UC Berkeley Now Arrested for Stabbing a Person Repeatedly," Law Enforcement Today, August 17, 2020, https://www.LawEnforcementToday.com/man-awaiting-trial-for-uc-berkeley-assault-stabbed-a-man-riding-his-bicycle/.

[6] Katie Mettler, "Police Have Arrested the Man They Say Punched a Conservative Activist at UC Berkeley," Washington Post, March 1, 2019, https://www.washingtonpost.com/education/2019/02/27/conservative-activist-was-punched-face-uc-berkeley-response-enraged-right/.

[7] Shuttershot45, "Trump Supporter Smashed in the Head with U-Lock by Masked Antifa Thug in Berkeley," YouTube.com, https://www.youtube.com/watch?v=9qKCl9NL1Cg, accessed June 25, 2021.

[8] Alan Feuer, "Antifa on Trial: How a College Professor Joined the Left's

Radical Ranks," Rolling Stone, May 15, 2018, https://www.rollingstone.com/culture/culture-features/antifa-on-trial-how-a-college-professor-joined-the-lefts-radical-ranks-630213/.

[9] Emilie Raguso, "Eric Clanton Takes 3-Year Probation Deal in Berkeley Rally Bike Lock Assault Case," Berkeleyside.org, August 8, 2018, https://www.berkeleyside.org/2018/08/08/eric-clanton-takes-3-year-probation-deal-in-berkeley-rally-bike-lock-assault-case.

[10] Charlie Kirk, @charliekirk11, tweet: "Leftist Violence . . . ," Twitter.com, July 9, 2019, https://twitter.com/charliekirk11/status/114866143804 8694272?s=20.

[11] Young America's Foundation, "Crazed Leftists Mob Conservative Students at Binghamton University," YouTube.com, November 15, 2019, https://www.youtube.com/watch?v=_X2-96gt9MI.

[12] Jennifer Kabbany, "SHOCK VIDEO: Aggressive, frenzied mob attacks conservative students, destroys their display," The College Fix, November 15, 2019, https://www.thecollegefix.com/shock-video-aggressive-frenzied-mob-attacks-conservative-students-destroys-their-display/.

[13] Jennifer Kabbany, "VIDEO: Unruly Campus Activists Shut Down Speech by 'Father of Supply-Side Economics' Arthur Laffer," The College Fix, November 19, 2019, https://www.thecollegefix.com/video-unruly-campus-activists-shut-down-speech-by-father-of-supply-side-economics-arthur-laffer/.

[14] Michael Curry, @curry3551, tweet: "Here is the video of the Battery today . . . ," Twitter.com, November 19, 2019, https://twitter.com/curry3551/status/1197020343405137920.

[15] Jeremiah Poff, "Semester of Violence: Physical Attacks on Conservative College Students Keep Piling Up," The College Fix, December 13, 2019, https://www.thecollegefix.com/semester-of-violence-physical-attacks-on-conservative-college-students-keep-piling-up/.

[16] David Aaro, "3 arrested in Tulane dorm room arson fire of YAL-member students," Fox News, March 24, 2019, https://www.foxnews.com/us/police-book-3-in-connection-with-reportedly-targeted-dorm-room-fire; Alana Mastrangelo, "Police: Three Arrested After Arson Attack on Tulane Turning Point USA President's Dorm Room," Breitbart, March 25, 2019, https://www.breitbart.com/politics/2019/03/25/police-three-

arrested-after-arson-attack-on-tulane-turning-point-usa-presidents-dorm-room/.

[17] Kaitlin Bennett, @KaitMarieox, tweet: "This deranged leftist and LGBT activist named Keaton Hill . . . ," Twitter.com, December 6, 2019, https://twitter.com/KaitMarieox/status/1203082233793384454.

[18] Benjy Egel, "Sacramento State Student Slapping College Republicans Ex-President on Video Goes Viral," Sacramento Bee, December 7, 2019, https://www.sacbee.com/news/local/education/article238146364.html.

[19] Charmaine Nero, "Viral Video Appears to Show Sacramento State Student Physically Confront Another Student," Fox40.com, December 7, 2019, https://fox40.com/news/local-news/viral-video-appears-to-show-sacramento-state-student-physically-confront-another-student/.

[20] Source: Telephone interview with Katie Daviscourt conducted August 25, 2021, plus subsequent phone and email exchanges.

[21] Hunter Harris, "Chuck Palahniuk Says the Right's 'Special Snowflake' Diss Came from Fight Club," Vulture.com, January 25, 2017, https://www.vulture.com/2017/01/palahniuk-snowflake-diss-came-from-fight-club.html.

[22] Wikiquote, "Jordan Peterson," https://en.wikiquote.org/wiki/Jordan_Peterson, accessed June 26, 2021.

Chapter 8: Foreign Influence on Campus

[1] Megan Henney, "Coronavirus Pandemic Could Cost the Global Economy $82 Trillion," Yahoo! Finance, May 20, 2020, https://finance.yahoo.com/news/coronavirus-pandemic-could-cost-global-161616535.html.

[2] Caitlin McFall, "Fauci Claims US Gave $600,000 to Wuhan Lab Research; Documents Show It Was More," Fox News, June 4, 2021, https://www.foxnews.com/politics/exclusive-fauci-claims-us-gave-600k-to-wuhan-lab-research-documents-show-otherwise; Brandon Gillespie, "Glenn Greenwald Mocks the Intercept for 'Accidentally' Unearthing Details on US Coronavirus Research in China," Fox News, September 7, 2021, https://www.foxnews.com/media/glenn-greenwald-intercept-details-us-coronavirus-research-china.

[3] Josh Rogin, "Opinion: State Department Cables Warned of Safety

Issues at Wuhan Lab Studying Bat Coronaviruses," Washington Post, April 14, 2020, https://www.washingtonpost.com/opinions/2020/04/14/state-department-cables-warned-safety-issues-wuhan-lab-studying-bat-coronaviruses/.

[4] David Acevedo, "The Thousand Traitors Program," National Association of Scholars, February 11, 2020, https://www.nas.org/blogs/article/the-thousand-traitors-program; Jason Mast, "Embattled Harvard scientist Charles Lieber goes on a counter-offensive, hiring high-profile lawyer and suing Harvard for abandoning him amid federal probe," Endpoints News, October 12, 2020, https://endpts.com/embattled-harvard-scientist-charles-lieber-goes-on-a-counter-offensive-hiring-high-profile-lawyer-and-suing-harvard-for-abandoning-him-amid-federal-probe/; Andy Z. Wang, "Lieber Prepares for Impending Trial on Federal Charges As He Battles Incurable Cancer," Harvard Crimson, April 7, 2021, https://www.thecrimson.com/article/2021/4/7/lieber-prepares-for-trial/.

[5] Department of Justice, Office of Public Affairs, "Harvard University Professor and Two Chinese Nationals Charged in Three Separate China Related Cases," Press Release, Justice.gov, January 28, 2020, https://www.justice.gov/opa/pr/harvard-university-professor-and-two-chinese-nationals-charged-three-separate-china-related.

[6] Department of Justice, U.S. Attorney's Office, Southern District of New York, "Senior Nasa Scientist Sentenced to Prison for Making False Statements Related to Chinese Thousand Talents Program Participation and Professorship," Press Release, Justice.gov, June 16, 2021, https://www.justice.gov/usao-sdny/pr/senior-nasa-scientist-sentenced-prison-making-false-statements-related-chinese-thousand.

[7] Department of Justice, U.S. Attorney's Office, Southern District of Ohio, "University Researcher Sentenced to Prison for Lying on Grant Applications to Develop Scientific Expertise for China," Press Release, Justice.gov, May 14, 2021, https://www.justice.gov/usao-sdoh/pr/university-researcher-sentenced-prison-lying-grant-applications-develop-scientific.

[8] Kristen Setera, FBI Boston, "FBI Special Agent in Charge Joseph R. Bonavolonta's Remarks at Press Conference Announcing Arrest of MIT Professor Gang Chen," FBI.gov, January 14, 2021, https://www.fbi.gov/

contact-us/field-offices/boston/news/press-releases/fbi-special-agent-in-charge-joseph-r-bonavolontas-remarks-at-press-conference-announcing-arrest-of-mit-professor-gang-chen.

9 Janet Lorin and Michael McDonald, "Harvard, Yale Under U.S. Investigation over Foreign Funding," Bloomberg-Quint, February 13, 2020, https://www.bloombergquint.com/onweb/harvard-yale-under-u-s-investigation-over-foreign-funding.

10 Department of Justice, Office of Public Affairs, "Researchers Charged with Visa Fraud After Lying About Their Work for China's People's Liberation Army," Justice.gov, July 23, 2020, https://www.justice.gov/opa/pr/researchers-charged-visa-fraud-after-lying-about-their-work-china-s-people-s-liberation-army.

11 Rachelle Peterson, "Documentary Pulls Back the Curtain On Communist China's Global Soft Power Outposts," The Federalist, April 26, 2017, https://thefederalist.com/2017/04/26/documentary-pulls-back-curtain-communist-chinas-global-soft-power-outposts/.

12 East Asia Research Center, "Confucius Institutes in South Korea Promote Chinese Communist Party's Propaganda," EastAsiaResearch.org, May 4, 2020, https://eastasiaresearch.org/2020/05/04/confucius-institutes-in-south-korea-promote-chinese-communist-partys-propaganda/.

13 Richard Herr, "The Role of Soft Power in China's Influence in the Pacific Islands," Australian Strategic Policy Institute, April 30, 2019, https://www.aspistrategist.org.au/the-role-of-soft-power-in-chinas-influence-in-the-pacific-islands/.

14 "How Many Confucius Institutes Are There in the United States?" National Association of Scholars, updated September 8, 2021, https://www.nas.org/blogs/article/how_many_confucius_institutes_are_in_the_united_states; Rachelle Peterson, "Confucius Institutes in the US That Are Closing," National Associate of Scholars, May 2020, https://www.nas.org/storage/app/media/Reports/Outsourced%20to%20China/confucius-institutes-that-closed-updated-may-1-2020.pdf.

15 Ethan Epstein, "How China Infiltrated U.S. Classrooms," Politico, January 17, 2018, https://www.politico.com/magazine/story/2018/01/16/how-china-infiltrated-us-classrooms-216327/.

[16] Dao News, "Details of 20 Billion RMB Universal Beijing Resort Revealed," DaoInsights.com, October 23, 2020, https://daoinsights.com/news/details-of-20-billion-rmb-universal-beijing-resort-revealed/.

[17] Maura Moynihan, "Disney's China Problem: West's Elite Covering up CCP's Misdeeds," The Asian Age, October 21, 2020, https://www.asianage.com/opinion/columnists/211020/maura-moynihan-disneys-china-problem-wests-elite-covering-up-ccps-misdeeds.html.

[18] Jack Nicas, Raymond Zhong and Daisuke Wakabayashi, "Censorship, Surveillance and Profits: A Hard Bargain for Apple in China," New York Times, May 17, 2021, updated June 17, 2021, https://www.nytimes.com/2021/05/17/technology/apple-china-censorship-data.html.

[19] Dave Gibson, "Was That New iPhone Made with Chinese Slave Labor?," US Incorporated, March 16, 2020, https://usinc.org/was-that-new-iphone-made-with-chinese-slave-labor/.

[20] Bill Gertz, "Joe Biden Ends Confucius Institute Disclosures," Washington Times, February 10, 2021, https://www.washingtontimes.com/news/2021/feb/10/joe-biden-ends-confucius-institute-disclosures/.

[21] Office of Senator Mitt Romney, "Romney, Rubio, Grassley, Portman Urge President to Implement Rule on Confucius Institutes," Press Release, Romney.Senate.gov, February 23, 2021, https://www.romney.senate.gov/romney-rubio-grassley-portman-urge-president-implement-rule-confucius-institutes.

[22] Office of Senator Susan Collins, "Senator Collins Applauds Decision to Close Confucius Institute at USM," Press Release, Collins.Senate.gov, April 13, 2021, https://www.collins.senate.gov/newsroom/senator-collins-applauds-decision-close-confucius-institute-usm.

[23] Office of Senator Tom Cotton, "Cotton Condemns Confucius Institute Rule Reversal," Press Release, Cotton.Senate.gov, February 9, 2021, https://www.cotton.senate.gov/news/press-releases/cotton-condemns-confucius-institute-rule-reversal.

[24] Christian Schneider, "Stanford Accepts $58 Million in Chinese Cash While Pushing Global Human Rights," The College Fix, July 2, 2020, https://www.thecollegefix.com/stanford-accepts-58-million-in-chinese-cash-while-pushing-global-human-rights/.

[25] Ryan Mauro and Alex VanNess, "Clarion EXCLUSIVE Report: Foreign

Influence Ops on US Universities—Clarion Project," ClarionProject. org, September 5, 2019, https://clarionproject.org/us-universities-foreign-funding-clarion-intel-exclusive/.

[26] Ibid.

[27] Ibid.

[28] Ibid.

[29] Arnon Gutfeld, "The Saudi Specter over the American Education System," Jerusalem Center for Public Affairs, September 3, 2018, https://jcpa.org/article/saudi-specter-over-american-education-system/.

[30] Ibid.

[31] JTA, Arutz Sheva Staff, "Student Who Threatened 'Zionists' Claims 'Trauma' From 1948," Arutz Sheva 7 IsraelNationalNews.com, August 5, 2018, https://www.israelnationalnews.com/News/News.aspx/250067.

[32] JTA, "Stanford Student Who Threatened 'Zionist Students' Resigns Post," Times of Israel, August 5, 2018, https://www.timesofisrael.com/stanford-student-who-threatened-zionist-students-resigns-post/.

[33] ZOA Campus, "Students for Justice in Palestine," Zionist Organization of America, no date, https://campus.zoa.org/students-for-justice-in-palestine/.

[34] Jason D. Hill, "The Moral Case for Israel Annexing the West Bank—And Beyond," The Federalist, April 16, 2019, https://thefederalist.com/2019/04/16/moral-case-israel-annexing-west-bank-beyond/.

[35] Jason Hill, Plaintiff, vs. DePaul University, Scott Paeth, and Salma Ghanem, case number 2020L004358, filed April 20, 2020, Cook County Circuit Court, Illinois, page 8, paragraphs 61 and 62, https://legalinsurrection.com/wp-content/uploads/2020/04/Jason-Hill-v.-DePaul-Univ-Complaint.pdf.

[36] DePaul Faculty Council, "Faculty Council Resolution on Academic Freedom and Responsibility," DePauliaOnline.com, May 1, 2019, https://depauliaonline.com/wp-content/uploads/2019/04/Agenda-9-Faculty-Council-Resolution-on-Academic-Freedom-and-Responsibility-1-1.pdf, accessed June 28, 2021.

[37] Doug Klain, "Depaul Students Claim Victory, Hill Vows to Continue Writing," DePauliaOnline.com, June 3, 2019, https://depauliaonline.com/41998/news/depaul-students-claim-victory-hill-vows-to-continue-writing/.

[38] Rifqa Falaneh, "OPINION: 8 Weeks Later: How the Student Coalition to #CensureHill Won," DePauliaOnline.com, June 3, 2019, https://depauliaonline.com/41912/opinions/opinion-8-weeks-later-how-the-student-coalition-to-censurehill-won/.

[39] Jason Hill, Plaintif, vs. DePaul University, Scott Paeth, and Salma Ghanem, case number 2020L004358, filed April 20, 2020, Cook County Circuit Court, Illinois, page 6, paragraph 44, https://legalinsurrection.com/wp-content/uploads/2020/04/Jason-Hill-v.-DePaul-Univ-Complaint.pdf.

[40] Ibid., 6–7, paragraphs 45–49.

[41] Jay P. Greene, Albert Cheng, and Ian Kingsbury, "Are Educated People More Anti-Semitic?," Tablet, March 29, 2021, https://www.tabletmag.com/sections/news/articles/are-educated-people-more-anti-semitic-jay-greene-albert-cheng-ian-kingsbury.

[42] Ibid.

[43] Ibid.

[44] Chelsea Hafer, "SJP Hosts 15th Annual Apartheid Week," The Hoya, April 5, 2019, https://thehoya.com/sjp-hosts-15th-annual-apartheid-week/.

[45] AP and TOI Staff, "Jewish Students Sue to Oust Pro-Palestinian Event at UMass, Citing Anti-Semitism," Times of Israel, April 30, 2019, https://www.timesofisrael.com/jewish-students-sue-to-oust-pro-palestinian-event-at-umass-citing-anti-semitism/; Resistance Studies Initiative, "Not Backing Down: Israel, Free Speech and the Battle for Palestinian Right," UMass.edu, (event date) May 4, 2019, https://www.umass.edu/resistancestudies/events/not-backing-down-israel-free-speech-and-battle-palestinian-right; Media Education Foundation, "Cornel West Speech at "Criminalizing Dissent" Palestinian Rights Panel at UMass," YouTube.com, December 5, 2019, https://www.youtube.com/watch?v=ngo1CiU4IIU; media education foundation, "Not Backing Down Panel: Israel, Free Speech & the Battle for Palestinian Rights," YouTube.com, June 27, 2019, https://www.youtube.com/watch?v=UuSPNo8yj28&t=4s.

[46] IfNotNow-Austin, "Join Us in Denouncing Texas Hillel's Israel Block Party," ActionNetwork.org, no date, https://actionnetwork.org/petitions/join-us-in-denouncing-texas-hillels-israel-block-party/;

IfNotNow-Austin, "Concerns with Texas Hillel's Israel Block Party on April 23rd," IfNotNow-Austin, March 15, 2019, https://medium.com/@ifnotnowatx/concerns-with-texas-hillels-israel-block-party-on-april-23rd-97953cbc9a86.

[47] Hosam Elattar, "Students Host Display Detailing Palestinian Struggle," Daily Titan, November 19, 2019, https://dailytitan.com/news/campus/students-host-display-detailing-palestinian-struggle/article_1293a54e-e8c3-5884-83be-69cb1046ad56.html; Jeremy Sharon, "ADL Blames Anti-Zionist Student Group for Anti-Israel Radicalism on Campus," Jerusalem Post, May 27, 2020, https://www.jpost.com/israel-news/adl-slams-students-for-justice-in-palestine-for-campus-radicalism-629487.

[48] Jeremy Sharon, "ADL Blames Anti-Zionist Student Group for Anti-Israel Radicalism on Campus," Jerusalem Post, May 27, 2020, https://www.jpost.com/israel-news/adl-slams-students-for-justice-in-palestine-for-campus-radicalism-629487.

[49] Students for Justice in Palestine at Vassar, "Vassar SJP's Statement on Hen Mazzig's Talk," Facebook.com, November 14, 2019, https://www.facebook.com/VassarSJP/posts/2640676409331100.

[50] Jeremy Sharon, "ADL Blames Anti-Zionist Student Group . . ."

[51] Strugglevideomedia, "Until Our Collective Liberation—NYC Demonstration for Palestine," ("Demonstration in Times Square New York City on 11/15/19"), November 17, 2019, https://www.youtube.com/watch?v=BcGsm5CUsVw.

Chapter 9: Woke and Weaponized

[1] Yaron Steinbuch, "Rep. Jerry Nadler Calls Violence from Antifa in Portland a 'Myth,'" New York Post, July 27, 2020, https://nypost.com/2020/07/27/jerry-nadler-calls-violence-from-antifa-in-portland-a-myth/.

[2] David Palumbo-Liu, "David Palumbo-Liu: Professor of Comparative Literature, Stanford University," Palumbo-Liu.com, no date, https://www.palumbo-liu.com/.

[3] John Rice-Cameron and Anna Mitchell, "Antifa Thugs Find a Champion and a Leader in Stanford Professor," January 15, 2018, https://stanfordreview.org/antifa-thugs-find-a-champion-and-leader-in-stanford-

professor-3/.

[4] Bill Mullen, "Homepage," BillVMullen.com, no date, https://www. billvmullen.com/.

[5] Bill Mullen, "Campus Antifascist Network," BillVMullen.com, no date, https://www.billvmullen.com/antifascist-network.

[6] Motion Church, "A Message from Our Senior Pastor regarding Our Event Entitled 'An Afternoon with Charlie Kirk,'" YouTube.com, April 23, 2021, https://www.youtube.com/watch?v=qCO-Yz_mwAo&t=1s.

[7] Wikipedia, List of Monuments and Memorials Removed during the George Floyd Protests, Wikipedia.org, https://en.wikipedia.org/wiki/List_ of_monuments_and_memorials_removed_during_the_George_Floyd_ protests#Others, accessed July 9, 2021.

[8] Jonathan Turley, "'Either You Are Anti-Racist or Racist': California Professor Put on Administrative Leave After Commenting on the Japanese Internment Camps," JonathanTurley.org, June 8, 2021, https:// jonathanturley.org/2021/06/08/either-you-are-anti-racist-or-racist- california-professor-put-on-administrative-leave-after-commenting-on- the-japanese-internment-camps/.

[9] Ibid.

[10] Ibid.

[11] Nick Welsh, "Santa Barbara City College Admin Put on Leave for Controversial Comments," Santa Barbara Independent, April 6, 2021, https://www.independent.com/2021/04/06/santa-barbara-city-college- admin-put-on-leave-for-controversial-comments/.

[12] UNCC Division of Student Affairs, "Mission, Vision and Values," UNC Charlotte, no date, https://studentaffairs.charlotte.edu/about-us/ mission-vision-and-values.

[13] Fairleigh Dickinson University, "University Mission, Vision and Values," FDU.edu, no date, https://www.fdu.edu/about/strategic-plan/mission- vision-and-values/.

[14] Clark University, "Our Mission," ClarkU.edu, no date, https://www. clarku.edu/who-we-are/our-mission/.

[15] University of Washington, "Vision and Values," Washington.edu, no date, https://www.washington.edu/about/visionvalues/.

[16] Cornell University, "University Mission," Cornell.edu, no date, https://

www.cornell.edu/about/mission.cfm.

[17] Ophelie Jacobson, "VIDEO: College Students NOT Proud to Be American," Campus Reform / The Leadership Institute, July 2, 2021, https://campusreform.org/article?id=17736.

[18] Margaret Hedeman and Matt Kristoffersen, "Art History Department to Scrap Survey Course," Yale News, January 24, 2020, https://yaledailynews.com/blog/2020/01/24/art-history-department-to-scrap-survey-course/.

[19] Abigail Thernstrom and Stephan Thernstrom, "Black Progress: How Far We've Come, and How Far We Have to Go," Brookings Institution, March 1, 1998, https://www.brookings.edu/articles/black-progress-how-far-weve-come-and-how-far-we-have-to-go/.

[20] James Lindsay, "How Not to Resolve the Paradox of Tolerance," New Discourses, January 26, 2021, https://newdiscourses.com/2021/01/how-not-to-resolve-the-paradox-of-tolerance/.

[21] Ibid.

[22] James Lindsay, "Critical Theorists as Grand Inquisitors: The Logic of "Repressive Tolerance," New Discourses, February 8, 2021, https://newdiscourses.com/2021/02/critical-theorists-as-grand-inquisitors-the-logic-of-repressive-tolerance/.

[23] Note: As Lenin and Mao showed, proletarian revolutions never take place unless they are instigated by what Lenin called "professional revolutionaries."

[24] Carlos J. Nan, "Adding Salt to the Wound: Affirmative Action and Critical Race Theory," Minnesota Journal of Law & Inequality, Volume 12, Issue 2, December 1994, page 558, https://scholarship.law.umn.edu/cgi/viewcontent.cgi?article=1456&context=lawineq.

[25] K. E. Kaplan, "Justice John Paul Stevens: Part Concurrence Part Dissent," The Civil Rights Movement, College of William & Mary, February 19, 2015, http://civilrightsmovement.blogs.wm.edu/.

[26] Ibram X. Kendi, How to Be an Antiracist, Extract by Penguin Books, June 9, 2020, https://www.penguin.co.uk/articles/2020/june/ibram-x-kendi-definition-of-antiracist.html.

[27] LeakSourceArchive, "Economist Thomas Sowell Talks about Harvard Obama & Derrick Bell," YouTube.com, March 9, 2012, https://www.

youtube.com/watch?v=KDeL-UK1p24.

[28] Thomas Sowell, "Racial Quota Fallout," Creators Syndicate, March 14, 2012, https://www.creators.com/read/thomas-sowell/03/12/racial-quota-fallout.

[29] Ibram X. Kendi, "Pass an Anti-Racist Constitutional Amendment," Politico, 2019, https://www.politico.com/interactives/2019/how-to-fix-politics-in-america/inequality/pass-an-anti-racist-constitutional-amendment/.

[30] Ibid.

[31] Christopher F. Rufo, "The Courage of Our Convictions," City Journal, April 22, 2021, https://www.city-journal.org/how-to-fight-critical-race-theory.

[32] Alexander James, "More Than Seventy-Five Colleges Host Blacks Only Graduation Ceremonies," Washington Examiner, May 21, 2019, https://www.washingtonexaminer.com/red-alert-politics/more-than-75-colleges-host-blacks-only-graduation-ceremonies.

[33] Ewan Palmer, "Fact Check: Is Columbia University Hosting Graduation Events Based on Race, Identity?," Newsweek, March 16, 2021, https://www.newsweek.com/fact-check-columbia-university-graduation-based-race-identity-1576567.

[34] Walter Williams, "Now Colleges Are Lowering Standards for This Program to Increase 'Diversity,'" Black Community News, September 25, 2018, https://blackcommunitynews.com/now-colleges-are-lowering-standards-for-this-program-to-increase-diversity/.

Chapter 10: The Professor Watchlist

[1] Jonathan McCormick, "Professor Worries Students Will Share 'Controversial' Recorded Lectures as Classes Move Online," Campus Reform, March 18, 2020, https://www.campusreform.org/article?id=14554.

[2] Greg Piper, "Coronavirus Prompts Professors to Hide Their Lectures from the Public as Everything Goes Online," The College Fix, March 25, 2020, https://www.thecollegefix.com/coronavirus-prompts-professors-to-hide-their-lectures-from-the-public-as-everything-goes-online/.

[3] Emma Pettit, "A Side Effect of Remote Teaching During Covid-19?

Videos That Can Be Weaponized," The Chronicle of Higher Education, March 24, 2020, https://www.chronicle.com/article/a-side-effect-of-remote-teaching-during-covid-19-videos-that-can-be-weaponized/.

[4] TPUSA, "Our Mission," Turning Point USA, no date, https://www.tpusa.com/ourmission.

[5] Emma Pettit, "A Side Effect of Remote Teaching . . ."

[6] TPUSA, "Julia Gruber, Tennessee Tech University," Professor Watchlist, Spring 2021, https://www.professorwatchlist.org/professor/juliagruber.

[7] Ibid.

[8] Campus Reform, "Penn State Professor," YouTube.com, July 22, 2021, https://www.youtube.com/watch?v=70iWl3b2y5o.

[9] Sergei Kelley, "'You May Have Oppressed Somebody:' Prof to White Student Who Said He Left His House That Day," Campus Reform, July 22, 2021, https://www.campusreform.org/article?id=17832.

[10] Campus Reform, "Penn State Professor . . ." (Emphasis in the original.)

[11] Sam Richards, "SOC 119: About," SOC119.org, no date, https://www.soc119.org/about.

[12] Campus Reform, "Penn State Professor . . ."

[13] SOC119, "Soc 119 Live Stream—Class #13: White Discomfort," YouTube.com, streamed live on Oct 8, 2019, https://www.youtube.com/watch?v=DKTUG02kTTg, at the 58:00 minute mark.

[14] Qur'an 8:12, English translation by Mohammad Habib Shakir, Three Translations of The Koran (Al-Qur'an) Side by Side, http://www.gutenberg.org/files/16955/16955.txt.

[15] SOC119, "Soc 119 Live Stream—Class 8—'Christian Sharia' (ENTIRE CLASS)," YouTube.com, streamed live on February 2, 2017, https://www.youtube.com/watch?v=AmzDnulSV_g, at the 25:35 minute mark.

[16] Isabel Wilkerson, "'African-American' Favored by Many of America's Blacks," New York Times, January 31, 1989, https://www.nytimes.com/1989/01/31/us/african-american-favored-by-many-of-america-s-blacks.html.

[17] Alissa Lopez, "Saying 'America Is a Melting Pot' Is a Microaggression, Purdue Class Teaches," The College Fix, April 14, 2016, https://www.thecollegefix.com/saying-america-melting-pot-microaggression-purdue-

class-teaches/.

[18] Ibid.

[19] Douglas Ernst, "Florida Professor Forbids Students from Using 'Euro-White Colonial' Phrase 'Melting Pot,'" Washington Times, August 11, 2016, https://www.washingtontimes.com/news/2016/aug/11/florida-professor-forbids-students-from-using-euro/.

[20] Patrick J. Hayes, editor, The Making of Modern Immigration: An Encyclopedia of People and Ideas, Volume 1 (Santa Barbara, CA: ABC-CLIO, 2012), 34.

[21] Ulrich Baer, "What 'Snowflakes' Get Right About Free Speech," New York Times, April 24, 2017, https://www.nytimes.com/2017/04/24/opinion/what-liberal-snowflakes-get-right-about-free-speech.html.

[22] Robby Soave, "So Brave: This University of Michigan Kid Selected 'His Majesty' As Personal Pronoun," Reason, September 29, 2016, https://reason.com/2016/09/29/so-brave-this-university-of-michigan-kid/.

[23] Emily Jashinsky, "Prof. Threatens to Punish Michigan Students Who Follow 'His Majesty's' Lead," YAF.org, September 30, 2016, https://www.yaf.org/news/prof-threatens-punish-michigan-students-follow-majestys-lead/.

[24] Clay Robinson, "UCSB Prof Uses Religion Class to Teach About 'Error' of 'American Exceptionalism,'" Campus Reform, June 5, 2020, https://www.campusreform.org/?ID=14987.

[25] William Nardi, "Professors Call Founding Fathers 'Terrorists,' Founding Ideals a 'Fabrication,'" The College Fix, November 16, 2016, https://www.thecollegefix.com/professors-call-founding-fathers-terrorists-founding-ideals-fabrication/.

[26] LNUC Concurrences, "S2S Interview with Nicholas De Genova on the Migration Crisis, Mobility and Postcolonial Studies," YouTube.com, June 27, 2017, https://www.youtube.com/watch?v=jkF0I1Z9eGo.

[27] Nicholas De Genova, "To the Editor," Columbia Daily Spectator, March 31, 2003, https://www.columbiaspectator.com/2003/03/31/letters-editorprofessor-qualifies-quotation-article-and-addresses-criticism/.

[28] Ibid.

[29] Jonathan Tannenwald and Inga Saffron, "Drexel Professor Reprimanded for 'White Genocide' Tweet Claims It Was Satire," Philadelphia Inquirer,

December 26, 2016, https://www.inquirer.com/philly/news/Drexel-officials-Professor-George-Ciccariello-Mahers-White-Genocide-tweet-was-utterly-reprehensible.html.

[30] Ibid.

[31] George Ciccariello-Maher, "Riots Work: Wolf Blitzer and the Washington Post Completely Missed the Real Lesson from Baltimore," Salon, May 4, 2015, https://www.salon.com/2015/05/04/riots_work_wolf_blitzer_and_the_washington_post_completely_missed_the_real_lesson_from_baltimore/.

[32] Sara Taylor, "Leftist Professor Publicly Calls for All Cops to Be Strangled with 'Intestines of the Last Capitalist'—Then Says He Got Death Threats," The Blaze, September 30, 2020, https://www.theblaze.com/news/leftist-professor-strangle-cops-death-threats.

[33] Colin Brewer, "Testament by Jean Meslier," New Humanist, February 15, 2010, https://newhumanist.org.uk/articles/2234/testament-by-jean-meslier.

[34] Herbert McCullough, "Speakers Fight Against Hatred Through Rally," The Wichitan, September 5, 2017, https://thewichitan.com/40707/news/speakers-resist-hate-rally/.

[35] Prescott College, "Patrisse Cullors MFA," Prescott.edu, no date, https://www.prescott.edu/faculty-staff-directory/patrisse-cullors.

[36] Joshua Rhett Miller, "BLM Site Removes Page on 'Nuclear Family Structure' amid NFL Vet's Criticism," New York Post, September 24, 2020, https://nypost.com/2020/09/24/blm-removes-website-language-blasting-nuclear-family-structure/.

[37] Karl Marx, The Communist Manifesto, LibreTexts, etext posted by Allison Hurst, April 6, 2021, https://socialsci.libretexts.org/Bookshelves/Sociology/Introduction_to_Sociology/Classical_Sociological_Theory_and_Foundations_of_American_Sociology_(Hurst)/01%3A_Marx_and_Engels/1.12%3A_The_Communist_Manifest.

[38] Jeff Magalif, "Weathermen, Police Scuffle in Cambridge," Harvard Crimson, November 20, 1969, https://www.thecrimson.com/article/1969/11/20/weathermen-police-scuffle-in-cambridge-pweathermen/.

[39] The Real News Network, "A Short History of Black Lives Matter,"

YouTube.com, July 23, 2015, https://www.youtube.com/watch?v=Zp-RswgpjD8&t=337s, at the 7:00 minute mark.

[40] Columbia School of Social Work, "Anthony Zenkus," Columbia.edu, no date, https://socialwork.columbia.edu/faculty-research/faculty/adjunct/anthony-zenkus/.

[41] Prof Zenkus, @anthonyzenkus, tweet: "Odd how you forget the millions . . . ," Twitter.com, January 15, 2018, https://twitter.com/anthonyzenkus/status/952967568851111937.

[42] Prof Zenkus, @anthonyzenkus, tweet: "Hitler was a capitalist . . . ," Twitter.com, January 15, 2018, https://twitter.com/anthonyzenkus/status/953040573857976326.

[43] Prof Zenkus, @anthonyzenkus, tweet: "The American flag is a symbol . . . ," Twitter.com, October 16, 2020, https://twitter.com/anthonyzenkus/status/1317083235797565440.

[44] Dr. Asatar Bair, @asatarbair, thread: "People say I 'idolize' Stalin. . . ," Twitter.com, June 26, 2021, https://twitter.com/asatarbair/status/1408953211361239042.

[45] Cynthia Haven, "Stalin Killed Millions. A Stanford Historian Answers the Question, Was It Genocide?," Stanford News, September 23, 2010, https://news.stanford.edu/2010/09/23/naimark-stalin-genocide-092310/.

[46] Dr. Asatar Bair, @asatarbair, tweet: "I'd like to comment on what is perhaps . . . ," Twitter.com, June 10, 2021, https://twitter.com/asatarbair/status/1403004114351521797.

[47] Dr. Asatar Bair, @asatarbair, tweet: "The UN Committee on the Elimination of . . . ," Twitter.com, February 25, 2021, https://twitter.com/asatarbair/status/1365184988396748802.

[48] Dr. Asatar Bair, @asatarbair, tweet: "I'm a huge fan of Mao . . . ," Twitter.com, June 22, 2021, https://twitter.com/asatarbair/status/1407490614300602373.

[49] Discover the Networks, "John Bellamy Foster," DiscoverTheNetworks.org, no date, https://www.discoverthenetworks.org/individuals/john-bellamy-foster.

[50] Discover the Networks, "Norman Markowitz," DiscoverTheNetworks.org, no date, https://www.discoverthenetworks.org/individuals/norman-markowitz.

[51] Colleen Flaherty, "Correcting the Record," Inside Higher Ed, July 19, 2017, https://www.insidehighered.com/news/2017/07/19/cal-state-fullerton-reinstates-lecturer-after-arbitrator-finds-no-evidence-most.

[52] Sarah Wolstoncroft and Brandon Pho, "Cal State Fullerton Peaceful Protest Ends in Altercation," Daily Titan, February 8, 2017, https://dailytitan.com/news/campus/cal-state-fullerton-peaceful-protest-ends-in-altercation/article_7a1802ca-4293-5038-893b-e3fde6e09940.html; Ariana Rowlands, "Police Investigate After Fullerton Lecturer Allegedly Assaults College Republican," Breitbart, February 8, 2017, https://www.breitbart.com/tech/2017/02/08/college-republican-makes-citizen-arrest-fullerton-professor-assaults-student/.

[53] Ariana Rowlands, "Police Investigate After Fullerton Lecturer Allegedly Assaults College Republican," Breitbart, February 8, 2017, https://www.breitbart.com/tech/2017/02/08/college-republican-makes-citizen-arrest-fullerton-professor-assaults-student/.

[54] Hayley M. Slye, "California Faculty Association 'Outraged' by Cal State Fullerton Lecturer's Suspension Following Altercation," Daily Titan, February 24, 2017, https://dailytitan.com/news/campus/california-faculty-association-outraged-by-cal-state-fullerton-lecturer-s-suspension-following-altercation/article_ea7c6e03-044b-5d59-886a-ae49f3e3647a.html.

[55] Cal State Fullerton, "College of Humanities and Social Sciences, Division of Anthropology: Lecturers and Visitors," California State University, Fullerton, no date, https://anthro.fullerton.edu/People/PartTime_Faculty.aspx (accessed September 3, 2021).

Chapter 11: Only in America

[1] Mark Burnett, Jump In! (New York: Ballantine Books / Random House, 2005), 23.

[2] Ibid., 27–29.

[3] Library of Congress, "Article I Section 9 | Constitution Annotated," Congress.gov, no date, https://constitution.congress.gov/browse/article-1/section-9/.

[4] All Lee Rizzuto quotes are based on a conversation between Lee and the author.

[5] Ibid.

[6] All Ambassador Fischer quotes are based on a conversation between Fischer and the author.

Chapter 12: How to Succeed without a Degree
[1] The dialogue in this story is not verbatim, but is reconstructed and paraphrased from the author's recollection of the event.
[2] eMediaMillWorks, "Text: President Bush Speaks at Yale Graduation," Washington Post, May 21, 2001, https://www.washingtonpost.com/wp-srv/onpolitics/transcripts/bushtext052101.htm.
[3] M0rganFReelance, "Dr Jordan Peterson Exposes Education System in Joe Rogan Interview," YouTube.com, December 12, 2016, https://www.youtube.com/watch?v=V26ABKDwssM, accessed July 12, 2021.
[4] Emma Green, "The Clarence Thomas Effect," The Atlantic, July 10, 2019, https://www.theatlantic.com/politics/archive/2019/07/clarence-thomas-trump/593596/.
[5] Adam Harris, "America Is Divided by Education," The Atlantic, November 7, 2018, https://www.theatlantic.com/education/archive/2018/11/education-gap-explains-american-politics/575113/.
[6] M0rganFReelance, "Dr Jordan Peterson Exposes Education System . . ."
[7] Ibid.
[8] For more information on the nine work colleges, see https://www.workcolleges.org/colleges.

Epilogue: Take Action!
[1] Kenny Stancil, "Poll Finds Socialism Increasingly Seen as 'Badge of Pride' in US," CommonDream.org, June 25, 2021, https://www.commondreams.org/news/2021/06/25/poll-finds-socialism-increasingly-seen-badge-pride-us.
[2] Matt Taibbi, "On 'White Fragility,'" TK News by Matt Taibbi, June 28, 2020, https://taibbi.substack.com/p/on-white-fragility.
[3] Gabe Stutman, "Stanford Diversity Programs Are Creating a 'Hostile Climate' for Jews in the Workplace, Staffers Charge in Federal Complaint," Jewish Telegraphic Agency, June 15, 2021, https://www.jta.org/2021/06/15/united-states/stanford-diversity-programs-are-creating-

a-hostile-climate-for-jews-in-the-workplace-staffers-charge-in-federal-complaint.

[4] Erin L. Thompson, @artcrimeprof, tweet: "I'm a professor who studies the deliberate destruction . . . ," Twitter.com, June 10, 2020, https://twitter.com/artcrimeprof/status/1270869001745432578.

[5] Herbert Marcuse, Marxism, Revolution and Utopia: Collected Papers of Herbert Marcuse, Volume 6 (New York: Routledge, 2014), 336.

[6] For these insights on the "credentialing pipeline," I am indebted to a conversation with James Lindsay.

[7] Jason D. Hill, "A Professor's Call to Shut Down Our Nation's Universities," The Hill, July 16, 2018, https://thehill.com/opinion/education/396764-a-professors-call-to-shut-down-our-nations-universities.

For the latest releases and news
from Winning Team Publishing,
please visit 45Books.com

WINNING TEAM
PUBLISHING

To learn more from Charlie Kirk

and Turning Point USA, visit TPUSA.com